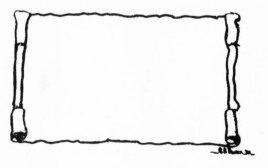

Talking at the Gates

TALKING
AT THE GATES

A Life of James Baldwin

JAMES CAMPBELL

VIKING

VIKING
Published by the Penguin Group
Viking Penguin, a division of Penguin Books USA Inc.,
375 Hudson Street, New York, New York 10014, U.S.A.
Penguin Books Ltd, 27 Wrights Lane,
London W8 5TZ, England
Penguin Books Australia Ltd, Ringwood,
Victoria, Australia
Penguin Books Canada Ltd, 2801 John Street,
Markham, Ontario, Canada L3R 1B4
Penguin Books (N.Z.) Ltd, 182–190 Wairau Road,
Auckland 10, New Zealand

Penguin Books Ltd, Registered Offices:
Harmondsworth, Middlesex, England

First American Edition
Published in 1991 by Viking Penguin,
a division of Penguin Books USA Inc.

1   3   5   7   9   10   8   6   4   2

Page xiii constitutes an extension of this copyright page.

LIBRARY OF CONGRESS CATALOGING IN PUBLICATION DATA
Campbell, James, 1951–
Talking at the gates : a life of James Baldwin / James Campbell.
p.   cm.
Includes bibliographical references and index.
ISBN 0-670-82913-7
1. Baldwin, James, 1924–1987—Biography.   2. Authors,
American—20th century—Biography.   I. Title.
PS3552.A45Z63   1991
818'.5409—dc20
[B]   90-50744

Printed in the United States of America

To my mother and father

Contents

Illustrations

Author's Note

James Baldwin frequently changed or modified the title of a book while he was writing it. *Go Tell It on the Mountain*, for example, was previously 'Crying Holy' and, before that, 'In My Father's House'; *Giovanni's Room* was 'One for My Baby', then 'Backwater', and then something different; *Another Country* began life as that, changed to being 'The Only Pretty Ring Time', and changed back to *Another Country* again. Sometimes the title came to him first and the book would grow to fit it, and sometimes a title existed in his mind for a decade or more without a book being written for it. For a novel which he planned to set on Emancipation Day in 1863 on a Southern slave-holding plantation, Baldwin conjured the title 'Talking at the Gates'. For almost twenty years, on and off, he talked about the book, but never wrote it.

Many people have shared their views and reminiscences with me in the writing of this account of Baldwin's life and work. In the text, the statements of an interviewee are signified by use of the present tense, or by the introductory phrase 'According to . . .', but seldom otherwise. Thus, 'John Brown says,' etc., or, 'According to John Brown', indicates that his remarks were made in an interview with me; but 'John Brown *said*' (recalled, complained, etc.) means that the statement is taken from a book or an article, which the reader will find referred in the Notes.

As regards the sensitive issue of the words 'Negro', 'black', 'Afro-American', etc., I ought to say that I have in general followed Baldwin himself. After about 1972, the term 'Negro' passed out of common usage, and it does so at roughly the same stage in this book.

This portrait of James Baldwin is offered not as a definitive picture but as a host of sketches and perceptions aiming towards a definition, yet finally backing down from one. No one, Baldwin used to say, can be described. In my view, it is more true of him than anyone.

James Campbell, June 1990

Acknowledgements

I am grateful in particular to Vera Chalidze and Caryl Phillips for their consistent help and advice, and to many other people, including Ernest Allen of the University of Massachusetts at Amherst, Gidske Anderson, David Baldwin, Gloria Baldwin, Richard Baron, Ann Birstein, Mary Blumenau (née Keen), Eugene Braun-Munk, Emile Capouya, Engin Cezzar, William Rossa Cole, Robert Cordier, Frank Corsaro, the staff of DeWitt Clinton High School, Fanny Dubes, Fern Marja Eckman, Michel Fabre, Eileen Finletter, Jamey Gambrell, Stanley Geist, Richard Gibson, Michael Greenberg, Lucien Happersberger, Bernard Hassell, Jim Haynes, Gordon Heath, Cathy Henderson of the Harry Ransom Humanities Research Center, University of Texas at Austin, Kenton Keith, Yashar Kemal, Ann Kjellberg, Jim Lesar, Norman Mailer, Bertrand Mazodier, Sheila Murphy, Leonard Nelson, Richard Newman of the New York Public Library, Barbara Nordkvist, Zeynep Oral, Edward Parone, E. M. Passes, William Phillips and *Partisan Review*, Norman Podhoretz, Michael Raeburn, David Ross, William Shawn, Leslie Schenk, Jim Silberman, George Solomos (a.k.a. Themistocles Hoetis), Will Sulkin, Gulriz Sururi, Raleigh Trevelyan, Diana Trilling, Bosley Wilder, Ellen Wright. I am also grateful to the Authors' Foundation and to the US Information Service for generous assistance towards the costs of travel.

Publisher's Acknowledgements

The publishers gratefully acknowledge permission to reprint copyright material:

The James Baldwin Estate for permission to quote the following: the poems 'Black Girl Shouting' and 'To Her'; the extract from the short story 'Peace on Earth'; the extract from the director's notes for *Fortune and Men's Eyes*; the extract from 'Giovanni's Room: A Screenplay'. All this material remains copyright of the James Baldwin Estate.

Doubleday, New York, for permission to quote from the following works by James Baldwin: *Go Tell it on the Mountain*, copyright © 1952, 1953 by James Baldwin; *Nobody Knows my Name*, © 1954, 1956, 1958, 1959, 1960, 1961, The James Baldwin Estate; *Going to Meet the Man*, copyright © 1951, 1957, 1958, 1960, 1965 by James Baldwin; *The Fire Next Time*, copyright © 1962, 1963 by James Baldwin; *Blues for Mister Charlie*, copyright © 1964 by James Baldwin; *No Name in the Street*, copyright © 1972 by James Baldwin; *Tell Me How Long the Train's Been Gone*, copyright © 1968 by James Baldwin; *If Beale Street Could Talk*, copyright © 1974 by James Baldwin; *The Devil Finds Work*, copyright © 1976 by James Baldwin; *Just Above My Head*, copyright © 1978, 1979 by James Baldwin.

Beacon Press, for permission to quote from *Notes of a Native Son*, © 1953, renewed 1955, by James Baldwin.

The lecture 'The Position of the Negro Artist and Intellectual in American Society' by Richard Wright, copyright © the Estate of Richard Wright.

The correspondence of Langston Hughes, copyright © George Houston Bass, Surviving Executor of the Estate of Langston Hughes.

The diaries of Richard Burton, reprinted from *Richard Burton: A Life 1925–1984*, by Melvyn Bragg, copyright © 1988 by Sally Burton.

The Grave of Alice B. Toklas and Other Reports from the Past by Otto Friedrich, copyright © 1989 by Otto Friedrich, published by Henry Holt and Company, Inc.

It was a severe cross, and I took
it up reluctantly. The truth was,
I felt myself a slave, and the idea
of speaking to white people weighed
me down. I spoke but a few moments,
when I felt a degree of freedom, and
said what I desired with considerable
ease. From that time until now, I have
been engaged in pleading the cause of
by brethren . . .

Narrative of the Life of Frederick Douglass,
an American Slave, Written by Himself, 1845

How many heartfuls of sorrow shall
balance a bushel of wheat?

W. E. B. DuBois
The Souls of Black Folk, 1903

PART I

No Story, Ma

'At some point in my history I became Baldwin's nigger. That's how I got my name.'

James Baldwin, London, 1968

Chapter One

'I never had a childhood,' James Baldwin told a French interviewer in 1974. To a journalist ten years earlier, he proclaimed, 'I did not have any human identity.' To his French interviewer he added, for good measure, 'I was born dead.'

He was in fact born in the Harlem Hospital at 135th Street and Lenox Avenue, New York City, on 2 August 1924, illegitimate, James Arthur to Emma Berdis Jones. She was not yet twenty years old and lately arrived in New York City from Deals Island, Maryland, caught in the northward drift which was sweeping thousands of her race and generation out of the strictly segregated Southern states. Emma Berdis knew the name of her first child's father, but she would not tell her son, and he never found out. 'I never had a childhood' means, partly, 'I never had a father.'

Before embarking on the story of a writer's life, it is customary to offer some discussion of his ancestry; but what to do about this writer's? His mother had conceived her son 'in sin' – as she herself, a devout Christian woman, would have felt – and then closed the door on the subject. The name Jones was within three years changed to Baldwin, which never felt properly his own: passed on to James through his mother's husband David, who was not his father, through *his* father, who had been born a slave.

If it was necessary to isolate a single, dominating impulse driving James Baldwin's work, it would be the need to defeat the silence which lies behind slavery and his people's first forced arrival in America – the Land of the Free, as Baldwin never tired of ironically repeating. The voice of his ancestors echoes through his pages, filtering black biblical rhetoric and blues and gospel lyrics through the autobiographical mode he adopts to tell his own singular story – the story of all his race – again and again, from first to last.

'I was born,' Baldwin also said, 'in the church', meaning not only that his mother was devout and his stepfather a preacher, but that the moral world in which he grew up was fortified and sanctioned by generations of deep believers. He learned something of the power of language in the church – in the pulpit, as a boy-preacher. He would turn his back on his faith by the time he was seventeen, but although he left the church, the church never left him. Would he have reiterated that he was 'born in the church' if it had? The prophesy of wrath and the quest for salvation shaped his imagination, just as the vocabulary and cadence of the King James Bible and the rhetoric of the pulpit were at the heart of his literary style.

In 1927 Emma Berdis had married David Baldwin, a labourer and a Baptist minister who preached in New Orleans and later in Harlem. Born in the small town of Bunkie, Louisiana, he had come north in 1919. According to his stepson,* writing in 1955, David Baldwin had left the South partly because of an inability to communicate with people, to establish ordinary social relationships, and also because his puritan soul recoiled at the prospect of New Orleans, with its vaudeville associations, as a new-world Sodom and Gomorrah.

This is a convincing 'domestic' explanation of a difficult personality acting to resolve a spiritual crisis. Later on, however, Baldwin would reinterpret his father's problems and say that he had fled the South because 'lynching had become the national sport'.

Here we come upon the first instance of a recurring characteristic: an interpretation of events which is not quite a misinterpretation, but, rather, a heightened reading, made in retrospect, but with the benefit of what might be termed 'hind-second-sight'. This reading uses facts somewhat as a poet might treat them; that is not to say it abuses them, but that it attempts to forge them into the kind of truth which goes beyond matters of fact. It is less dramatic (though perhaps no less disturbing) to say that a forebear changed his locale out of personal difficulties than to suggest that he was fleeing the lynch mob. Yet Baldwin is most certainly not lying or romanticizing: lynching was indeed the terror of the South. In 1919, when David Baldwin left, lynchings were commonly reported in New Orleans newspapers, were not greatly condemned, and were divided into 'good lynchings' and 'bad' – the latter being those deemed unduly brutal.

---

* Baldwin usually referred to David Baldwin as his father, and to himself as David's son; from now on, that is how their relationship will be described here.

Nevertheless, Baldwin's father probably left New Orleans, as he himself would later quit New York, for a complex of reasons, the general lawlessness towards blacks having as much to do with it as anything else. What is a traditional literary device – compression, the arrangement of details in a certain order so as to charge them with significance – commonly becomes in Baldwin's hands a way of re-reading and re-telling his own life story.

David Baldwin was much older than Emma Berdis Jones. His mother, Barbara, who lived with the family in New York and died when James was seven, had been a slave, and David himself was born possibly before the Emancipation in 1863. His son did not know exactly how old he was, only that he was 'very, very old when he died', but the younger of David's two brothers, George, was born in 1866.

David had been married previously and had had children. There was a daughter who was as old as his new wife. His youngest son from his first marriage, Samuel, was eight years older than James and also lived with him and Berdis as part of the family in New York. Another son from the earlier marriage was called David, and the same name was given to his fourth son by Berdis. David Baldwin senior was very dark – 'like pictures I had seen of African tribal chieftains' – although he had a half-brother who was, in effect, 'white', conceived by Barbara and her white master: 'Daddy's distant eyes, the same tension in the mouth ... Strange, to see your father in whiteface.' The implications of this aspect of miscegenation meant a great deal to Baldwin and came to occupy a place at the centre of his philosophy: American racism was a sin against the blood.

Although the Baldwins stayed at a number of different addresses in New York, it was always in Harlem: Lenox Avenue on the west, the Harlem River on the east, 135th Street on the north and 130th Street on the south. 'We never lived beyond those boundaries; this is where we grew up.' In 1924, the year of Baldwin's birth, Harlem was still a mixed district. The 'turning over' of white to black in the new corridors of tenements from 130th Street upwards had begun only ten years earlier. Germans, Greeks, Irish, Jews and others still shared the stairways with black neighbours, though the influx from the South was rapidly giving the blacks a majority.

Many of these tenements are gone now, and in their places stand redbrick blocks of flats which have themselves already shaded into the tones of the ghetto. The six blocks between 130th and 135th Streets, where Baldwin grew up, have deteriorated into one of the worst slums in the Western world, where the scars of poverty, drug and alcohol addiction, violence and racism show on almost every face in the street. Even as a child, Baldwin claimed, he was conscious of a distinction between his kind of life and the other. 'When you go downtown you discover that you are literally in the white world. It is rich ... People walk about as if they owned where they are – and indeed they do ... You know – you know instinctively – that none of this is for you.'

If he went downtown, instinct could give way to explicit instruction. 'Why can't you niggers stay uptown where you belong?' a policeman was heard to mutter as Baldwin was on his way to the public library on 42nd Street. Once, when out in his own neighbourhood collecting firewood, he was taken to a vacant lot by two white policemen and questioned about a crime; they searched him, then left him, a ten-year-old boy, flat on his back on the waste ground.

The first house he remembered was on Park Avenue – 'which is not the American Park Avenue,' he told the sociologist Kenneth Clark in 1963, pointing to the gulf between the image suggested by the grand street name and the reality of its uptown squalor (adding, with typical bitter humour, 'or maybe it *is* the American Park Avenue'). Dressed formally in a Homburg hat and dark suit, David Baldwin travelled out to Long Island every day throughout the 1920s and 1930s to work at a soft-drinks bottling factory. On Sundays or in the evenings he preached sermons in Pentecostal storefront churches. He gave little to his wife's son, in terms of affection or otherwise: 'If it ever entered his head to bring a surprise home for his children, it was, almost unfailingly, the wrong surprise'; and in turn James Baldwin grew to hate the man whom he believed, until his teens, to be his father. What paternal love existed in the household was reserved for David Baldwin's son by the earlier marriage, Samuel, but this also went unrewarded: in 1932, Sam, then seventeen, left home vowing not to return until his father's funeral, a vow which he kept.

'*As for me and my house*,' David Baldwin preached, '*we will serve the Lord.*' He could serve little else. A man with few friends and no money, he was an ineffective head of household, and the sight of his two eldest sons going out to work as shoeshine boys, and of his wife cleaning the houses and doing the laundry of well-off whites, did nothing for his morale. Unable to pay the rent, or to make the landlord carry out basic repairs to their crumbling apartments, forced to send Jimmy to buy day-old bread at discount prices, about the only thing David Baldwin seemed capable of producing was yet another mouth to feed. Finding it impossible to impose his authority on the world outside, he exercised tyrannical power under his own roof. His wife addressed him as 'Mr Baldwin'. Dressed in bathrobe and slippers, he moved around the house, one of Baldwin's schoolfriends recalled, 'like a dark cloud. I remember one instance when he ordered Jimmy to do something and Jimmy said he had to study. His father looked at him and said, "Cease studying."' There were beatings, insults, furious arguments between husband and wife, and between David and his sister Barbara, who also shared their cramped, cold-water flats. Baldwin remembered his father 'locked-up in his terrors; hating and fearing every living soul including his children ... his long silences punctuated by moans and hallelujahs and snatches of old songs while he sat at the kitchen window'. Finally, in the early 1940s, blinded by paranoia and refusing to eat – he thought his family was trying to poison him – David Baldwin went mad.

Baldwin wrote much about his childhood, and almost without exception his memory speaks of misery and confusion. As the family increased in number – eventually there were nine children – the labourer's wages brought home less and less. It was almost barefoot poverty. Baldwin felt that he had 'scarcely ever' had enough to eat, and his resentment of his father veered between hatred and contempt. He believed himself to be ugly because his father told him so and called him 'frog eyes'. Equally hurtful, he thought his mother was ugly too, again because David Baldwin said so. One day, leaning out of the window, he saw a woman with thick lips and big eyes on the street, and excitedly called out to his mother to come to the window and see: 'Look, there's someone who's uglier than you and me.'

David Baldwin hated white people, and his devotion to God was mixed with a hope that God would take revenge on them for him. But in his children's eyes, his bitterness and suspicion seemed like cruelty, directed at them.

Baldwin grew up helping his mother as she brought each of her children into the world, feeding and changing them, using one hand to support a baby and the other to hold a book. He read a mixture of the prescribed and the proscribed; the former was the Bible, naturally, and the latter just about everything else. Reading was viewed with suspicion by his father, but Jimmy, constitutionally and culturally unfitted for the Harlem street corner, found that he was good at other things, that he could score points with his sharp mind and clever tongue, and that being talented in this way could help him win acceptance in the world beyond Harlem. A white teacher from his elementary school, Orilla Miller, spotted his promise and gained his parents' permission – grudging in David's case, grateful in Berdis's – to take their son to see *Macbeth* and other plays in downtown theatres. He was reading Dickens, Dostoevsky and Harriet Beecher Stowe's *Uncle Tom's Cabin* before he reached his teens, and with such concentrated intensity that his mother tried to hide the books; even then he was attempting to write himself. He was recognized, he told his French interviewer in 1974, as being '*doué*' (gifted).

David Baldwin's disapproval stemmed mainly from religious convictions, but there was another reason: bright black boys with ambition, his experience in the South had taught him, could be a menace to themselves and those around them. The element of concern buried in his father's authoritarianism became visible to Baldwin only as he grew into a man himself. At the time it seemed that each forbidding stricture was a darkening of the oppressive shadow, deepening and hardening their mutual dislike.

Harlem streets today are as full of churches with colourful names as they were fifty years ago: the Little Widow's Mite Church, the Holy Ghost Pentecostal Church, the Revival Time Pentecostal House of Prayer, the Rock Church, the Holy Tabernacle Church, Church of the Holy Agony, etc. Some are above shops, others in basements; all but a few look like anything but a church – like a sweetshop or a warehouse or a take-away. These churches are a direct transplant from the rural districts of the pre-First World War segregated South, and their religion is the fundamentalist Protestant sect called Pentecostalism. Among its practices and beliefs are faith healing, speaking in tongues and a ritual which in black churches is known as 'pleading the blood', a state of rapture characterized by trance as a prelude to salvation.

When the sinner fell on his face before the altar, the soul of the sinner then found itself locked in battle with Satan: or, in the place of Jacob, wrestling with the angel. All the forces of Hell rushed to claim the soul which had just been astonished by the light of the love of God . . . Only the saints who had passed through this fire – the incredible horror of the fainting of the spirit – had the power to intercede, to 'plead the blood', to bring the embattled and mortally endangered soul 'through'.

The black immigrants who came north in droves after the First World War brought their religion with them. For some, there was nothing else to bring. They were leaving the bloodstained earth of the South for the more liberal, more industrialized – if not always more prosperous – cities of the North. 'I was born into a Southern community displaced into the streets of New York,' Baldwin said. 'And what did we bring with us? What did my father bring with him? He brought with him his Bible. He, and others like him, with their Bibles and their hymn books, managed to rent a space which had been a store, and took out the fixtures, built a pulpit, got a piano, a tambourine – and it became a church.'

David Baldwin loved to sing:

> I want to be ready
> To walk in Jerusalem,
> Just like John.

The children, though they found it hard to love *him*, loved to sing too. Baldwin's sisters, when they were old enough, could form themselves into a gospel quartet, playing the piano and harmonizing in thirds and sixths:

> I want to go through, Lord,
> I want to go through.
> Take me through, Lord,
> Take me through.

The first black church in Harlem was the Gothic St Philip's Episcopal Church on West 134th Street, which was built around 1912. As a child, Baldwin went with his father to the famous Abyssinian Baptist Church on 138th Street, which was headed for many years by Adam Clayton Powell. David Baldwin never preached there, though. As his reputation dwindled, he was not much in demand, going 'from church to smaller and more improbable church'. And at the same time, his precocious son began to compete with him, becoming a preacher himself at the age of fourteen.

In 1937 Baldwin had joined the Mount Calvary of the Pentecostal Faith Church on Lenox Avenue (now demolished), known locally as Mother Horn's Church. His best friend in junior high school, Arthur Moore, worshipped there with his parents, and when he introduced Baldwin to the pastor, Mother Horn, she asked the question: 'Whose little boy are you?' –

the same question with which the dealers and racketeers on street corners had confronted and frightened him. But on this occasion, he replied simply and with his heart, 'Why, yours.'

Shortly afterwards, he followed the Moores to another church, smaller than Mother Horn's, the Fireside Pentecostal Assembly on 136th Street and Fifth Avenue (also now demolished), and it was here that, at the age of fourteen, Brother Baldwin entered the pulpit and became a Holy Roller preacher.

'There's nothing I want to do more than preach,' he had told his mother, greatly to her satisfaction. We cannot know what David Baldwin was like in the pulpit when he was at his best, but his son was described by Arthur Moore as 'good ... inspired ... very hot'. Baldwin declared candidly: 'I was a great preacher.'

In the pulpit of the Fireside Pentecostal Assembly he learned that he had authority as a speaker and could do things with a crowd. He knew the Bible so well that he coloured his phrases with Old Testament rhetoric and poetry, with full conviction. God's assistance during the preaching of a sermon – heard as a voice from heaven – was more important than its careful preparation beforehand. The ability to command an audience – to make it answer the preacher's call and move to his rhythm – counted for everything in the black churches. Inspiration, in this comparatively unsophisticated pulpit, meant more than ordination.

Just as he extemporized his sermons, so Baldwin put little or no preparation into his later public appearances, yet many of those who saw him speak will say he was the greatest orator they ever heard. Sometimes he kept a set of notes to hand when giving a lecture, but more often he had just a finishing post in mind, perhaps something freshly understood which he wished to clarify for himself as much as for his audience. The oratorical delivery also lies behind his style of writing, and the echo sounds back to the day when he became a Young Minister in the Fireside Pentecostal Assembly.

The two books which are often taken as his best – the novel *Go Tell It on the Mountain* and the essay *The Fire Next Time* – centre on this moment. Indeed, both novel and essay introduce it in the opening paragraph. The hero of *Go Tell It on the Mountain*, John Grimes, is introduced to us on his fourteenth birthday – 'Everyone had always said that John would be a preacher when he grew up' – while *The Fire Next Time* begins, 'I underwent, during that summer that I became fourteen, a prolonged religious crisis', and follows the steps which Baldwin took to the pulpit.

As a young man, Baldwin became vividly aware of the wickedness all around him, and of the temptations infesting the streets he walked every day. They were filled with junkies, winos, pimps, pickpockets, girls in shiny dresses – girls who, only a year before, had been singing beside him in church. At the time, he saw the evil which surrounded him not as an emanation of injustice, as he did later, but as a warning. Life posed a choice between salvation and damnation: to a boy born into a fundamentalist household, these were not abstractions but actualities. If it was a choice between heaven and the flames, then he would take the former. For three years he righteously spurned the pleasures – greedily pursued by his contemporaries – of cigarettes, alcohol, the cinema, sex, and the Harlem dance floor, which was only a rehearsal for sex.

As Brother Baldwin's reputation as a preacher grew, he accepted success graciously and conducted himself as a Young Minister should. But there was a growing realization that the passion of his sermons came not from a pure heart, but from vanity and ambition. For there were two preachers in the house now, and youth made him a bigger crowd-puller than his father. He pushed his advantage ruthlessly, 'for it was the most effective means I had of breaking his hold over me'.

Thus he made his 'father' into a mere 'father-figure' and, for the time being, disposed of him. By the time David died in 1943, James Baldwin, living away from home, had turned his hatred into indifference; but both the active and the passive emotion shielded him from a feeling he never lost, of having missed a father's approval – which implanted in him a lifelong yearning for it. 'The son must slay the father' become one of his mottoes, drawn, like so much of his personal theology, from the Bible. He went on to adopt another father-figure in David's place, and then another. And he slew those too.

Chapter Two

At each of the three schools he attended, all in New York, he is remembered as having been exceptionally, even uniquely, intelligent. Yet his formal education was over by the time he was seventeen. This was not by choice: he had planned to go to college, Baldwin was apt to tell people some years after leaving high school. Family economics played a major part in his decision not to, but it was also a matter of temperament. Baldwin's intellect was not the sort to store useless information or to pursue disinterested inquiry: what quickened his mind was passion, and a passionate involvement was necessary before he would pick up his pen. He wrote about other writers, for example, only when they or their books had made a profound impression on him; he could speak about historical or political events with scant regard for facts and figures but with an eye for subtle implications which escaped the orthodox historian. At the same time he could exhibit a surprising ignorance: 'Is Scotland *joined* to England?' he asked during his first visit north of the border.

He was below average height and slightly built, with small feet and fine, elegant hands and forearms. A gap showed between his two front teeth, and his head, from a certain angle, seemed to rise upwards to a point of tufted hair. Out of his dark brown complexion bulged two enormous eyes.

His father had told him he was ugly, but that was incorrect. Baldwin may not have been tall and handsomely formed, like so many of his Harlem peers, but he had a face which was animated and magnetic, and often tender. The photographic record shows a remarkable range of portraits, from a teenage gargoyle to a black James Dean.

The Principal of his first school, Public School 24, on 128th Street between Fifth Avenue and Madison, was a woman named Gertrude Ayer, the only black person of that rank in New York City. She remembered him as slim, with 'haunted eyes': he remembered her as the one who proved to him that he need not be defined by colour. 'I remember too his mother

NO STORY, MA 13

above all other mothers,' Mrs Ayer said. 'She had the gift of using language beautifully. Her notes and her letters, written to explain her sons' absences, etc, were admired by the teachers and me. This talent transmitted through her is surely the basis of James' success. It is said that he too writes like an angel, albeit an avenging one.' More important personally to Baldwin was Miss Orilla Miller, the young mid-Westerner who introduced him to Shakespeare and who proved to be a staunch friend to the Baldwin family in adversity. She earned from Mrs Baldwin the ultimate tribute: she was 'a Christian'.

For a writer who made so much use of childhood and adolescence in other respects, Baldwin wrote surprisingly little about his actual schooldays. Of his early formative experiences, school was the least important. It had nothing like the effect on him that the church did, or his realization of the downtown/uptown divide. When he spoke about his schooldays, it was likely to be with detestation: 'I was physically a target. It worked against me, y'know, to be the brightest boy in class. And I suffered. So I really *loathed* it.'

In 1936 he enrolled in Frederick Douglass Junior High, where the poet Countee Cullen taught French and played the forward-looking role of literary advisor to the English department. Another teacher, Herman W. Porter, remembered the thirteen-year-old Baldwin as being able to write 'better than anyone in the school – from the principal on down'. Porter was faculty advisor to the school magazine, the *Douglass Pilot*; for the autumn 1937 issue the theme was to be 'The School and the Community', and Baldwin was made editor.

On a Saturday morning Porter went to the Baldwin apartment, which at the time was on Fifth Avenue. He was met at the door by the 'unbelievably poverty-stricken' household, an overwhelming swell of noise and clutter, a 'gaggle of youngsters' swarming under Mrs Baldwin's feet. Consent from the father, grudging as always, was given for the boy to accompany the teacher to the main branch of the public library on Forty-second Street, to research an article on 'the community' for the school magazine. On the bus downtown, noticing that his pupil seemed tense and drawn, Porter opened a window; when they got off the bus, Baldwin vomited all over his teacher's shoes.

Once he had recovered he was left in the library with his brief, and from an afternoon of reading turned in the article 'Harlem – Then and Now', which duly appeared in the *Douglass Pilot*.

I wonder how many of us have ever stopped to think what Harlem was like two or three centuries ago? Or how it came to be as it is today? Not many of us. Most of us know in a vague way that the Dutch lived in Harlem 'a long time ago', and let it go at that. We don't think about how the Indians were driven out, how the Dutch and English fought, or how finally Harlem grew into what it is today ...

The essay, which continues for several pages, tracing the development of Harlem from the seventeenth century to the present, is remarkable for its professional fluency and the absence of the words 'white' and 'Negro'. Although the streets of Harlem were more mixed than they are today, the private world of the Baldwins was almost exclusively black – determined by the church, by the bitter resolve of his father, and by school, Miss Miller's intercession apart.

High school was different. DeWitt Clinton High is situated not in Harlem but in the Bronx, on a long, tree-lined avenue called Moshalu Parkway. It takes a train-ride to get there from Harlem, which for Baldwin meant a daily trip out of the ghetto into a world populated by immigrants of all types, many of them Jewish, almost all of them white. The names in the graduation year-book of 1941 display the varied ethnic backgrounds of the students: Aronds, Arohnson, Asch, Aschenbrenner, Avonda, Azznara ... Of the fourteen graduates' portraits on the first page, only one – Baldwin's – is black.

His years at DeWitt Clinton coincided with his years in the pulpit. But although a young clergyman, Baldwin was not overburdened with piousness. His friends in high school were the literati, among them Richard Avedon, then an aspiring poet and later a successful photographer (and collaborator with Baldwin on *Nothing Personal*, 1964), and Emile Capouya, later to become literary editor of the *Nation* and now a New York publisher. Together, the three worked on the school magazine, the *Magpie*. Baldwin was assistant to Avedon in 1940, and in 1941 Capouya was assistant to Baldwin.

'It was perfectly apparent that he was an extraordinary kid,' says Capouya; another schoolfriend, Burton Benbow, recalls him as being 'very nervous and very witty'. Baldwin was always the maverick, always the exception, but as well as being the brightest boy in the school, he was also the poorest. He came from a family fired not by a desire for upward mobility but by religious zeal, ruled by a father who could command his son, 'Cease studying,' and tell his son's friends that they were in league with the devil. Baldwin's studying, when he got down to it, was leading not to university and a professional career but to a chain of menial jobs of the sort reserved for blacks in Northern cities.

More than twenty years after his graduation, in response to articles she had read by the now-famous Baldwin which contained uncomplimentary remarks about his native city, Marcella Whalen, a teacher at DeWitt Clinton in the 1930s and an advisor to the editors of the *Magpie*, wrote a letter to a magazine advising her old pupil to douse his radical fire and cheer up. 'I have been disappointed by your repeated harsh criticisms of New York,' Mrs Whalen said in the *National Review*, unimpressed by the eloquence of the recently published *Fire Next Time* (1963). She quoted him as saying he 'hated' the city, and as asking, 'What did I ever do to deserve so ghastly a birthplace?'

Mrs Whalen produced 'character cards' to prove how highly she and other teachers at DeWitt Clinton thought of him. Her own read:

Feb 19, 1941 – James Baldwin shows outstanding character in unselfish work as Editor of the *Magpie*. A talented and modest boy who will surely go far.

Another teacher praised the hours of work he put into reading and suggesting improvements in the work of other young writers, while Gertrude Lavery had written (May 1941):

James Baldwin was outstanding for his modest, unassuming attitude in a class where he was an intellectual giant.

Mrs Whalen had another card to play: in 1942 Baldwin had interviewed the black poet Countee Cullen for the *Magpie*, and he reported back optimistically:

'Have you found,' I [Baldwin] asked, 'that there is much prejudice against the Negro in the literary world?'
Mr Cullen shook his head. 'No,' he said, 'in this field one gets pretty much what he deserves.'

Marcella Whalen was naïve, but she was correct in one particular: Baldwin flourished on the staff of the *Magpie*. The magazine was a splendid production: well-printed, on high-quality paper, with many of the

contributions enhanced by illustrations, some of which are of a professional standard. Between 1940 and 1942, in addition to the interview with
Cullen, Baldwin published poems, short stories and short plays in the
Magpie. Here takes place the primary development of Baldwin the writer,
conscious of his proper subject-matter and already displaying a sophisticated grasp of literary devices.

Of his poems in the *Magpie*, the best is 'Black Girl Shouting', remarkable for its technical assurance and its subject:

> Stomp my feet
> An' clap my han's
> Angels comin'
> To dese far lan's.
>
> *Cut my lover*
> *Off dat tree!*
> Angels comin'
> To set me free.
>
> Glory, glory,
> To de Lamb
> *Blessed Jesus*
> *Where's my man?*
>
> Black girl, whirl
> Your torn, red dress
> Black girl, hide
> Your bitterness.
>
> Black girl, stretch
> Your mouth so wide.
> None will guess
> The way he died
>
> Turned your heart
> To quivering mud
> While your lover's
> Soft, red blood
>
> Stained the scowling
> Outraged tree.
> *Angels come*
> *To cut him free!*

Comparisons between this and the other poems Baldwin published in the *Magpie* make one wonder why he so seldom used a vernacular that came to him naturally, and within which he so ably commanded a rhythm and expressed his concerns (black protest; divine salvation). His other poems – 'To Her', 'The Dream', 'Paradise', 'Sonnet' – are plagued by the usual apprentice's inversions, archaic diction, poetical subjects and the like. Compare, for example, the clever and subtle expression of Negro reaction to cruelty in 'Black Girl Shouting' – 'stretch/Your mouth so wide./None will guess/The way he died' – with the romantic platitudes of another poem of the same date, 'To Her':

> How did we reach this Fairyland
> Of our love?
> How ventured we to soar so high
> This world above?
> How did we reach it, dearest?
> Obscure, yet clear.
> A road went winding glory-ward
> And led us here.

One answer to the question of why Baldwin did not follow the path he seems to have cleared in the former poem is contained in a letter he wrote in 1953 to Langston Hughes, the best-known Negro poet of the time and an expert in the literary employment of black dialect. Replying to an admiring note from the older man, Baldwin genially confessed that he had written a great deal of poetry while in junior high and had shown some of it to the school's literary adviser Countee Cullen. All Cullen had said was, 'It's an awful lot like Hughes.'

Baldwin's stories of the time, though they have a black content, nevertheless strain for a prose which is untouched by black speech. 'Aunt Tina' and 'The Woman at the Well', both published in the *Magpie*, foreshadow, in a minor way, his first novel. In 'Aunt Tina', a household of 'devout Christians' is disturbed by the narrator's father's sister, as the Grimes family in *Go Tell It on the Mountain* are by Aunt Florence (and as the Baldwin family were in life by David's sister Barbara). 'The Woman at the Well' has an adult preacher in Alabama remembering 'the time he had first "got religion" – two weeks after his thirteenth birthday', which recalls the later novel's opening lines: 'Everyone had always said that John would be a preacher ... Not until the morning of his fourteenth birthday did he really begin to think about it.' The story moves to a brutal conclusion, with the preacher beaten to death in an assault involving one Frank Johnson, 'chief deputy of Cullen County, Alabama, and member of the KKK'. As he dies, the preacher sees the water in the well beside which he had been attempting to convert a friendly white woman 'leaping up and springing into eternal life'.

The best of these juvenile short stories is 'Peace on Earth'. It is set in wartime, at Christmas. Three young Negro soldiers and their white comrade wait in a dug-out for the shelling to begin: 'Stan, Pete, Johnny and I were part of that much-ridiculed class of people known as "Holy Rollers" ... the only way to be entirely consecrated was to possess His Holy Spirit ... dancing, smoking, gossiping, moviegoing, and living loosely all came under the heading of sin.'

'Peace on Earth' does not sink under the weight of its religious portent and autobiographical reference, however; it contains some authentic dialogue and climaxes with an intermingling of the sounds of battle with a reading by Johnny from the Ninety-first Psalm which recalls (perhaps too vividly) Hemingway's story of less than a decade before, 'A Clean, Well-lighted Place':

Johnny read: 'He that dwelleth in the secret place of the Most High shall abide under the shadow of the Almighty.'
O, Lord, I thought, help me always to dwell in Thy secret place.
Screams, bullets, shells – far away the noise of battle. The voice went on:
'I will say of the Lord – .'
Somewhere a man was screaming – 'In him will I trust.' I trust you, Lord – help me trust you –.
'Thou shalt not be afraid' – in the darkness – the danger – your comrade's arms about you – your head on his shoulder – thou shalt be not afraid –
'For He shall – keep – thee – '

The story ends with the death of one of the soldiers, and a questioning by the narrator, Scotty, of his own faith: '"Stan," I asked miserably, "why is there no peace on earth? Christ came to bring peace."' Stan has no answer, and the final 'greater vision' is awarded to the white comrade, Johnny, who 'knew that Christ would never be recognized until the sky cracked and the earth trembled with the power and glory of His return.'

For the moment, the faith is intact. But Baldwin's scepticism was growing, and he was being drawn away from the pulpit. When the moment of his anti-conversion arrived, a white comrade again would play a crucial part – not sustaining the doubter in his faith, but helping him to break with it completely.

The boom years of the 1920s – the era of the consumer revolution, of mass production and the assembly line, of great building in New York and fortunes on the stock market – scarcely touched America's 16 million black citizens. Moreover, a population the size of Canada's could look in vain to find itself represented in national literature, art, drama or the cinema, unless to serve as nannies, doormen or grinning entertainers ('Black girl, stretch/Your mouth so wide'). Out of this determined anonymity in the 1920s emerged an abstraction called the New Negro, who embodied the aspirations of the rising generation. Simultaneously, but not coincidentally, the cultural phenomenon known as the Harlem Renaissance came into being. Among its leading lights were James Weldon Johnson, Langston Hughes, Countee Cullen, Jean Toomer and Claude McKay. Encouraged in some cases by white editors and patrons, such as Carl van Vechten and Joel and Amy Spingarn, they and others produced a stream of novels, poems, plays and essays reflecting the experience of the modern American black.

The main activity of the Harlem Renaissance took place in the years immediately before and after James Baldwin's birth. In 1924 Alain Locke was preparing an anthology to be published under the title *The New Negro*. Yet the mass of blacks in Harlem were as little affected by the so-called renaissance in their midst as they were by the 'boom' they might hear in the downtown distance. 'The ordinary Negroes hadn't heard of the Harlem Renaissance', Langston Hughes remarked in his autobiography *The Big Sea* (1945). 'And if they had, it hadn't raised their wages any.'

The Baldwin family certainly had at once more basic and more lofty concerns – food and worship – and even when he came to artistic consciousness in the early 1940s James Baldwin showed scant interest in the cultural movement which had flourished in the neighbourhood during his childhood.

The puritanical regime which his father exercised under his roof was one reason for Baldwin's lack of interest in the black renaissance; but what is more important is that from the moment he first knew he was going to be a writer – a writer or nothing at all – Baldwin set his course for the mainstream. The conditions were, to say the least, unfavourable. When he began to write in earnest in the mid-1940s, only one black writer in the history of America, Richard Wright, had been treated to national acclaim. But for Baldwin the important thing was to become an artist; to make oneself into a 'Negro writer' was to accept the patronage of the literary world, and one's place in the second rank.

While his subject-matter, even in his juvenilia, was more often than not black, like Wright and a majority of American writers of the time he looked to Europe for formal models. The evidence contained in 'Black Girl Shouting' apart, he left behind scarcely a hint that he even held an opinion about the prime movers of the Harlem Renaissance: Toomer, Johnson and McKay he never mentioned in print; Hughes was to be the subject of a scathing review in the *New York Times* in 1959; as for Cullen, who had been a teacher at Frederick Douglass Junior High School, Baldwin passed no opinion on his poems and was later unable to recall which subjects he had taught.

The first artist to exert a strong personal influence on him was not a writer at all, but a painter. By the time Baldwin met him, Beauford Delaney was already a respected and admired figure among the artistic community of Greenwich Village. Henry Miller wrote a long essay extolling the painter, 'The Amazing and Invariable Beauford Delaney', which speaks – like all accounts by those who knew him – of Delaney's gentleness, kindness and ready friendship: 'Beauford retains the green vision of a world whose order and beauty, though divine, are within the conception of man. The more men murder one another, bugger one another, corrupt one another, the greater his vision becomes.'

Born into a poor black family in Tennessee in 1901, Delaney had come north in the 1920s. To Baldwin, who met him five years before Miller paid homage, he was to prove a teacher; in the young would-be writer, more than twenty years his junior, Delaney found a willing pupil and a friend for life. Addressing a group of women prisoners at Riker's Island, New York, over three and a half decades later, Baldwin said: 'The most important person in my life was and is . . . Beauford Delaney.'

Recalling the day when he first knocked on Delaney's door in Greenwich Village in 1940, Baldwin wrote:

He had the most extraordinary eyes I've ever seen. When he had completed his instant X-ray of my brains, lungs, liver, heart, bowels, and spinal column (while I said usefully, 'Emile sent me') he smiled and said, 'Come in,' and opened the door.

He opened the door all right.

Cullen apart, Delaney was the first genuine artist Baldwin had met. His attitude towards the Harlem Renaissance poet was one of schoolboy to schoolmaster, whereas he found Delaney warm and friendly, with a gift for instruction by example. In his studio at 181 Greene Street, Baldwin heard recordings of Ella Fitzgerald, Fats Waller, Bessie Smith – all forbidden at home – and listened to the older man talk about painting. 'I learned about light . . . he is seeing all the time; and the reality of his *seeing* caused me to begin to see.'

Delaney was important not only for his aesthetic teaching, but for the precedent Baldwin found in his way of living. Delaney was neither famous nor rich; yet he was incontrovertibly an artist. And although he was a black artist, his work was not complicated – or simplified – by matters of protest. He tried above all to do his duty as a painter: to see clearly and to put down what he saw, to bear witness.

In the same year that Baldwin met Delaney, an important event took place in American letters: the publication of *Native Son* by Richard Wright, perhaps the first novel by a black American to be regarded in the literary world as a work of major significance. These two encounters – with Delaney in person, with Wright through his novel – together form the most profound influence on Baldwin in his teens. His career at the *Magpie* had already helped him chart a route to his proper subject: his people, seen through the lens of his own self. Now Beauford Delaney opened the door on a way of seeing. And Richard Wright showed that a black writer need have no fear of competing with whites on equal terms.

These meetings also had their effect on Baldwin the preacher. The sacred, it turned out, was not the only domain to scrutinize in search of the 'everlasting life'; looked at another way, perhaps the Holy Ghost might be identified here on earth, among human beings, in works of art (Baldwin had not reached the stage where salvation would be pursued via the profane). Beauford Delaney taught him that art was a way of celebrating the material world, of transcending it and returning to it something of itself in coherent, meaningful form.

Another person who played an important role in Baldwin's life at this time was his schoolfriend, Emile Capouya. It was Capouya who introduced him to Delaney, and Capouya who told him, when he was sixteen and undergoing a crisis of faith, that it was cowardly to remain in the church only because he was afraid to leave it.

By 1941, according to Capouya, Baldwin was 'in the church but not of it. He said that it was socially impossible for him to leave the church.' When the Young Minister finally summoned the courage to prise himself away, it was with Capouya's help, and the symbolic lever was art.

'There was no love in the church', Baldwin wrote later:

It was a mask for self-hatred and despair. The transfiguring power of the Holy Ghost ended when the service ended, and salvation stopped at the church door. When we were told to love everybody, I had thought that meant *everybody*. But no. It applied only to those who believed as we did, and it did not apply to white people at all.

This decisive moment was recounted in different versions and at different times, once again displaying Baldwin's tendency to shade or highlight a detail, for dramatic effect.

In 1964 Baldwin told Fern Marja Eckman, who was interviewing him for a book-length portrait, how, after his final sermon, he sneaked out of the Fireside Pentecostal Assembly before the end of the service and never went back. The text for his sermon was 'Set thy house in order . . . ' – it was a sermon to himself, Baldwin said. He tiptoed away from his seat in the front row, met a friend and went to a matinée of *HMS Pinafore*.

To a reporter from *Life* magazine the year before, he had given roughly the same story, with the same matinée. But when he came to write about the incident in his 1976 study of the role of blacks in American film, *The Devil Finds Work*, Baldwin touched it up for dramatic purposes. The friend is named as Capouya, who challenged him to leave the church, saying that he would buy two tickets for a Broadway matinée on Sunday and that the two should meet on the steps of the public library on 42nd Street in time for curtain-up. However, here the matinée is not Gilbert and Sullivan but Orson Welles's stage version of Richard Wright's *Native Son*, which opened on Broadway on 25 March 1941. Baldwin introduces this new ingredient tentatively – 'I am fairly certain that the matinée, that Sunday, was *Native Son*' – but from there rushes forward to insist on the moment's importance to him: 'I will not forget Canada Lee's performance [as Bigger Thomas, in the leading role] as long as I live . . . his physical presence gave me the right to live.'

Half a century later, Capouya is unable to confirm either version, believing that he was taken to see both productions by his sister: 'Working-class kids around 1941 could not manage the price of two matinée tickets ... Going under my own steam – and buying two tickets – seems out of the question.'

It is possible that the event has simply slipped Capouya's mind, of course; but what matters is the way Baldwin reworked his autobiography for self-dramatization. It is no accident that by 1975, when the *Native Son* 'red herring' – as Capouya now refers to it – turns up, Baldwin was a more self-consciously black writer than he was in 1963–4. How much more appropriate, how much more just, for a budding young Negro writer to be converted by means of the greatest black novel of the time than by an English comic operetta.

In any case, the moment was crucial, liberating him from a crutch and bringing new personal freedom, but also causing a severe breach within the family. What's more, it bred a contradiction, for in a sense Baldwin never left the church. Although his faith was made secular, he retained his belief in the philosophy to which the church had first introduced him, but in which, in his eyes, the church had failed: *love thy neighbour as thyself* – or, translated into the mature Baldwin's humanist terms, 'People will only face in your life what they are prepared to face in their own.'

In the DeWitt Clinton graduation year-book, beside his photograph and nickname, Baldy, Baldwin's ambition is given as 'Novelist-playwright'. All students were asked to make a comment upon graduating: Baldy's is 'Fame is the spur and – ouch!'

When he left school in the summer of 1941, it was with the intention of continuing to City College, New York, a free school attended mainly by less-well-off students. But college was not for him: as the eldest child in the family and the first to be able to earn a wage, he had to help his parents feed the seven other children. Among many labouring jobs he took in the following years was one in the employ of the United States Army in New Jersey in 1942. It was the second year of US involvement in the war, and it was to help build the Army Quartermaster Depot at Belle Mead, near Princeton, that Baldwin took a job as a railroad hand, laying track.

Once again, Capouya was the agent. He and Baldwin stayed at the home of Capouya's friend Tom Martin, a foreman at the plant, in a tiny place called Rocky Hill. The wages were good – $80 a week, compared to the $30 or so he could expect to find in New York – but the work was hard, and when it came to being a railroad hand, Baldwin, though described by friends of the time as 'wiry' and 'muscular', was not an enthusiastic worker. 'He was lazy,' Capouya recalls. 'He used to walk trailing his shovel behind him, and the people who ran the place soon got fed up with that.'

It was in New Jersey that the event took place to which Baldwin, looking back in his 1955 essay 'Notes of a Native Son', ascribed another conversion. It was, however, the reverse of the spiritual coin, and an important stage in the quest which now concerned him: not for a place at the feet of Jesus, but for his own identity. What kind of American was he if America confined him to a poverty-stricken slum? What kind of man would he become if he was not free to pursue his true vocation? What kind of future could he expect if he lived, like his father, at the mercy of racism and the hatred it excited inside him?

In so far as he ever forced these questions to a resolution, the process began one night in Belle Mead early in 1943. Highly strung and of an edgy disposition at the best of times, Baldwin was on the point of leaving the Belle Mead depot following a series of firings and rehirings. When he finally got the sack, it was ostensibly for taking too long a lunch-break. This he admitted was true, but there was also a racial element in the sacking.

Or was there? The tension which determined Baldwin's perceptions and movements nowadays was caused by genuine experience of racism, but it inevitably resulted in a heightened sensitivity which was apt to respond to racial injury where none existed. This was precisely the bind that was killing his father.

Segregation existed there in New Jersey, however, and, with mainly white friends, Baldwin was always coming up against it. 'We don't serve Negroes here,' a young black man or woman entering a cafeteria could be told. 'It was the same story all over New Jersey,' he wrote, 'in bars, bowling alleys, diners, places to live. I was always being asked to leave.'

Until his final day at work, he had succeeded in treating this social perversity with a mixture of pained amusement and forced contempt. On what was supposed to be a last-night fling, however, he entered a place called The American Diner – the irony was not lost on him – with a relative of Tom Martin's. When he was greeted by the old refrain, 'We don't serve Negroes here', something snapped in him. He parted from his friend and wandered into the night, eventually entering a restaurant so plush that 'not even the intercession of the Virgin would cause me to be served':

I rather wonder, until today, what I could possibly have looked like. Whatever I looked like, I frightened the waitress who shortly appeared, and the moment she appeared all my fury flowed towards her. I hated her for her white face, and for her great, astounded, frightened eyes. I felt that if she found a black man so frightening, I would make her fright worthwhile.

She did not ask me what I wanted, but repeated, as though she had learned it somewhere, 'We don't serve Negroes here.' . . . Somehow, with the repetition of that phrase, which was already ringing in my head like a thousand bells of a nightmare, I realized that she would never come any closer and that I would have to strike from a distance. There was nothing on the table but an ordinary water-jug half full of water, and I picked this up and hurled it with all my strength at her. She ducked and it missed her and shattered against the mirror behind the bar.

With a mob at his back he left the restaurant, and managed to escape. On reflection, he saw that he had been a step away from destroying not just another person, but himself. He realized, as he wrote in 'Notes of a Native Son', the essay which charts his passage from boyhood to maturity, from service in an exhausted church to the revelation of a spiritual humanism, 'that my life, my *real* life, was in danger, and not from anything other people might do but from the hatred I carried in my own heart'.

'Notes of a Native Son' was Baldwin's first *tour de force* in the genre in which he was to excel, the autobiographical essay. It uses the Belle Mead incident only as a prelude to two events of yet greater significance: the death of his father and, on the same day, 29 July 1943, the birth of his baby sister. David's funeral took place on 2 August – the day of Jimmy's nineteenth birthday and also the day of a savage race riot in Harlem. In the opening paragraph of the essay, Baldwin skilfully dovetails the death, the birth, the birthday and the riot, to show how it seemed, in the conscience of the young former clergyman, that God himself 'had devised, to mark my father's end, the most sustained and brutally dissonant of codas', that the violence all around was meant 'as a corrective for the pride of his eldest son'.

Some of these events are treated in contemporary correspondence, with an occasional difference in shading in the detail. Writing to a friend Stephen D. James, who had been drafted into the army at the turn of

1942–3, Baldwin makes it plain that, while it left him without a job, his dismissal from the depot was hardly a cause for regret. From where he was sitting, he told James on 14 February 1943, everything was fine. He was living in Princeton, with plenty of time for writing, although the poems he had produced lately were for the most part 'junk'. The details of his last night in Belle Mead are not mentioned.

Baldwin's true subject, he had begun to realize even by 1943, was his difficult history, but he had not yet gained the confidence to place himself at the centre of that history and treat himself as its prime representative. Much of his best writing concerns things which happened in his family, or close to it, up to the time of his father's death. But it would need a dozen or more years and the space of an ocean before these events could be persuaded to yield up the stuff of myth in essays such as 'Notes of a Native Son'.

David Baldwin had been unwell for a year and had lost his mind. One night he wandered out of the house and Jimmy had to go searching for him in the streets; he was found sitting on a low wall in the darkness, staring at nothing. Now he was confined to an institution on Long Island and, according to his doctors, his condition was serious.

Writing again to Stephen James in December, Baldwin said that he thought, quite impersonally, that his father would probably die. 'He had never meant very much to me.' They had never succeeded in being father and son. Once his father was taken to hospital, however, he learnt something which did rouse him: his mother was expecting another child – her ninth. The head of the family was dying, financial and domestic matters had reached a desperate pass, and now – another baby! It seemed like a mocking last exit.

He found a job in a New York meat-packing factory, at the paltry rate of $29 a week – a reduction of more than 150 per cent on his Belle Mead earnings. It was obvious, he told his friend, that, failing an inheritance, he could do nothing for the family. And as long as he was trying to aid the family, he could do nothing for himself.

On Wednesday 28 July, Baldwin made his only visit to see his father on Long Island. Whatever he expected, it was not what he saw: a skull with deep eye sockets pressed into it; black skin making a ghoulish contrast against white sheets; the mouth slightly foaming, the eyes glazed. A skeleton more than a man, connected to life by a tangle of tubes.

Together with the aunt who had accompanied him, he left the hospital in shock and went home. Next morning a telegram arrived to say that David Baldwin had died. He was over eighty years old. Berdis Baldwin had hysterics. She went into labour, and produced her ninth child, a girl – amazingly, born alive and healthy.

Her eldest son, now twice-fatherless, went out and tramped the streets of the city, wondering how on earth to bury a body and nourish a baby – not to mention seven other children, the eldest of whom was fourteen – on $29 a week, less tax.

With the help of relatives, the money for the funeral was eventually raised, and the family gathered in church on 2 August. While they were there, a riot broke out in Harlem. In the lobby of the Hotel Braddock on 125th Street, a well-known hang-out for soldiers and girls who wanted to meet soldiers, a black serviceman had been fired at by a white policeman. Word spread that the soldier had been shot in the back and was dead (both untrue), and a mob congregated in front of the entrance to the hotel before spreading out along 125th Street and up Seventh, Eighth and Lenox Avenues, setting Harlem on fire. The following morning the family took the coffin to the graveyard for burial. They drove, Baldwin wrote in 'Notes of a Native Son', taking the metaphor of divine retribution a step further, 'through a wilderness of plate glass'.

Baldwin returned to work at the meat-packers but on his first day back passed out; he left the building and didn't return. He started a new job a few days later, but something alarming was happening to him: the very sight of a factory, the knowledge that he had to be there eight or ten hours a day, filled him with revulsion. There began a period of drifting. He told Stephen James that he passed most of his nights in Village bars and cafeterias, sleeping during the day and prowling the streets at night. Another friend from the time, the poet Harold Norse, recalled his first encounter with Baldwin, in the small hours of a night in 1943:

As we left the cafeteria in the fog and bitter cold, a small black youth loped swiftly towards us through the mist, a woolen Navy watch cap pulled down around his ears, his wild eyes bugging out alarmingly, giving him the crazed look of a junkie about to kill for a fix. Wearing only a torn blue sweater over a thin shirt, he was shivering. He looked as if he'd gladly cut our throats for a quarter.

By the winter of 1943, he had recovered sufficiently to take yet another job – elevator boy in Wannamaker's department store – and to lead as close to a normal life as possible. Putting a brave face on the daily grind, he made the best of his artistic impulses, so various and powerful that he must have felt overwhelmed as much by their revelations as by the darkness of his domestic chaos.

He was reading Shakespeare, Milton's 'Lycidas', Thomas Wolfe, T. S. Eliot; he urged Stephen James to seek out and read Eliot's poem 'The Love Song of J. Alfred Prufrock'. Encouraged by what he had discovered in the studio of Beauford Delaney, he was learning about the line and balance of painting – in particular, he loved Rembrandt and Degas. He was even thinking of enrolling in drama school, once he had the money. He joked, in a rare allusion to colour in his correspondence with James, that he might get to play Othello – quipping that that would be a real break for Shakespeare.

'Jimmy had a concise, accurate way of putting things, with a rapid delivery', Harold Norse wrote, recalling the ragamuffin whose acquaintance he made in Greenwich Village in 1943. 'His mind was nimble . . . he sounded like an educated white man.' In his letter of December 1943 to Stephen James, he enclosed a number of recent poems and asked for his friend's opinion. But '1st Person Singular: Lament', 'On Hearing Handel's *Messiah*' and '3 a.m.' show only that he had failed to build on the technical success of 'Black Girl Shouting'. Surprisingly, given his admiration for Eliot, he was still a victim of archaisms and stilted rhyme-schemes. '1st Person Singular', however (which Baldwin told James was written in the early morning in an all-night cafeteria), contains a comment on the recent events. The world's 'booming voice' speaks into the young poet's ear, commanding him to go out and provide for 'those ill-begotten', assuring him that he will outgrow the 'nonsense' of poetry and art in good time.

It is doubtful that he ever again spoke of his eight brothers and sisters as ill-begotten. But his despair is easily understood. His idea of himself as an artist was lost in the murk of the ghetto. Yet it was the only idea of himself he had.

Chapter Three

A year and some months after the funeral, at the end of 1944, Baldwin met the man he had already appointed to be his father's deputy: Richard Wright.

His longing for someone to look up to and learn from, who could exercise authority without cruelty, who would approve effort, and even more success, was complicated by the discovery that the man he called father, and with such bitterness, was not his father after all. The discovery took place before David died, while Baldwin was still at school; Capouya recalls him sitting on a park bench, relaying the news through tears.

It is less likely to have been the stigma of illegitimacy that troubled him – though, since he was a Christian at the time, that would have mattered – than the shock of realizing that a central plank of the deck was no longer there, had never existed. Although at times he had hated the man, hatred was mitigated by blood: after all, he *is* my father.

Beauford Delaney, older and much respected though he was, was by temperament unsuited for a paternal role, and Baldwin regarded him more as a friend. But Wright, at thirty-six, was the famous and successful novelist Baldwin was hoping to be. As he had competed and quarrelled with his stepfather, so he would compete with Wright – on the page – and, eventually, quarrel with him too. The relationship deepened in complexity when the two men were reunited in Paris in 1948; soon after that it became sour, and, at least according to Wright, vicious. This might have been because the adoption process which Baldwin had set in motion was not mutually acknowledged: to Wright, Jimmy Baldwin was just a talented boy whom he was pleased to help.

In the three years between their meeting and Wright's final departure for France in 1947, relations between him and Baldwin were quite frank and simple. Baldwin had read the novel *Native Son*, in which the brutish hero Bigger Thomas murders the white girl Mary, and he had also – whether on the day of his defection from the church or on another day – seen Canada

Lee's arresting performance in the stage version, which struck him as 'terrifying'. When he knocked on Wright's door in Lefferts Place, Brooklyn, where the novelist lived with his wife Ellen and their baby daughter, he expected to be greeted by a similarly intimidating figure. Instead Wright met him with a smile, 'faintly, mockingly conspiratorial', a salute of 'Hey, boy!' and a bottle of bourbon.

In one of the trio of memorial pieces which he wrote after Wright's death, Baldwin recalled this first encounter:

I did not drink in those days, did not know how to drink, and I was terrified that the liquor, on my empty stomach, would have the most disastrous consequences. Richard talked to me or, rather, drew me out on the subject of the novel I was working on then. I was so afraid of falling off my chair and so anxious for him to be interested in me, that I told him far more about the novel than I, in fact, knew about it, madly improvising, one jump ahead of the bourbon, on all the themes which cluttered up my mind. I am sure that Richard realized this, for he seemed to be amused by me.

For Baldwin, the real purpose of the meeting was to persuade Wright to read the extant pages, numbering about fifty, of an early version of *Go Tell It on the Mountain* called 'Crying Holy'. Wright, generous then and always with younger authors, agreed to do so. He did better: in the new year he helped Baldwin obtain a grant of $500 from the Eugene F. Saxton Memorial Trust – the first tangible recognition, outside the pages of the school magazine, of Baldwin's aspiration to become a writer.

'Crying Holy', which had the alternative provisional title of 'In my Father's House', was worked and reworked until it died – almost. Like the stories in the *Magpie*, it provided the kindling for Baldwin's first published novel.

Two days after Christmas 1945, he wrote to Wright from upstate New York where he was then living, having been forced out of the city by what he calls 'the housing shortage', a curiously discreet phrase given his (and Wright's) experience with landlords and property agents. It would not be unusual, for example, for a friend of Baldwin's to rent a place and move in first, establishing a confident relationship with the superintendent; only then would Baldwin follow. The superintendent might or might not object; or the neighbours might protest directly to the owner. If so, then Baldwin would have to leave.

His book, he told Wright, was completing itself: it still lacked a great deal, but he felt that he could do no more to it once this final draft was finished. It takes a long time to learn how to write a novel, Baldwin admits with engaging candour: he had scarcely begun. In the meantime, though, he had the money. The award, he said, was one of the most wonderful things that had ever happened to him. He gave some of it to his mother, and then, in a 'fine careless rapture', and with a recklessness concerning finance that was to remain constant, spent the rest as quickly as he could.

The master–pupil relationship at this point can be gauged from the fact that, one year after their introduction, Baldwin is still addressing him as 'Dear Mr Wright'. He saw Wright once more before the latter left for a visit to Europe, which led to greater familiarity. 'Dear Richard' he begins his next letter, and immediately apologizes for troubling him. What he is after is a literary contribution to a foundling magazine with which he is associated. An enclosed sheet sets out the magazine's prospectus. He is taking the liberty of contacting Wright in Paris, Baldwin explains, because (a) he is one of the group of people mentioned in the opening paragraph ... and (b) because he has never before had the opportunity of writing to anyone in France. His novel was being discussed at Harper's, who administered the Saxton Trust, and he was developing drafts and sketches of another under the provisional title 'Still Life', which was to be an 'intense study' of a New England spinster.

He assured Wright that the people involved in setting up the magazine – which leaves no sign of having progressed beyond its proposal – were without marked political affiliations. This shows respect towards the older writer's sense of propriety (he was already at that time, and from then on, under investigation by the FBI for Communist ties) but does not reflect Baldwin's own concerns; these were years when he himself was flirting with socialist groups and standing on picket lines.

Mention of colour is absent from his letters to Wright, but the problems of colour were very much present in his life, and in Wright's. In 1945 the Wrights had failed to buy a house in Vermont, and only succeeded in gaining the title to an apartment in Charles Street, New York, by means of a ploy which involved paying in cash and having the deeds signed before the vendors realized they were selling to a black person. From May 1946 until January 1947, Wright and his family stayed in France as guests of the newly liberated French government, and the interlude had a refreshing and purgative effect, expelling the horrors of racism from his mind and soul. Their return brought renewed anxiety about his own and his family's safety, however (as a black spokesman with a white wife, Wright was especially conspicuous and vulnerable), and in August 1947 the Wrights left America again, this time to settle in Paris for good.

On hearing the news of Wright's sponsored trip during the second half of 1946 Baldwin gaily declared, 'It's a very wonderful thing to have happened.' The only other person he would have liked it to happen to, he jokes, is himself. He has dreamed of visiting France since he was twelve, he says, and he signs off with love to Paris and Le Havre. The lack of mention of colour problems seems almost wilful, for within eighteen months Baldwin would follow in his mentor's footsteps and his departure would be for the same reasons.

Although he had by now quit Harlem he had not abandoned his family. But supporting them on wages drawn from the sorts of job he could find was just not possible. So he took a second job, which meant he was running Wannamaker's elevator during the day and sweeping its floors at night. Writing under these circumstances was very difficult. The Saxton money was gone and his novel, in its current version, could not find a publisher (his main hope, Harper's, had rejected it). What free time he had, Baldwin spent hanging round bars in Greenwich Village, the San Remo and the Riviera, getting drunk, sometimes belligerent, always, by the end of the night, penniless.

'Desolate demoralization' was the phrase he used to describe his situation. These were the sorts of pressures that killed his friend Eugene Worth. One night in 1946, at the age of twenty-four, Worth hurled himself from the George Washington Bridge. The irony of the bridge's name was not lost on Baldwin, and sixteen years later he resurrected his friend for the character of Rufus in *Another Country*.

As if there was not enough to cope with that year, he also faced a different kind of trouble, personal and confusing. He dropped a hint, though no more, in a letter to Stephen James: he was 'screwed up'; he had lost his bearings. At the root of it was sex.

Baldwin had had girlfriends: Jessie, a Jewish girl with whom he was in love when he was eighteen and she twenty-four; Grace, a black girl to whom he became engaged to be married around the time of the death of Eugene Worth; and there are casual mentions of others. But it was at this time that he faced up to his homosexual desires. Emile Capouya recalls him expressing some doubts about his sexual proclivities: 'But he said he'd resolved them. I thought he meant he'd had some kind of fling with a man but had sorted it all out. I didn't realize that it was the other way round – what he was trying to say was that it was mostly boys rather than girls from now on.'

Baldwin declared his homosexuality more or less immediately to new acquaintances. It was a way of getting the worst over with at once. He would force himself to say, at the outset of a friendship, 'I am a homosexual', he told his diary, so that if the other person wished to leave he could do so at once. This he knew was childish, but it derived from a fear of rejection. A friend from the time, Stan Weir, corroborated this. One night in Greenwich Village, Baldwin challenged him: 'It took you months to become fully aware that I develop relationships that include what is sexual, with men. You had known it, and did not know it, because you buried it. "Homosexual" is a hard word to accept.' This is precisely why Baldwin urged himself to own up to it, to confess, confession being the spirit's cleansing operation. 'He'll have to go through life confessing over and over,' another friend said with foresight at the time. Baldwin was determined not to treat his homosexuality like a skeleton in the cupboard – if you can't be frank about that, then until it's in the open you can't be frank about anything else.

It would not be long before, in a similar spirit, he would give a homosexual content to his writing. By 'going public' in this way, he pre-empted the shame which was usually attendant upon a homosexual life in those days. Baldwin had grown up to the shocking discovery that the colour of his skin stood between him and the possibility of life lived to its full potential – between him and life itself, in fact. He made up his mind not to allow his sexual orientation to fortify the barrier. Love is where you find it, he would say; gender, and certainly not race, is not its determinant.

Few of Baldwin's essays deal with the subject of homosexuality. One that does is 'Here Be Dragons', a series of speculations on androgyny, written towards the end of his life, but dealing chiefly with his adventures in Greenwich Village in the 1940s. Most of the white girls he had been involved with, he writes, 'had paralyzed me, because I simply did not know what, apart from my sex, they wanted'. This seems particularly hard on Jessie, the Jewish girl six years his senior about whom he had written so feverishly to Stephen James in 1943: she was wonderful, she had a brilliant mind and a brilliant personality. She was sincere. His powers of description would fail her, but he added, in a curiously tender postscript, that she was not in the least pretty . . . 'She's a swell kid.'

In any case, romantic liaisons with the opposite sex tapered off soon afterwards, though his desire for women, or perhaps for the sense of normality and orthodoxy which relationships with women conferred, was not extinguished altogether. Even in Paris he would sleep with women, though less frequently than before, and with little heart. Women always numbered among his closest friends, and he continued to attract them, but the less he made love to women the more redundant his challenging declaration of 'I am a homosexual' became.

Chapter Four

At the turn of the year 1946–7, Baldwin was an apprentice writer with a desire to prove himself, a young man in a white belted raincoat, an *habitué* of Greenwich Village with a longing to participate. And not only in writing: he wanted to act as well; he had an interest in painting; and, of course, he loved music.

The first music he discovered – the only kind that was allowed to reach his ears while his father was alive – was the music of the church. 'There is no music like that music', he wrote, referring to his days as a preacher,

no drama like the drama of the saints rejoicing . . . their pain and their joy were mine, and mine were theirs – they surrendered their pain and joy to me, I surrendered mine to them – and their cries of 'Amen!' and 'Hallelujah!' . . . sustained and whipped my solos until we all became equal, wringing wet, singing and dancing, in anguish and rejoicing . . .

When, in Beauford Delaney's studio in the Village, he began listening to Ma Rainey, Louis Armstrong, Paul Robeson, Bessie Smith, he understood how that music also had its roots in spirituals, and that many of those singers and musicians, like him, had a background in the church and had first discovered music there too. When at last he went to dance-halls, to hear his favourite jazz bands or their local equivalents, he saw how not only the music but the 'dancing . . . and rejoicing' had filtered down from sacred to secular: worshipping at the temple of the spirit or the body, Southern blacks in a Northern street were driven by the same tambourine and piano, the same rhythm and the same beat.

It was in the Village that Baldwin met Theodore Pelatowski, an artist of his own age, of Polish extraction from Connecticut. Pelatowski's main interest was painting, but he also took photographs and worked with Baldwin's old schoolfriend Richard Avedon. Together with Pelatowski,

Baldwin made a second attempt at writing a publishable book – not the improbable study of a New England spinster he had mentioned to Richard Wright, but something closer to home and, formally speaking, more original. It was non-fiction – his first proper excursion in the mode which fitted him best – and it was set in Harlem: Pelatowski's photographs of Harlem churches and dance-halls, accompanied by Baldwin's text.

The photographs survive. One is of Baldwin's first church on Lenox Avenue, above the Yo Yo Dance Club and a tailor's shop. A smartly dressed woman in a hat and spectacles is walking by, her back to the camera. Like everyone in the photograph – like everyone in all the photographs – she is black. On the windows of Mother Horn's church are printed variations, in English, French and Spanish, on the theme 'Jesus Saves'. Another church is located above the Pick-a-bone barbeque, yet another beside a Chinese laundry. There are many pictures of interiors, and an astonishing series of action shots of the church service.

Here stands Sister Reece, a grey-haired woman preacher in a silken robe and sash, one arm outstretched to point her delivery of the Lord's word. Her congregation is made up of boys and girls between the ages of eight and fifteen (including two of Baldwin's sisters). Soon they are roused to dance and sing; now they are in ecstasy, now some are rolling on the floor in what seems to be agony but is actually the next stage in their transcendant passage. One of them is unconscious, her eyes clenched shut, 'with the spirit', on 'the threshing floor', while around her other little pairs of feet continue their pattern of rejoicing. All the while, an old man plays on at the piano.

As one looks at these pictures from the turn of 1946–7, phrases more evocative of the American rock 'n' roll days of the 1950s come to mind: 'I'm gone,' 'It sends me.' The expressions, like the music, come out of the black church, however – even the phrase 'rock and roll' was born there. Baldwin's intention was to point up the vitality of the church, and show how it permeated all zones of black life. In Pelatowski's pictures of dance-halls, the same anguish and joy is visible as in those of the church, the same hands and feet responding to the same rhythm, the same embrace, the same call-and-response, from the bandstand to the dance-floor – even, it seems, the same pianist.

There are many other photographs: of church doorways, church entrances with snow on the ground, Harlem bars, the inside of the Baldwin home on 131st Street; in one picture sits the baby who was born three-and-a-half years earlier, beside an elderly woman, David Baldwin's sister. But images of the church predominate. For Southern blacks displaced on to the streets of New York, the church was where life began and ended.

It is possible that the inspiration for this book came directly from Richard Wright. Five years earlier, in 1941, Wright had published just such a compilation of text and photographs; the latter were taken from the Farm Security Administration files and were by a variety of hands, including Walker Evans. The images in Wright's *Twelve Million Black Voices* include not only run-down Southern farms but also dance-halls and Harlem storefront churches: 'On the plantation our songs carried a strain of other-worldly yearning which people called "spiritual",' Wright wrote; 'but now our blues, jazz, swing, and boogie-woogies are our "spirituals" of the city pavements.'

Baldwin and Pelatowski's attempts to sell their own set of city-pavement spirituals met with no success. Although his failures did not cause Baldwin any lasting damage as a writer, they gnawed at his morale, like all failures. In between jobs he had managed to complete 'Crying Holy', but Harper's had said no, Doubleday had said no, Vanguard had said no, and there was little to do except take it back and see what, if anything, could be salvaged. His second book had required less of the writer than the first, but that didn't make its rejection any easier to face.

This apprenticeship was eventually to bear fruit, however. During the half-decade spanning 1950–55, when Baldwin would produce highly successful writing, the church was to be his major inspiration, providing the background to fully realized work in each of the genres he favoured.

He had failed at the level which seemed most important, but Baldwin nevertheless became a professional that year. His first contribution to a major journal appeared on 12 April 1947: a review in the *Nation* of *Mother* by Maxim Gorki. It was commissioned by Randall Jarrell. Brief though it is, the mature voice of James Baldwin can be heard in it:

He is concerned, not with the human as such, but with the human being as a symbol; and this attitude is basically sentimental, pitying rather than clear . . .

This review was followed by another, of a book about Frederick Douglass, *There Once Was a Slave*, by Shirley Graham. Setting the standard as an uncompromising critic which he was to keep up during his eighteen-month stint as a regular reviewer, Baldwin roundly condemned this book about one great black leader by a woman who was the wife of another – W. E. B. DuBois. Miss Graham, Baldwin said, had made no contribution whatever to 'interracial understanding', being so 'obviously determined to Uplift the Race that she makes Douglass a quite unbelievable hero and has robbed him of his dignity and humanity alike.' The preacher's voice is being transformed into a writer's style: 'Relations between Negroes and whites ... must be based on the assumption that there is one race and we are all part of it.'

At twenty-two, Baldwin was a critic of some quality. Book-reviewing was not well paid, but to be paid at all for writing was gratifying. There was an irony in his situation: the editors who commissioned his first reviews and articles – Jarrell, Saul Levitas of the *New Leader*, Robert Warshow and Elliot Cohen of *Commentary*, Philip Rahv of *Partisan Review* – were all white. 'I had been to two black newspapers before I met these people and had simply been laughed out of the office.' And yet, what they wanted him to review mainly concerned the 'Negro problem', on which he was auto-matically assumed to be an authority by virtue of the colour of his skin. Six years on, as part of the pre-publicity for his first novel, Baldwin explained to a journalist on the *Michigan Chronicle* his reasons for giving up book-reviewing, saying that he 'baulked' at the assumption that he was a 'born expert' on the Negro problem. He wasn't necessarily claiming expertise in any other area, but he resented the specialization being so 'irresistibly' imposed on him – the limitations thus created might not, after all, be *his* limitations.

The point is well-argued; but it would appear that more often than not he left the office with a different book from the one they had offered him, for the evidence suggests that his complaints about being restricted to the 'Negro problem' are unfounded. For the *Nation*, the score was one apiece: Gorki and Douglass. For the *New Leader*, however, where Saul Levitas was the literary editor and where Baldwin did most of his reviewing, he tackled only a few books with a black content, in a list which includes, among others, an account of the Brooklyn Jewish gang the Amboy Dukes, a study of Catholic philosophy, the latest Erskine Caldwell, Hodding Carter's *Flood Crest*, *The Portable Russian Reader* and two books about Robert Louis Stevenson.

On re-reading Stevenson for the purpose of writing his review, Baldwin was surprised to find 'an element faintly disturbing' lurking beneath what he had previously seen as delightful, ornamental surfaces. It was a discovery he could relate to himself:

The relationship between David and Alan on which much of [*Kidnapped*] turns, is far more than a friendship and is certainly not the traditional Anglo-Saxon friendship. Alan is for David a father-image, a lover, a foe, a child, and, over and above all, a symbol of romance . . . Stevenson exhibits in the relationship of these two a richness and complexity of insight which does not anywhere – until Kirstie and Archie in *Hermiston* – characterize his studies of men and women.

V. S. Pritchett, editor of one of the volumes under review (*Novels and Stories*), had also observed this (as have other critics since) and Baldwin hastily expresses agreement that this does not at all indicate 'that Stevenson was homosexual', just that men, being the movers and makers of the world, were to him 'less of a riddle' than women.

His work was beginning to give him a reputation. The note appended to his scathing review of *Flood Crest* in the *New Leader* of 24 April 1948 reads 'James Baldwin is the author of the much-discussed article-review of *Raintree County*'. This refers to his notice of Ross Lockridge's highly successful novel in the issue of 10 April. Baldwin took an adverse view of the book's popularity, pouring scorn on its 'superficial sunlight' and mocking its dreamy praise of America as 'the last best hope on earth'. He rounded up his disgust at the book's avoidance of reality by saying '*Raintree County*, according to its author, cannot be found on any map: it is always summer there. He might also have added that no one lives there anymore.'

The review was handed in, but not published, before the news arrived that Ross Lockridge had committed suicide. Declining to withdraw the piece out of discretion, Saul Levitas simply asked his reviewer to add a postscript. In this, Baldwin, far from modifying his stern comments, charged full-steam ahead, explaining why he refused to tolerate Lockridge's 'affirmative' vision, whose ethics came out of 'Sunday School and Boy Scout Meetings'. If we cannot understand ourselves, Baldwin concluded, adapting his own principal ethic to form the wretched author's epitaph, 'we will not be able to understand anything.'

This first, small taste of notoriety rather shocked Baldwin, but it tested his resolve to stand his moral ground when under pressure to withdraw. He was becoming well-known among New York's intelligentsia for his range of reading and an intellectual certainty beyond his years. Mary McCarthy, who met him at this time at a lunch given by William Phillips of *Partisan Review*, found him extremely knowledgeable about literature. His reading, McCarthy recalled, was 'not coloured by colour – this was an unusual trait. He had what is called taste – quick, Olympian recognitions that were free of prejudice.'

Other people who knew Baldwin better, including Phillips himself, could adjust the focus of that perception, and see that Baldwin talked articulately, even brilliantly, about many things but not the one that preoccupied him: the rage that burned beneath his black skin.

Following his success in the Trotskyite *New Leader*, he was picked up by *Commentary*, the journal of the American Jewish Committee, edited by Elliot Cohen and Robert Warshow. It was the latter who encouraged him to write his first full-length essay, a discussion of Negro anti-Semitism entitled 'The Harlem Ghetto', which appeared in *Commentary* in February 1948. The essay 'won national comment', according to Baldwin's billing in a future issue. *Partisan Review*, probably the leading journal of the time, was also interested in him, but nothing appeared under his name until the following year, by which time he was in Paris.

Not only were the editors of these journals white; their heritage and beliefs, their entire outlook, connected them firmly with the old world. They might willingly give heed, and column space, now and then to the 'twelve million black voices' in their midst (in reality, nearer sixteen), but their radicalism, broadly speaking, was directed at problems of class and not race. At the same time, they were seriously concerned with matters of culture, especially literature, and it was in their pages, not the pages of the poetry magazines and journals of 'Negro writing' that had been open to his Harlem Renaissance forebears, that Baldwin wanted to be published.

In spite of the example of Wright, it was a somewhat freakish alliance. During the war which had just ended, for example, black and white troops had been segregated, and if it was still unusual to see a black person mixing with whites in New York, it was even more surprising to find a young Negro with no formal education beyond the age of seventeen contributing regularly to the nation's top intellectual magazines. But Baldwin impressed his employers as being reliable and bright; what's more – something editors appreciate – his articles were talked about.

He was alert to the developing conundrum of his situation. If, in spite of his ambitions, Baldwin felt that he did not really fit in with the Greenwich

Village set, no one could really say of him now that he belonged in Harlem. He had never quite been part of its street life, judging it 'wicked' while younger, and a waste of time when he grew up. His energy was reserved then for the church and now for art. A visit home these days meant returning to a cramped apartment with children underfoot and perhaps a carping relative asking when he was going to outgrow this artistic 'nonsense'. Also, his homosexuality was quite open now, and was more likely to draw base comment in Harlem than in the Village. It is not surprising, then, that he preferred to spend his time among people who at least gave the appearance of sharing his concerns.

Baldwin was later heard to complain in a general way that his early acceptance was a form of tokenism. But while there might have been an element of good will at the outset of his career, the interest which Rahv and others took in him was certainly genuine, for Baldwin was genuinely talented; men of their experience would not have tolerated a third-rater for long, even if the original appeal had been to their conscience.

Following his modest success with 'The Harlem Ghetto' in the spring of 1948, the *New Leader* published another essay in October. 'Journey to Atlanta' was based on a diary kept by Baldwin's youngest brother David during a trip to the South with a gospel quartet. This was also admired, but it was not what he wanted to do. Such pieces were more 'serious' than his book-reviews, but he really thought of himself as a writer of fiction.

Philip Rahv did him the favour of recommending his new novel – in the form of a few sample chapters and an outline – to a senior editor at Random House, but the response was no more encouraging than the previous ones had been. The editor, Robert Linscott, showed scant enthusiasm for what would eventually become *Go Tell It on the Mountain*, judging the characters and situations 'not sufficiently strong, compelling or even realized to carry the weight of the author's intention'.

It is hard to write a novel, Baldwin had admitted to Richard Wright three years before; it did not seem to be getting any easier.

There was consolation, however, during the same month: in October 1948 his first short story, 'Previous Condition', was published in *Commentary*. According to the editors, it heralded the arrival of 'an important new talent on the literary scene'. Like most of Baldwin's early work, it is indeed precocious, displaying a controlled narrative flow and an assured tone of voice, even if the voice is not yet the author's own.

The story is related in the first person, and concerns Peter, a young actor out of work in New York. Peter is the first of many artist-heroes to appear in Baldwin's fiction: often they are actors; he also created musicians, singers, writers, painters and a sculptor. Peter is down on his luck:

The show I had been in had folded in Chicago. It hadn't been much of a part – or much of a show either, to tell the truth. I played a kind of intellectual Uncle Tom, a young college student working for his race . . . here I was, back in New York and hating it.

What 'Previous Condition' succeeds so well in doing – apart from sustaining the tough, disciplined, Hemingwayesque tone already encountered in the juvenile 'Peace on Earth', which Baldwin was never to adopt again – is dramatizing the dilemma in which its author was then trapped: between two hemispheres, one black and one white.

Part of the story involves Peter's eviction from a Greenwich Village apartment, where his Jewish friend Jules has had to smuggle him in in the first place. Peter only leaves the house when the other tenants have gone to work, and returns after dark, when they are asleep. One day, inevitably, the landlady knocks on the door:

'Who are you? I didn't rent this room to you?'
My mouth was dry. I started to say something.
'I can't have no coloured people here,' she said. 'All my tenants are complainin'. Women afraid to come home at night.'

A moment later, in the face of Peter's stubbornness, she screams that she doesn't let rooms to 'coloured people':

'Why don't you go uptown, like you belong?'
'I can't stand niggers,' I told her.

In the bitterness of the ironic retort lies the rub. Peter does, at last, move out, and that night, after seeing Jules and then having dinner with his (white) girlfriend, he goes up to Harlem where, in the eyes of the white world, he belongs but from which he feels himself alienated. He immediately gets involved in a touchy exchange in a bar, rejecting a pass made by a worn-out black woman. 'You must think you's somebody,' she reprimands him tartly, and turns away. Peter longs for something 'to make me part of the life all around me', but there is nothing, 'except my colour'. A white stranger coming in and seeing a young black man drinking in a Harlem bar would assume he was at home, but 'the people here knew differently, as I did'.

The story ends on a note of fleeting reconciliation, with Peter offering to buy the women a drink:

> 'I'll take a beer,' the young one said.
> I was shaking like a baby. I finished my drink.
> 'Fine,' I said. I turned to the bar.
> 'Baby,' said the old one. 'What's your story?'
> The man put three beers on the counter.
> 'I got no story, Ma,' I said.

The ending is superbly controlled, without a surplus word of dialogue or descriptive phrase. Even the use of 'the man' to introduce the barman is fully considered, for the barman – as Pelatowski's photographs of Harlem bars show – would have been white, and 'the man' is one way black slang refers to whites. The man serves up his narcotic; the black woman crumbles; and the enlightened boy looks around and tries to sum himself up.

The original manuscript of his first published story exposes the heat of Baldwin's temper at the time, and shows how, for literary purposes, he reined it in – with the help of some rigorous editing. Many changes were made in the typescript submitted to the magazine before it appeared in print, most significantly concerning the deletion of obscenities. In 1948, it was unwise, legally – and also, as far as the American Jewish Committee was concerned, commercially – to use taboo words in print. The largest cut is made in the eviction scene. The manuscript reads:*

Alright. Alright. You can have the goddam room. Let me get dressed. I watched her face. Unless you want to come in and help me. I almost said, Let's go to bed together, you maggot-eaten bitch, because I knew that in the back of her mind she was recalling every rape story she had ever heard, every dirty darky story ever told, getting hot between her dried up legs. I could have taken her then and raped her in the filthiest way I knew just because I hated her; and because she was white . . .

I slammed the door.

---

* In both manuscript and magazine versions Baldwin dispensed with quotation marks, restored for book publication – *Going to Meet the Man* – in 1965.

In the published version, all of the material which is certain to have struck the editors of *Commentary* as too risky has been deleted. Peter is allowed to say, in the paragraph before this one, 'You wanna come in and watch me' (get dressed), but instead of the outburst quoted above, the scene is controlled:

'All right. All right. You can have the goddam room. Now get out and let me dress.'
She turned away. I slammed the door.

There are two sets of revision marks on the manuscript. One is in Baldwin's handwriting, but the other has been made by a *Commentary* editor, probably Warshow, who was one of Baldwin's favourite editors. As well as paying heed to the obscenity laws, he was giving the young writer a lesson in keeping violence contained, in classic Hemingway style. The story does not need the 'obscene' material. Its violence and ugliness are packed in between the lines, increasing the tension in Peter's narrative voice and assuring the reader that even though Peter, at any moment and with justification, might run out of control, his creator will not.

'I'll blow my fuckin' top' on page 10 of the manuscript is simply, in the published version, 'I'll blow my top.' The paragraph in which this occurs ends in manuscript, 'Now when I go to a strange place I wonder what will happen, will I be accepted, if I'm accepted, can I accept? Jesus, I feel like somebody had cut off my balls.' In the published version, this speech ends: '. . . if I'm accepted, can I accept?'

'Previous Condition' was published just a few weeks before Baldwin left America, beginning a period of self-exile that was to last, in all, nine years. And in the pressures closing in on Peter we can read the reasons for his flight.

His second book project, with Pelatowski, had failed to catch the fancy of a publisher. But, like the first, it did secure him an award. This time the money – $1,500 – came from the fund established by the early-twentieth-century philanthropist Julius Rosenwald. As with the Saxton money, Baldwin put a portion aside for his mother and spent liberally from the remainder. Before it was all gone, however, he made a decision to move.

Richard Wright, a man who had grown up on Southern plantations, come north and won acclaim as a writer, had had similar experiences, which had almost broken him. Before that could happen, he took the white woman he had married, and their daughter, to Paris, where his life would not be treated as dirty and his love as a dirty joke. Baldwin followed. He was no longer the awkward ex-evangelist out of school who had knocked on Wright's door in Brooklyn. His religion, and his race, had given him a literary style; his native city had given him a subject; but it would not, he feared – in spite of the encouragement of Levitas, Warshow and others – give him a career.

'I got no story, Ma.'

Unless he wrote his own.

PART II

Lord, I ain't No Stranger Now

Being a problem is a strange experience –
peculiar even for one who has never been anything
else, save perhaps in boyhood and in Europe.

W. E. B. DuBois, *The Souls of Black Folk*, 1903

Chapter Five

'Why did you leave America?'

Baldwin seldom refused a request for an interview, and once he was famous and 'Paris' had become part of his legend, he was asked this question many times. He gave different answers on different occasions, but his replies are all basic variations on the explanation he sent to William Phillips early in 1949, a few months after settling in to St-Germain-des-Prés. Paris seems to have at once unwound him and disclosed his deepest fears and hurts. The discretion over 'the housing shortage', the polite phrasing, the innocent need to convince himself that what Countee Cullen had told him was true – that there was no 'prejudice against the Negro in the literary world' or any other world – have all but been abandoned: at home, he told Phillips, he had worked himself into such a state that he scarcely knew where he was going or what he wanted. As causes, he mentions race, calvinism, sex, a 'violent, anarchic, hostility-breeding' pattern which, once one has discovered that it has 'turned inward', then seems invested with the power to kill.

This is a remarkable moment in Baldwin's development; for he is seeing himself from the outside, as someone who can say *I did not know who I was.* Yet, by detaching himself from his own dislocation, he has started to transcend the condition. The past months in recently liberated Paris, he adds in his letter to Phillips, though probably inexcusable from a practical point of view, have been the saving of him; it was 'the best move' he could have made.

However, he still felt guilty about deserting the family. Even though the next eldest, George, and some of the others were now of an age to earn money, Baldwin found it hard to justify running away. Emile Capouya remembers him admitting desperately that he could not go on trying to support them. 'I suppose if he was going to write anything, he couldn't do it at the same time as running elevators and sweeping floors.'

Baldwin felt that his flight from home 'stank of betrayal'.

The price of getting to Paris by aeroplane in 1948 was $660, or about half a year's wages for a New York labourer. Once he had paid for his ticket, he was left with only $40 out of the Rosenwald Fellowship to sustain himself. But money meant nothing when he was faced with his own negation: 'I did not know who I was.' The flight to Paris was a leap into visibility.

When Baldwin first set foot in Paris on 11 November 1948, it had not yet recovered from the depredations of the war; the city was running on bicycles and enduring food rations. It was possible for a foreigner to eat and sleep frugally, however, and the large number of young Americans living there on the dispensations of the GI Bill provided the basis of a social circle.

The $40 lasted about three days, then he was broke. Poverty in Paris is part of the mythology of the expatriate American writer, but in Baldwin's case it was truly dire. He stayed broke for most of the next nine years. The odd jobs which had supported him in New York were not available here. Hateful though those jobs were, they provided quick money. But waiting on tables in Greenwich Village did nothing to equip one for the job of being a waiter in Paris. His earning potential from writing was also reduced, since the journals he had contributed to at home were unlikely to take the trouble of shipping books for review across the ocean in expectation of receiving a notice two months later. Writing for French journals, on the other hand, was badly paid, and involved obstacles of a linguistic and social sort which he was not yet ready to confront.

The American magazines would be prepared to look at longer, more considered pieces, however, and Baldwin now set his mind to this. On leaving New York he gave his occupation to the passport office as 'Foreign Correspondent', citing *Partisan Review* even though he had never written a word for them. Foreign Correspondent: it must have sounded grand to the young man with half a book in his bag. And yet he could not have been unaware that it was tempting fate to give himself titles he had scarcely earned.

He had a new range of subjects before him: Paris, the Americans who lived there, the effects on them, and on himself, of being refugees from the New World in the Old. As always, his predominant desire was to write fiction, but practical constraints – money, displacement, lack of time and space to settle into long work – directed him towards the form which suited his talent best: the essay.

His only means of support was his pen, but his main asset for survival was not his pen as such but his literariness. Baldwin was well-read by the time he quit New York, not only in English and American literature but in Russian and French as well – 'Baldwin had read *everything*', said Mary McCarthy – and his reading, which had drawn him towards France in the first place, also helped prepare him for life there. He had read Balzac, for example, who taught him a lesson about the place of French institutions, from the universality of bureaucracy to the role of the concierge; from Flaubert he learned about the play of morality and hypocrisy, and the importance of conventional behaviour; Hemingway advised him about food, drink and waiters; Henry Miller revealed the secrets of sex in districts which, once only places of legend, now became his haunts: Montmartre, Montparnasse, St-Germain-des-Prés.

Paris had already been imagined by him before he entered France; and when it came to walking on real pavements, this made him more comfortable, and less of a stranger.

In the course of recovering from the Nazi occupation, Paris was still putting its various departments back in order, its intellectual department as much as any other. Many writers were guilty of collaboration with the Germans: some were tried and imprisoned; one, Robert Brasillach, was executed; others, such as Drieu la Rochelle, committed suicide before the readjusted state could take its own revenge. A blacklist was drawn up, and magazines and publishers were encouraged to boycott the names appearing on it. There was debate over whether this advice should be followed, or whether writers shouldn't better make peace and get back to work.

None of this meant much to Baldwin. In America, he had experienced the war at more than arm's length, and he never showed much interest in the perils of French colleagues under German rule. French (and other foreign) intellectual life he was happy to leave alone, his interest in such things extending no further than the interest taken in him. He could write only about subjects and ideas which affected him personally. Thus his 1954 essay on Gide – the only French writer he discussed at length in print – focused on Gide's homosexuality; occasional comments on Camus were directed at Camus's concept of justice. He later dismissed the tenets of existentialism as 'obvious', without offering much indication that he had fully absorbed them, and although he met both Sartre and de Beauvoir, they left little impression on him, just as he – young, barely published and non-French-speaking – meant nothing to them.

French intellectual life was not generally the concern of American blacks in Paris, who had enough to do in trying to define their slot in a foreign culture, and, from this new perspective, revising their place in their own. For them, the journey to Paris was not so much a flight to an intellectual capital or to gay and cheap living as an escape from the daily enormities of racism. Living in the City of Light meant less to them than being somewhere that would not penalize them for being dark.

A black man marrying a white woman in New York in the 1940s had to accept the possibility of violence day by day; in Paris mixed marriage between black and white was acceptable. Baldwin moved, as he had moved in New York, among white society, black society and mixed society, but on the Left Bank each group did not feel alienated or menaced by the other groups. Here no one particularly cared if a black man went into a white woman's room and left the next morning, or if two men were known to be sleeping together. The French didn't necessarily approve; they just regarded it as none of their business. 'Every Negro in America,' Richard Wright told an interviewer from *Ebony* magazine in 1953, 'carries all through his life the burden of race consciousness like a corpse on his back. I shed that corpse when I stepped off the train in Paris.'

Racism there undoubtedly was, encountered at unexpected moments in unlikely places, but it wasn't the stubborn, ugly racism of 'We don't serve Negroes here', or 'I don't rent rooms to coloured people', nor the institutionalized racism of the South with its segregated buses and lunch-counters. Europe offered a certain freedom from that, and an older, deeper vision of life. There was some consolation, to New World eyes, in ancient stones and customs. Baldwin might not wish to live by the conventions he had imbibed from Balzac and Flaubert, but he understood the reasons for their existence.

And, being the city of artists, Paris attracted other artists. Several black writers were already there or would follow: the novelists William Gardner Smith, Frank Yerby and Chester Himes; the journalists Ollie Harrington and Richard Gibson; Herbert Gentry, a painter, and Gordon Heath, an actor and singer, were also there. Beauford Delaney arrived in the early 1950s. Many jazz musicians came to Paris too, some because they were unable to work in America. And, of course, Richard Wright was in Paris.

When Baldwin's plane touched down at the airport after circling above the city for what seemed to a first-time flier like hours, a train took him to the centre of town. There he was met by a friend from Greenwich Village who led him straight to St-Germain and the café Deux Magots. Richard Wright was seated at a table with another man. His face brightened when he saw his young protégé, and he greeted him as he always did – 'Hey, boy!'

Baldwin and Wright were still friends at this point. Baldwin might have felt that he needed Wright in Paris, but, knowing that Wright scarcely needed *him*, he might also have felt his arrival in his mentor's city as an embarrassment. And, kicking against his sense of shame, he also kicked Wright.

But that came later. For the moment he was glad to see the great man, and equally pleased to be introduced to some other young writers who congregated at their table. Someone showed him to a small hotel across the Boulevard St Germain, on rue Dragon, and he stayed there a few nights before moving to a more sociable place near the river, on the rue de Verneuil.

*

Give the Dumonts my love. And tell Jimmy that I'll get to Cannes and cash the money, send him some and he will pay off my February rent and laundry and please come down to this delightful place as soon as he can. I know he'd like it . . . and he can work peacefully.

The letter from which this is taken was sent in February 1949 to Mary Keen, an English woman, by one of her American friends. They were two of several young people Baldwin met at the Hôtel de Verneuil, a small place seven storeys high, on the corner of rue de Verneuil and rue du Beaune, near the Seine, in St-Germain-des-Prés. In hotels such as this, one could live cheaply – though never cheaply enough for Baldwin – cook in the rooms, which was not strictly allowed, and stay more or less as a permanent resident. The Dumonts were the Corsican family who ran the hotel.*

A couple of weeks later, though he had evidently promised to join his generous American companions in the Midi, there was still no sign of him. Mary's friend wrote:

We expect Jimmy momentarily, don't leave the house without posting notes for him, put hash-hish on the table beside his bed, buy extra veal chops for supper, etc etc.

* Baldwin later gave the name Mme Dumont, with roots, like the real Mme Dumont, 'somewhere in Corsica', to the nanny in his 1958 story 'This Morning, This Evening, So Soon'. In 1990 Mme Dumont was still running the Hôtel de Verneuil.

And still he doesn't come. If he's still there by the time this gets to you – cut him dead for me!

He did not make it to the Côte d'Azur on that occasion, but he did travel across the English Channel in May 1949 in a attempt to forge magazine contacts in London (a '*heavier* city' than Paris, he wrote to Mary Keen) and on 26 October he set off on a trip which was projected to end in Tangier. 'About midnight at the Gare de Lyon, where they were all leaving', Otto Friedrich, a young New Yorker also lately arrived in Paris, recorded in his journal –

Themistocles, with a homely but very expensive-looking American girl, and Jimmy and Schaef at the *degustation* having cognac, so I had one too. I asked where Gidske was. They said she was guarding the baggage, because this was really a train to Toulon, not the Riviera, and all full of sailors, and there were two tough characters in the compartment, so they didn't want to leave the baggage alone.

The party for the trip included Gidske Anderson, a Norwegian journalist to whom Baldwin had become fairly attached, and Themistocles Hoetis, a small, shaven-headed man with bright eyes and a beret, from Detroit. He was of Greek origin and had changed his name to save the family honour. He too had ambitions to write – he would in fact publish a novel before Baldwin did – and at the time was involved in setting up a little magazine called *Zero*. The trip was also to have included Asa Benveniste, another aspiring writer and *Zero*'s co-editor, and his wife-to-be Pip, a painter; but in the end they postponed their departure.

'So finally it came to train time', wrote Otto, 'and everybody piled on board, and there were fond farewells, and the engine began puffing forward . . .'

By this time, Mary Keen's American correspondent was on the other side of the Atlantic. When she got news of the grand trip from Mary Keen, she wrote with exasperation:

I hope that it will prove a good thing and that Jimmy will be able to write once in Tangiers. But cannot see him doing so, or it turning out as it should, surrounded with Al, Pip, Themistocles and Gidske. Jimmy, I have come to the conclusion (probably a temporary one but nevertheless) is a complete, absolute, and assinine *FOOL*. His one charm and single saving grace is that he always listens to you, agrees with you, seems intelligently interested in whatever you're saying to him (especially if it's something about him) and thereby passes and is even sought out as a charming, pleasant, extremely intelligent person. Also a 'lovable' one through that knack of his of wearing all his possible troubles on his sleeve and then brushing them off on you like so much dandruff – only Jimmy's problems are always put so that it is vaguely and vainly flattering to have to deal with them and help him solve them etc etc. Just *look* at this trip . . . What in the name of heaven does he think he's doing? How does he paint this ridiculous and sordid business to himself? He lies. Day in and day out, he spends his time lying about reality, about what he is, about what he can do and will do, about everyone around him.

There was to be no Tangier, however; not on this occasion. For one thing, Themistocles had got the boat-schedules mixed up, and they discovered they would have to wait a week in Marseilles before sailing. For another, the price of a ticket was greater than expected, and would have left them with scarcely a penny to spend once they got there. More seriously, Baldwin fell ill. So while Themistocles hung on in Marseilles and then continued to Tangier, Baldwin and Gidske Anderson retreated to nearby Aix-en-Provence, where they found cheap accommodation at the Hôtel Mirabeau. Otto Friedrich put down the sequence of events in his journal:

November 9 . . . Schaefer got a letter from Gidske which says that Jimmy is sick. At first they thought it was a bite by what Gidske calls a 'bedbog', but then it got worse and he had to go to the hospital. They said it was an inflamed gland, which had to be opened.

November 14 . . . Gidske writes now that Jimmy is better, but they still don't know whether he needs an operation. She says they have given up on Tangier . . . Her English continues to be miraculous. She describes Jimmy's hospital as 'croded, dirty, unafficient, and smelling like a hors stable'.

Gidske was tall and blonde, Baldwin dark and diminutive, and they used to tell people that she was his 'fiancée'. He was the first black person she had ever met, and at first he seemed to her like 'a figure out of a curious adventure land'. Soon she grew to like and admire him, his charm, his seriousness, and his small collection of personally chosen books – so different from the nonchalant acquisitiveness of the more affluent Americans. He read Shakespeare and the Bible, it seemed to her, over and over again.

Gidske wrote her own account of their stay in Aix many years later, and it paints an endearing, if sometimes harrowing, picture. In Paris, Baldwin had bought an old office typewriter, 'as big as a threshing machine', which was very heavy and difficult to move from one place to another. He insisted on taking it on the trip, however, and once installed in the Hôtel Mirabeau, set it up on a rickety old table in his room. When he let go on the keys, 'the rattle could be heard all over the hotel'.

The management was tolerant, and Baldwin got back down to work on 'Crying Holy', but then the owner of the hotel fell seriously ill, and Baldwin was asked not to hammer on his machine until the old man died, which he duly did. There was then no one in the hotel who would be bothered by noise, simply because, the rooms being unheated, the place was empty all day.

We tried hard to get some work done, sitting down in front of our desks in full winter gear, but in the end we gave up, and spent our days sitting in cafés, talking and waiting.

They were waiting for money to arrive from Paris, and until it did, being entirely penniless, they could not eat. Eventually, they found a Provençal restaurant prepared to give them credit, and when Baldwin was admitted to the dreadful municipal hospital, the bountiful restauranteurs sent Gidske to visit him with bread and fruit. While the doctors operated on him, she waited in the corridor, and when she saw him being carried back to his bed by the 'monstrous' hospital orderlies, she had the feeling that he was some sort of 'king', who had landed by accident in hell. A fortnight later, he was back in Paris, though not yet completely recovered.

A king in hell – Baldwin left this impression on many people. An aristocrat in intelligence, sensitivity, manners, he endured the worst pains and humiliations of poverty and prejudice. Most of the Americans in Paris were there on an adventure, or as part of their education. Baldwin saw it as literally a matter of saving his life.

It caused warps in his character. Unpredictable, undependable, erratic, hysterical, self-dramatizing – all this and more was characteristic of Baldwin. 'Jimmy was fundamentally an actor,' says Gordon Heath, who had also fled New York racism and landed in Paris shortly before, 'both in the theatre and out of it.' Baldwin himself once made reference to 'all those strangers called Jimmy Baldwin', suggesting confusion at being asked to play a variety of roles, from poet to speech-maker, from exotic to underdog. Friends often found themselves wondering when he was acting a part and when not, and with which of the 'strangers' who inhabited him he was most familiar, and with which were they.

Baldwin had, and always would have, a love of performance, particularly when in the starring role. In Paris, this was restricted to bars and restaurants; later on, he would fill TV screens with a presence which, paradoxically, was completely convincing. He harboured a desire to work in the theatre, and had a fantasy of owning a 16 mm camera and making experimental films. Otto Friedrich even recorded in his journal a date – 15 September 1949 – when Baldwin was supposed to open as a singer in a nightclub in the Arab Quarter (nothing more was ever said about it, so it seems that he never did).

And yet this prima donna exhibited an endearing humility and vulnerability. Mary Keen, who was working as a translator at the World Federation of Trades Unions, remembers Baldwin's tenancy at the Hôtel de Verneuil as being characterized by illness and anarchy. The previous year he had fallen sick, and the elder Mme Dumont had tended him while allowing free board at the hotel, an act of kindness he never forgot. His chaotic style of living was becoming notorious. He borrowed things and never returned them; he failed to turn up for appointments; he could not pay the rent in his own room, but took up residency in Mary's and used her bed for assignations; he was every bit as irresponsible with other people's money as with his own. 'He could never afford to buy cigarettes or drinks, not to mention meals. He would borrow and then, of course, be unable to pay back,' says Mary Keen.

His habits of borrowing and of not keeping appointments were not charming, but the moment he was seated opposite a friend with a drink in his hand, he would become animated and humorous, intimate and brilliant – and would be forgiven.

The Verneuil crowd comprised, in addition to Mary Keen, other aspiring writers such as Elliott Stein, Fred Moore, Asa Benveniste and Herbert Gold; Gidske Anderson, and her friend Bosley Brotman; and a French anarchist called Charlie. All were white.

Mary Keen claims that Baldwin's friends in the hotel and at the Café de Flore, where they spent many evenings, did not think of him as a black person. But although Baldwin made no show of being the odd one out, he was forced to see himself as black and incorporated the self-deprecatory tricks of the inferiority trade into his wit. Mary Keen remembers that strangers assumed he was a jazz musician – their definition of a black man in Paris – and one of the mock titles for a book she and Baldwin concocted for fun was 'Non, nous ne jouons pas la trompette' ('No, we don't play the trumpet').

Words commonly used to describe Baldwin by those who knew him during this period are 'intense', 'unreliable', 'comical'. Another acquaintance of the time recalls him as being 'very ugly': 'Put a bone through his nose and it would've made sense,' says Ann Birstein, herself now a novelist in New York, then a frequent visitor, like Baldwin, to the literary gatherings held in the rue de Verneuil apartment of Eileen and Stanley Geist. 'If there was bad luck going, he would get it. But Jimmy was laughing all the time. He was very funny.' The business of dreaming up titles for books that would not get written seems to have been popular. 'I remember,' says Birstein, 'that the one we thought of for Jimmy was "A Negro looks at Henry James", which was a big joke at the time.'

More of a joke for some than others. Baldwin laughed along, giving a public show of acceptance of himself as a figure of fun, no doubt perceiving beneath the jests a genuine affection. But he was also making the effort to be released from the description 'young Negro writer', and even 'young Negro'. Unsympathetic perceptions of him as a savage with a bone through his nose could only fortify the category. And Baldwin knew well the workings of the process whereby you internalized others' invidious views of you. Baldwin understood why the 'Black girl' stretched her mouth wide in his poem, but his understanding was not always shared.

After leaving the Café de Flore, the company might move on to Gordon Heath's folk club in rue de l'Abbaye, where audiences showed appreciation by snapping their fingers rather than applauding. Or else Baldwin would go off to La Reine Blanche, a bar on the south side of Boulevard St-Germain patronized mainly by what he called at the time 'ambivalent men'. But Baldwin liked to waive distinctions, between white and black, between men and women, and, typically, he took his girl-friends to La Reine Blanche. Baldwin enjoyed female company and, with five sisters, made friends with women easily. Bosley Brotman, one year older than him and from New York, was one. They were briefly lovers, according to Bosley Brotman (now Wilder). Of their relationship, Baldwin confessed to his typewriter, 'I for the first time shook myself free of the notion that no white American could really comprehend my fears.'

'Jimmy could laugh to the depths of his being,' wrote Gidske. Women were attracted to him for his sense of humour and his intelligence, but many also appreciated his trait of speaking openly about his feelings. What's more, he was frequently in need of nursing, and was 'mothered' by women as various as Mme Dumont, Gidske herself, and Mary Keen, who had a fond reputation at the Hotel de Verneuil for feeding hungry writers with an English stew.

After returning from Aix, however, Baldwin had to find a new room, as his place at the Verneuil was taken. He went to stay in a dark and gloomy hotel on rue du Bac, with rooms, Gidske Anderson wrote, 'as large as ballrooms in a castle, where the stairs and floors made creaking noises when you stepped on them, and a mildewy smell pervaded the corridors'. Christmas was coming, and the 'affianced' couple dreamt of a celebration, with a tree and a big Christmas dinner – to be cooked, alas, 'on our little primus burner'.

Compared with how things turned out and what he got, Baldwin would have regarded that as a feast fit for a king indeed. A few days before Christmas, Gidske passed by the Hôtel du Bac in search of him.

The man who owned the hotel sat as always bent over some mysterious books he was writing in, and as always replied to me without lifting his head. Jimmy was not in. This was not so very strange. But when the next day he gave me the same laconic answer – 'Il est sorti', in the evening, the next morning and several more times – I began to be worried. I tried to find out from him whether Jimmy had been back at the hotel at all, if he had seen him, but the man always replied in such a way that he made it seem as if Jimmy had just gone out the door ... At five o'clock one afternoon I met a mutual friend of ours who told me that Jimmy was in jail, and that he had been inside for several days already.

The charge was as petty as the events that led to it were farcical. Baldwin had been detained on suspicion of being in possession of stolen property: namely, a bedsheet. It had been offered to him by a new-found American friend who had filched it from a hotel on the Right Bank, and it quickly found its way on to Baldwin's bed, as a way, he wrote, of forcing 'on the attention of the Grand Hôtel du Bac the unpleasant state of its linen'.

Once the police had been alerted by the proprietors of the original hotel, a rapid investigation led to rue du Bac and the room of the young white American who had recently made Baldwin's acquaintance. This led in turn to Baldwin's own room. They were cordially invited by the ignorant occupant to continue the search – and instantly found what they were looking for.

Baldwin protested his innocence, but was whipped off to prison anyway – Fresnes, a Gothic pile on the outskirts of Paris, where he spent Christmas, 'hanging in a kind of void between my mother's fried chicken and the cold prison floor'. A week later, the case was brought to court and, the butt of much festive merriment, he was acquitted.

In the essay 'Equal in Paris', Baldwin casts himself as a Charlie Chaplin figure, always on the losing end, enduring accumulating misfortunes with an optimism founded on the belief that nothing worse can happen than this – though it always does. It is his funniest piece, but the humour does not obscure the essay's serious purpose. The adventure in Fresnes was deeply uncomfortable and humiliating, yet it taught him a valuable lesson about the frailty of his European refuge: the laughter of the court upon hearing the story of the stolen bedsheet was the laughter of those

who consider themselves to be at a safe remove from all the wretched, for whom the pain of living is not real. I had heard it so often in my native land that I had resolved to find a place where I would never hear it anymore. In some deep, black, stony, and liberating way, my life, in my own eyes, began during that first year in Paris, when it was borne in on me that this laughter is universal and can never be stilled.

One should perhaps assume some benefit of hindsight in this account of the painful, 'liberating' rite of passage, since the essay was written five years after the events described ('Equal in Paris' was first published in *Commentary*, March 1955). In yet another way, also metaphorical but more immediately felt, life indeed 'began' in the days after his release from prison: he fell in love.

Lucien Happersberger, a Swiss, was seventeen years old when he met Baldwin in La Reine Blanche at the turn of 1949–50. He had left his home in Lausanne and come to Paris without his parents' approval, living there on his wits, being 'kept', at one time or another, by both men and women.

Baldwin instantly took a liking to his good looks, his devil-may-care hedonism, his healthy appetite for pleasure. Lucien was not bookish but he was quick-thinking and witty, and his canny sense when it came to

sizing up others complemented Baldwin's all-embracing, sometimes naïve, trustfulness. Lucien's disregard for the lines of gender was instinctive: he loved women, but he liked men as well; most of all, he liked making love.

Baldwin accepted Lucien first as a friend, then as a younger brother, and then as a lover. But Happersberger insists that the first of those was the main nourishment of their relationship. It was to sustain it over the next forty years, with Happersberger playing a role in each Act of Baldwin's future life. 'We were buddies,' he says. 'We accepted each other exactly as we were. That's rare. We were not lovers as if we were living together.'

However much of a bohemian and sexual outlaw he might have seemed at times, Baldwin held on to an ideal of love. 'Jimmy was very romantic,' Happersberger says. 'He had a dream of settling down. There seems to be a myth that I was someone whom he lived with like that in Paris in the 1950s – he talked that way to other people later on himself, I heard him – but I wasn't. We saw each other every day but we never lived together in Paris at all.'

Both continued to have lovers, and in the summer of 1952, Lucien's girl-friend told him that she was expecting a baby. 'I went to Jimmy and said, she's pregnant, what should I do? And he, good Protestant that he was, said "Marry her".'

When, in due course, the new Mrs Happersberger presented her husband with a son, he was baptized Luc-James, twinning the names of father and godfather.

Chapter Six

The person who was sitting with Richard Wright at the Deux Magots on the day that Baldwin first set foot in Paris was Themistocles Hoetis, the founding editor of *Zero* magazine. Inspired by news of the impending arrival on the Left Bank of the young black writer, Hoetis had called on Wright and brought him to Boulevard St-Germain for a rendezvous.

Wright had once edited a little magazine himself, and had agreed to contribute a story to *Zero*. It was Hoetis who took Baldwin to a cheap hotel on rue Dragon once the reunions had been effected at the Deux Magots. The two men liked each other. Hoetis was small, with mischievous eyes, willing to try anything. He too was writing a novel. Their meeting resulted in friendship and also in Baldwin's first literary commission in Paris: 'Everybody's Protest Novel'.

The essay was included in the launch issue of *Zero* – Spring 1949 – and is one of the reasons why the magazine is remembered today. The same issue had contributions from Christopher Isherwood, Kenneth Patchen, William Carlos Williams and Wright himself, whose story 'The Man Who Killed a Shadow' precedes Baldwin's essay in the list of contents.

Baldwin felt closely involved in the running of the magazine, even using the editorial 'we' in a letter of 1953, but he had little to do with either the editing or the business side. His place was to be a contributor. A second essay was published in the next issue; 'Notes of a Native Son', started in 1952 but not completed until 1955, was originally intended for *Zero* (it eventually appeared in *Harper's*); and an early draft of Act One of the play *The Amen Corner* was printed in issue no. 6, July 1954 (it was to be thoroughly revised for later performance), by which time the editorial office had moved to the United States.*

---

* *Zero* published a seventh issue – Spring 1956 – with Wallace Stevens, Paul Bowles, Gore Vidal and Ivy Compton-Burnett; the magazine then expired.

'Everybody's Protest Novel' is a discussion of protest fiction, focusing principally on Harriet Beecher Stowe's novel *Uncle Tom's Cabin*. Baldwin judges the book to be 'very bad'; its portrayal of black people is sentimental and dishonest. Black characters have had their skin lightened to signify gentility and, if they are male, their virility admonished; forbearance is presented as the main virtue a slave can possess. Mrs Stowe's novel leaves unanswered 'the only important question: what it was after all that moved her people to such deeds'.

At the end of the discussion, Baldwin introduces another novel with a black protagonist – Richard Wright's *Native Son*. Baldwin treats his mentor dispassionately; Bigger Thomas, Wright's hero, is nothing more than Uncle Tom's descendant, 'flesh of his flesh, so exactly opposite a portrait that, when the books are placed together, it seems that the contemporary Negro novelist and the dead New England woman are locked together in a deadly, timeless battle; the one uttering merciless exhortations, the other shouting curses.'

It is a cute twist in the argument, not much more than a coda, and the essay is today regarded as a classic statement on the literature of protest. It marks a graduation from Baldwin's book-reviewing career, though it is one of only a few attempts he made at writing longer literary criticism.

He sent a copy of the typescript to William Phillips, who accepted it for *Partisan Review* despite feeling faintly piqued that Baldwin had not given it to them originally. But 'Everybody's Protest Novel' came out in Paris first, and when Richard Wright read it he was confused – didn't *Native Son* stand as a monument and a measure of possibility in the eyes of all young black writers, especially Baldwin, who was being touted as 'the next Richard Wright'? Then he was angry.

'Wright was furious about the *Zero* affair,' says Hoetis. 'He thought we'd set him up. I said we didn't set anybody up. We just got a story from the old black writer and an essay from the new. That was all there was to it. But he was very angry.'

On the day the essay was published in the spring of 1949, Baldwin strolled into the Brasserie Lipp, on the other side of the Boulevard St-Germain from the Deux Magots. Wright was already inside. He called Baldwin over to his table.

Richard accused me of having betrayed him, and not only him but all American Negroes by attacking the idea of protest literature ... And Richard thought that I was trying to destroy his novel and his reputation; but it had not entered my mind that either of these *could* be destroyed, and certainly not by me.

Baldwin claimed that he hadn't meant to condemn Wright's novel; as far as he was concerned, he wrote, 'I had scarcely even criticized it.' This is more than a touch disingenuous, for almost as soon as he left the Brasserie Lipp after his discomfiting interview with Wright, he embarked on another essay, 'Many Thousands Gone', twice as long as the first and constructed around a sustained assault on the integrity of *Native Son*.

On the one hand Baldwin was simply doing his duty as a literary critic, clarifying his view of a work whose true worth might by now have been obscured by its plaudits: far from being a progressive work of black fiction, *Native Son* was *re*gressive. Baldwin deplored the author's moral wavering, his inability to decide if his hero was right or wrong; he felt it was this failure to make a choice that left *Native Son* 'trapped by the American image of Negro life'. Bigger Thomas – or his later incarnations, for Baldwin predicted with some accuracy that Wright could only repeat himself – was left with nothing more resolute or creative to do but commit one more bloody murder. Hence the equation with Harriet Beecher Stowe: Wright too has evaded 'the only important question: what it was, after all, that moved . . . people to such deeds'.

Baldwin cautiously told Philip Rahv, co-editor of *Partisan Review*, where 'Many Thousands Gone' was also published, that he did not intend his essay to be read as an attack on Richard Wright. Whether meant as an attack or not, the highly charged atmosphere between them could only be intensified by renewed criticism.

Why had a relationship that was once genial and fruitful developed into such a difficult 'social situation'? Wright was a touchy man, lacking Baldwin's sense of humour, and sensitive when it came to his own standing in the literary world. He considered it improper that Baldwin, sixteen years his junior and a *parvenu*, should venture to criticize his work at all. He took it as an insult, particularly in view of the fact that this was the same boy that he had sponsored for a fellowship four years earlier.

Baldwin had originally seen Wright as a father-figure, and as such Wright was a source of inspiration and assistance, but beyond a certain point he became an obstruction. The young preacher's 'father' had been a preacher; now the young writer's 'father' was a writer. Like David Baldwin, Wright obstructed the prodigy unknowingly, even while believing he was being helpful. He was the stick against which the world measured the growth of the younger man. Baldwin was later to accuse Wright of having left the next generation of Negro novelists with nothing to write about – a remark not meant as praise. It is not altogether surprising, then, that Baldwin – tense, ambitious, frightened, 'wearing all his possible troubles on his sleeve' as one friend put it – should have leaped to grab the measuring stick and beat the master with it.

Wright, nevertheless, might have brushed aside Baldwin's comments as the antics of an ungrateful and unscrupulous upstart. And although he did not do so, not being sufficiently detached from the 'social situation' that gave rise to them, we must at least consider the possibility that Baldwin exaggerated Wright's anger in his written accounts. 'Terrible warfare' Baldwin called it, but according to Wright himself, in the only record he has left of the relationship, it was warfare in only one camp. Indeed, he wishes to make it perfectly clear that Baldwin was far more angry at him than he was at Baldwin.

This side of the Baldwin–Wright story has never been explored before, for the simple reason that all the evidence was gathered by one side: six of Baldwin's essays contain extended discussion of Wright (four are devoted to him), while Wright never once mentioned Baldwin in print. He did, however, make reference to the younger writer in a public lecture given at the American Church in Paris on 8 November 1960, his last public appearance before his death at the end of that month. It is a discussion of the state of relations among black intellectuals in Paris, and it contains an account of an apparently vicious squabble with Baldwin.

The year is 1953; Wright is having a drink in the Deux Magots with the novelist Chester Himes, who was previously acquainted with Baldwin only through his writings. 'A third Negro writer joined us', Wright told his audience, in the company of 'a Mrs Putman'. Although the lecture was given when the two men had known each other for sixteen years and at a time when Baldwin had become quite famous, Wright throughout misspelled Baldwin's name in his script (as well as that of Mrs Putnam, wife of James Putnam, one-time secretary of the US chapter of the PEN club):

I must tell you that there existed between Chester Himes and me, on the one hand, and Balwin, on the other, a certain tension stemming from our view of race relations. To us, the work of Balwin seemed to carry a certain burden of apology for being a Negro and we always felt that between his sensitive sentences there were echoes of a kind of unmanly weeping. Now Chester Himes and I are of a different stamp. Himes is a naturalist and I'm something, no matter how crudely, of a psychologist. This tension between Balwin and me and Himes, until that evening, had never been mentioned or directly written about.

The four of us – that white lady, Balwin, Himes, and me, – sat sipping beers.

'I want to talk to you,' Balwin said to me.

'Sure. Why not. I'm here,' I said.

'What did you think of that article I wrote about you?' Balwin asked.

I recalled the article. I had not understood the points that Balwin had made about me or against me. His article had dealt with the subject of identification and I had been baffled about his being concerned with what identification he had. I felt I was a Negro, an American Negro. Balwin was questioning that hard fact.

'Balwin, I didn't know what you were talking about in that article,' I said softly, trying to smile to cushion the shock of my statement.

Balwin glared at me.

'Don't take me for a child,' he warned.

'What are you talking about?' I asked, laughing a bit. That did it. My laughter spurred him to rage.

He leaped to his feet, pointed his finger in my face and screamed:

'I'm going to destroy you! I'm going to destroy your reputation! You'll see!'

'What are you saying? What are you talking about?'

'I said that I am going to destroy you!' Balwin screamed.

'Tell 'im, Jimmy; tell 'im!' the white woman, Balwin's friend, egged him on.

'Why don't *you* tell me?' I challenged her.

'He's telling *you* for *me*,' the white lady said, her face excited with a kind of sensual hate.

'Jesus Christ,' Himes exclaimed, rising. He wiped sweat from his forehead and said: 'Excuse me. I'm going to take a walk around the block. I can't take this.'

He left. Since I was the object of the attack, I could not leave. I sat on, looking pityingly at Balwin.

'Look, guy, forget me,' I begged him.

'I'm going to destroy you,' he vowed hysterically, over and over again.

I said nothing. I let him empty himself of his abuse of me in public. Finally, Balwin and his white lady friend rose and left. Himes rejoined me.

'That was horrible,' Himes sighed.

'Well, I guess it's better for it to be said openly than just thought of in private,' I said.

'But he said that in front of that white woman,' Chester Himes voiced the heart of his and my objection.

'That was the point,' I said.

Reportage or revenge? As 'attacks' go, this is nastier than anything Baldwin ever committed to print, and the final quip is the last turn of the knife: Baldwin's resentment of, and ingratitude to, Wright is explained by black self-hatred.

But is the story accurate? Baldwin was certainly capable of throwing a violent tantrum, even of being vindictive. His admitted feelings about Wright declined from hero-worship to pity, and the two writers' difficult relationship was well-known in Paris. But no one else suggested that their quarrel had become lethally poisonous. According to Wright's widow, Ellen, the older novelist retained an affection for Baldwin until the end of his life, and often came home with agreeable reports of having met him in the street. Baldwin himself wrote to his publisher at the turn of 1952–3 that Richard Wright should be sent a copy of his forthcoming novel – 'Why the hell not? We're perfectly pleasant to each other.' And towards the end of his life, Baldwin encouraged the view that relations were never as dramatically adversarial between him and Wright as they had been made out to be: asked by an interviewer about Wright in 1984, he referred to 'our early hostile period, which I thought was ridiculously blown out of proportion'.

So let us have the view of someone else who was present: Chester Himes, who also wrote an account of the meeting. Himes, who had begun his writing career in prison while serving a sentence for armed robbery, came to Paris only in 1953. He and Baldwin became close friends much later, but they had not met before this incident. This and other details tell us that the time and place are the same as that described by Wright, notably the arrival on the scene of Mrs Putnam. There are substantial differences between the two accounts, however, beginning with the fact that in Himes's version the meeting at the Deux Magots was not accidental but had been set up by Baldwin who had telephoned Wright at his home (Himes was present) and asked for a loan of ten dollars. According to Himes, Mrs Putnam was not merely Baldwin's 'white lady friend' but a mutual friend of Baldwin and Wright's; and going to the Deux Magots to meet Baldwin meant Wright postponing his arranged trip to a cocktail party – being given that evening by none other than Mrs Putnam herself.

We hurried to the Deux Magots and found Baldwin waiting for us at a table on the terrace across from the Eglise Saint-Germain. I was somewhat surprised to find Baldwin a small, intense young man of great excitability. Dick sat down in a lordly fashion and started right off needling Baldwin, who defended himself with such intensity that he stammered, his body trembled, and his face quivered. I sat and looked from one to the other, Dick playing the fat cat and forcing Baldwin into the role of the quivering mouse ... Then suddenly a large group of people approached us. I looked up and was startled to find Mrs Putnam among them ... It wasn't long before Mrs Putnam and all her friends had gotten to the heart of the matter and taken sides. All of the women and the majority of the men took Baldwin's side – chiefly, I think, because he looked so small and intense and vulnerable and Dick appeared so secure and condescending and cruel. But in the course of time they left us to go to dinner, and still Baldwin and Dick carried on while I sat and watched the people come and go. Later we went down the boulevard to a Martiniquan café. It had grown close to midnight, and we had not eaten, but still the discussion went on. It seemed that Baldwin was wearing Dick down and I was getting quite drunk. The last I remember before I left them at it was Baldwin saying 'The sons must slay their fathers.' At the time I thought he had taken leave of his senses, but in recent years I've come to better understand what he meant.

The two versions were written long after the events they describe. Given the discrepancies between them, it is even possible that Baldwin himself was referring to the same occasion when he wrote, in 'Alas, Poor Richard', 'Once, one evening ... Richard, Chester Himes, and myself went out and got drunk. It was a good night, perhaps the best I remember in all the time I knew Richard.' But perhaps we should best trust Chester Himes, since he is the disinterested party and his account has a vividness and clarity of detail which Wright's story lacks.

When it came to writing 'Alas, Poor Richard' after Wright's death, Baldwin's main concern was to explore the nature of the dissensions between himself and Wright. This he did by a tortuous route. He accepted the son–father parallel, which so much has been made of since, and the second part of the three-part essay, 'The Exile' (originally Wright's obituary), ends on a note which is very similar to the memorial essay on Baldwin's own father, 'Notes of a Native Son'. The latter concludes:

I wished that he had been beside me so that I could have searched his face for the answers which only the future would give me now.

Compare that with the ending of 'The Exile':

Whoever He may be, and wherever you may be, may God be with you, Richard, and may He help me not to fail that argument which you began in me.

Which is a far cry, even allowing for the passage of time (seven years had gone by since the meeting described by Wright) and the softening effects of death, from 'I'm going to destroy you.'

'Alas, Poor Richard' is in places a mocking piece, even cruel; but its principal motor is not malice. As usual, Baldwin is striving to make sense out of confusion, and to put something on record. If this involves leaving a few bruises on other people's shins along the way, so be it. The cool temper of 'Alas, Poor Richard' frequently struggles with the powerful emotion which prompted it, but that emotion is not venomous.

Baldwin lists a catalogue of complaints – his own and others' – about Wright: he did not understand jazz; he did not understand Africa; he thought he was white; he inflated his own importance in the eyes of the French writers, whom he courted; he harboured illusions about prejudice against blacks by other expatriate Americans; he was out of touch with the reality of the race problem in the United States; he bored the younger writers who had once revered him, and so on. Here we can see that the gulf separating Baldwin and Wright was more than simply that between a son and a father. The old charge of slaying the father is sometimes cited by critics as if it explained *everything* about the relationship between these two highly complex men. It contains a certain amount of truth, but it is, in fact, no more than a proverbial crime, a supposition. Their quarrel, at the nitty-gritty, was actually over something more tangible – the social and artistic responsibilities of the writer.

Wright and Baldwin were of different generations and each had his own conception of the proper role of the writer in society. Wright emerged from the generation which had produced the 'committed' left-wing writers of the 1930s. Once a member of the Communist Party, he would still, when the occasion demanded, join an organization or even found one, or arrange a protest action, or make a speech. He had suffered years of FBI surveillance, and American government interference in his life continued even in Paris. In November 1951, for example, the American Embassy informed the Department of State that Wright was 'willing to go to any length to attract attention to the problem of racial discrimination in general and to its manifestation in the United States in particular'. He was identified by an FBI agent as one 'who contended that the Communist

Party had the choice to champion civil rights', that the same party 'had helped the Negro in such fields as labour and the law', and that there was 'a need for a revolutionary party in the United States'.

According to Chester Himes, on the very day of the meeting with Baldwin, Wright had received an unwelcome visit at home from Senator Joseph McCarthy's investigators for the Senate committee on un-American activities, David Schine and Roy Cohn. Even Baldwin, unknown to himself, was conscripted by an FBI informant to discredit Wright: at a meeting of Wright's Franco-American Fellowship on 16 December 1951, the informant reported, the main public opposition to Wright was voiced by James Baldwin, who 'attacks the hatred themes of Wright's writings'.

Wright's response to Baldwin's criticism of him in *Zero* must be seen in the context of this larger insecurity. After a lifetime of harassment and discrimination he was embattled; he took sides instinctively; he knew who his enemies were – the FBI, the CIA, McCarthy, Cohn – but when his friends and disciples turned against him as well, his emotional network short-circuited.

As for Baldwin, he was by comparison an aesthete (his own realization of the power of the government's security services would not come until later). In the 1940s and 50s he saw the writer's place as being not on the platform but at the desk. His role was to probe the hidden laws which govern behaviour and hence change, and to translate his perceptions into works of art. He should strive to be 'one of those people on whom nothing is lost', a motto adopted from his new idol, Henry James. 'Here you come again with all that art for art's sake crap,' Wright would rebuke him, insisting that all literature was protest. All literature may be protest, Baldwin replied, but not all protest is literature.

Had he kept his all too understandable paranoia in check, Wright might have chosen to disregard Baldwin and his criticism. But Baldwin could not disregard Wright. Once a symbol of what he could achieve, Wright appeared to him now as a writer gone astray – out of fashion and out of touch. Once an idol, he had diminished so much that Baldwin could see in him only an object lesson. '*Be careful*,' he warned himself, in 'Alas, Poor Richard'. '*Time is passing for you, too, and this may be happening to you one day.*'

Chapter Seven

When Richard Wright complained of 'a kind of unmanly weeping' echoing from Baldwin's 'sensitive sentences', we can take it that he is referring to Baldwin's homosexuality. According to Mrs Wright, her husband harboured no intolerance of homosexuals in general, yet in at least one letter Wright expressed 'disgust' at Baldwin's homosexuality. A lifelong friend of Baldwin's, Bernard Hassell, recalls a remark made by Wright in Paris when an advance excerpt from *Go Tell It on the Mountain* was published in a magazine, to the effect – Yes, he can write. But he's a faggot.

Baldwin had had his share of labels: 'a Negro', 'a boy from the ghetto', 'a holy roller', 'a bastard', 'a homosexual'. No label would stretch further than to limit the person so described. Whatever the maze of Baldwin's sexuality, it could not be summed up in the derogatory term 'faggot'. Baldwin was never a closet homosexual; nor did he make his homosexuality into a political stance. He simply insisted on the freedom to be himself, rejecting the orthodoxy that would define him as, variously, a queer, a pervert, a fairy, or the victim of some sort of genetic imbalance, or a disease – or, later on, 'gay' . . . definitions which, if one accepted them, corrupted one's experience and understanding of oneself.

He first tackled the subject in fiction in *Giovanni's Room*, but many years before that he opened a remarkably bold discussion of the manifestation of homosexuality in American literature – in mainly repressed forms – in an essay written for *Zero*. 'Preservation of Innocence', a little-known companion piece to 'Everybody's Protest Novel', appeared in the Summer 1949 issue. It constructs a defence of the homosexual against the common charge that he is 'unnatural' because he has 'turned from his life-giving function to a union which is sterile'.

Part I of the essay is a philosophical speculation on this concept of 'nature', and the distortions suffered by it in order that it exclude the homosexual. In Part II, Baldwin changes tack and embarks on a literary discussion. The American 'tough guy' novels of James M. Cain and Raymond Chandler are brought in to illustrate the proposition that the homosexual's 'present debasement and our obsession with him correspond to the debasement of the relationship between the sexes'. The very popularity of the tough guy provides the evidence:

it is impossible for a moment to believe that any Cain or Chandler hero loves his girl; we are given overwhelming evidence that he wants her, but that is not the same thing and, moreover, what he seems to want is revenge ... The woman, in these energetic works, is the unknown quantity, the incarnation of sexual evil, the smiler with the knife.

The essay was at first intended to be part of a longer project with the ambitious-sounding title 'Studies for a New Morality'. It got no further but, as a tandem, 'Everybody's Protest Novel' and 'Preservation of Innocence' make some crucial assertions: that colour and sex are the defining preoccupations of the American mind, and therefore, since it is individuals who make nations, of American history. Lying at the base of the troubled American soul is a denial of the blood (for Baldwin was of the belief that the United States was indeed a melting pot, and that 'integration' had already taken place – 'in the womb') and the repression of a primary factor in the erotic instinct.

These were the two great anti-themes of his country's history, which he was to pursue in future writing, fiction and non-fiction.

It was living in Paris that fired him with the confidence to express these subversive ideas. But while Paris might give him the spirit to write, it hardly gave him the space. Moving from one cold, cramped hotel to another, with little privacy and less money, Baldwin found it hard to settle down to his novel. Paris was great for living, great for *talking*, which was one of Baldwin's true skills, but less good for working. The problem was the pleasure. Left Bank society was mainly café society, and, flitting easily from one hang-out to another, Baldwin, if he happened to be without Lucien, could always be sure of finding company and, if he was without money, of finding a ready hand to buy him a drink.

There was the Deux Magots and the Flore, of course, rather expensive but at times containing a generous community of artists and students, and perfectly positioned in the centre of the Boulevard St-Germain. For after-hours, there was l'Echelle de Jacob, where Gordon Heath used to sing 'Pick a bale o' cotton' to the rhythm of the chef whipping up a soufflé in the kitchen behind him; or l'Abbaye, Heath's own club; or Chez Inez, run by the singer Inez Cavanaugh, which specialized in jazz and fried chicken; or La Reine Blanche, where the ambivalent men were to be found. In the afternoons, one could go to the Monaco, a little café round the corner from the Carrefour de l'Odéon, a stone's throw from the Wrights' apartment on rue Monsieur le Prince; or else to the Café Tournon, a cramped, poorly ventilated place on rue de Tournon, preferred by the black writers Chester Himes, William Gardner Smith and Richard Gibson. Wright habitually passed by the Tournon at four o'clock in the afternoon, according to Gibson, 'To have a coffee and play the pinball machine. He brought his distinguished visitors there and sometimes, rather pontifically, dispensed wisdom to the wayward black youths.'

Baldwin did not go often to the Tournon. Gibson remembers why. 'He did not feel comfortable in the leftist atmosphere of the place. And also, many of the Tournon habitués had little sympathy for homosexuality.'

During the summer of 1949, Otto Friedrich had described a typical day or two's 'work' in his journal:

August 17 ... Met Jimmy at the Royal at 7.30, and along came Lionel [Abel], and Jimmy said, 'Here comes my favourite intellectual.' Abel was pleased, and we all went to supper at the Basque place on the rue Mabillon. It was fairly expensive but very good – Jimmy and I had a faux filet, which was served with Madeira sauce and champignons, and Abel bought a bottle of rosé ... One trouble was that Abel and Jimmy had to talk about Richard Wright, a conversation I have heard about a million times. They are still rehashing Jimmy's article in *Zero* with Abel defending the older generation ... Abel was very charming, and in one of his explaining moods, so he explained Henry James, Flaubert, Faulkner, Cyril Connolly, Leslie Fiedler, Picasso's inability to sleep nights, and the absence of an influence of older French writers on younger French writers.

After dinner, Jimmy and I were going to a movie – *Back Street* with Boyer and Sullivan – but it was way out at the far end of the rue de Babylone, and by the time we got there, with Abel explaining things all the way, it turned out that the movie had started at nine and not ten, and now it was ten-thirty, so we came all the way back to the Royal, with Abel still explaining (Graham Greene, Sartre, Bernanos, etc, etc).

We were talking about Milton Klonsky, would-be poet, for whom Abel appropriated Lenin's term 'a gangster of the pen', and then there he suddenly appeared, trying to be important, so we all ignored him. And then a girl called Nina something, who had just heard Mahler's *Song of the Earth* and had just seen a bullfight and had to tell us all about them. And then somebody called Ted rode up on a tandem bicycle, the other half of which was occupied by someone called Siegfried, who had just got back his short stories that very afternoon from Mr Baldwin, who had told him to tear them up because they were terrible, especially the one about the world-famous pianist who had no little fingers because his manager, Mr Elbow, had made him cut them off for publicity (and he wasn't kidding) . . .

August 18 . . . Stephen, the one who wrote that awful novel, was complaining because he couldn't get his next book written, and he said, 'Why don't you sell me a manuscript?' And I said, 'I won't sell you one, but I'll write you one,' and Jimmy said, '*I'll* write you a manuscript.' Then we said we'd collaborate and write a quick best-seller for Stephen to sell to the movies. Stephen said he was very serious, and we said we were very serious. Stephen said he had already been paid an advance of $1,000, and he hadn't written a line, and what was he going to do? We said he should give us $400 apiece and we would write 100 pages to justify the advance, and then we would get half the royalties on the finished book. Stephen said, 'Dumas did it, so why shouldn't I?' . . .

After he left, Jimmy and I plotted out the great novel, which was to be called *The First Time I saw Paris*, the real and true story of Young Love . . . We parted, the master and I, solemnly swearing that we would really do it . . . I wrote six pages this afternoon. Jimmy read them and laughed, and Abel read them and laughed. Jimmy never wrote anything, and Stephen himself never showed up, the bastard.

This sort of caper was great fun, but it wasn't productive. While at his desk, Baldwin would be drawn outdoors by the alluring sound of café-banter; but once in the café, he knew he should be at his desk.

So, at the end of 1951, he and Lucien Happersberger decamped for Switzerland. Lucien's parents owned a small chalet in the mountain village of Loeche-les-Bains (or Leukerbad, in German), near Lausanne. Loeche-les-Bains was noted for its curative thermal springs, and at an altitude of 4,630 feet was permanently under snow in winter. Baldwin was trying to find a quiet space to finish *Go Tell It on the Mountain* at last, but in order to persuade his father to let them have the chalet throughout the winter months, Lucien had to play a trick. He brought his father a set of certified X-rays of a pair of lungs in the early stages of tuberculosis. The doctor had recommended mountain air, Lucien told his father. And no doubt he had – but the lungs did not belong to Lucien.

'I got X-rays of someone's lungs from a student in medicine, took Jimmy with me, and we left for Switzerland. I showed these X-rays of "my lungs" to my father, pretending that I had been cured of tuberculosis and needed convalescence in the mountains. That's how we got to Loeche-les-Bains, in my mother's family chalet. My father sent fifty Swiss francs a week. It lasted all that winter of 1951. Jimmy re-wrote *Go Tell It on the Mountain* and finished it.'

Baldwin was the first black person ever seen in this tiny village of a few hundred people, and the locals were not shy of showing their curiosity. They wanted to touch his hair, to see if it was prickly. They wanted to touch his skin, to see if the blackness rubbed off. They identified him with Africa and kept him up-to-date with their missionary work, whereby donations were deemed to 'buy' African children for God. Outside the church, charitable villagers would inform Baldwin proudly, 'We have bought six *nee-gers* this year.'

Not only had they never seen a black person in Loeche-les-Bains, they had never seen a typewriter either, and this added to Baldwin's peculiarity. Happersberger recalls that it made a great deal of noise for the people who lived down below, and he had to bring them upstairs to gaze on the wondrous machine and the strange little black man who operated it.

Before reaching Switzerland, Baldwin had come close to scrapping his novel. It had occupied him over eight years and, in different forms, had been rejected several times. This had sapped his confidence. But in the Happersbergers' chalet, its several parts suddenly fell into place. During the next three months in the snow-covered mountains, he hammered it into a final form, and posted it to his agent in New York at the end of February 1952.

When he typed out the new title page of the book – known until then as 'Crying Holy' – he had in mind of course the gospel song 'Go Tell It on the Mountain', but an experience which occurred in Switzerland added an extra dimension. Happersberger took Baldwin on a small mountain-climbing expedition; during the ascent Baldwin slipped and, according to Happersberger, nearly fell to his death. Lucien, an experienced climber, held him by the hand and talked to him while he remained stuck in a precarious position, until he was calm enough to be coaxed upwards to a sure footing. The side of the mountain on which they were climbing was in shadow – which was why it was frozen solid and dangerous – but as they reached the new landing in safety, the plateau was suddenly lit up by fabulous sunshine, reflected by a soft carpet of snow. It seemed heavenly.

'That's how *Go Tell It on the Mountain* got its title,' Baldwin would tell people. Happersberger feels that, typically, he needed the story, with its punchline, to justify the frightening experience on the mountainside. 'He talked about it as if it was some sort of a miracle. But these things happen all the time to climbers. He liked to tell stories like that about things he had been through.'

The opening page of *Go Tell It on the Mountain* strikes an autobiographical note: John Grimes, living in Harlem poverty with his parents and brother and sisters, pledges his allegiance to the Lord. He has been singled out to be a preacher when he grows up – 'just like his father'. He is already in obedience to the tyrannical Gabriel, who is not his real father, and is effectively cut off by a puritan regime from all the other boys and girls playing in the street around him. Gabriel Grimes favours Roy, his natural son, whereas John is 'a stranger, living unalterable testimony to his mother's days in sin'. Until his marriage with the church, John's main consolation is his mother's love.

It is a pernicious habit of critics to seek out autobiographical patterns in novels where none exists. Some readers, encouraged by the parallels with the author's own life drawn in the opening pages of *Mountain*, have gone on to read it as plain autobiography, even seeing in the character of Richard – John's real father, who died in the South – a proof that Baldwin knew his own father's identity and that the fate of Richard in the novel was *his* fate in life.

Such crude interpretations can be dismissed. But details apart – John is to be a preacher, like his father, his father calls him 'frog eyes', says that all white people are wicked, and so on – how far are we entitled to go in reading Baldwin's first novel as an account of his own experience? What did Baldwin himself have to say? Asked by the *Michigan Chronicle* in February 1953, a month before the book was published, he seemed to deny that there was any autobiographical content in *Mountain* at all:

I had been carrying [it] about with me since the day of my father's funeral. My father's funeral does not appear in the novel – had nothing whatever to do with it – and by this time my father had nothing to do with it, either. There's a great misapprehension abroad to the effect that writers take people out of life and put them into books, but nothing could be further from the truth ... If I had never known my father, if I had never lived in Harlem – I would never have written this book. That's obvious. But the novelist is not a portrait painter; he deals in distortions.

However, as if to provide a perfect illustration on the folly of taking an author at his word when speaking about his own work, Baldwin also said this:

I suppose that *Mountain* can be considered a kind of love song – a confession of love – for that David Baldwin it took me so many years to understand ... *Mountain* comes out of the tension between a particular father and a particular son. No matter that he was not my biological father.

The latter statement was made thirty-two years after the former, and the discrepancy is probably best resolved by saying that while *Mountain* retains its integrity as a work of fiction, it is informed by deep autobiographical feeling, from which Baldwin had distanced himself during the writing of the novel and in the months immediately following its completion.

The first section of *Mountain* links John's hatred of his father and his sense of sin: 'His father had always said that his face was the face of Satan ... He stared at his face as though it were, as indeed it soon appeared to be, the face of a stranger, a stranger who held secrets John could never know.' This part of the novel is set in Harlem, between home and the family's storefront church, the Temple of the Fire Baptized. Part II reaches back in time to the South and gives compact histories of John's ancestors, including his mother and stepfather, while the third part of the novel is largely devoted to John's long night in church, 'on the threshing floor', as he pleads with Jesus to 'take him through', to save him.

Lord, I ain't
No stranger now!
Yes, the night had passed, the powers of darkness had been beaten back. He moved among the saints, he, John, who had come home, was one of their company now.

Go Tell It on the Mountain is Baldwin's most accomplished novel, technically, and his most disciplined. It is without the idealizations, the sentimentality, the jarring tones and overlong conversations, even the moral fervour, which, separately or all at once, were to mar, in part or whole, his later novels. It has a cool perfection, the flip side of which is that it is somewhat stiff and formal in manner. John is sympathetic but he lacks vitality, and the landscape of his Southern forebears – where Baldwin had not yet been – is short of colour and atmosphere. The prose is peppered with biblical allusions and the words of Negro spirituals, a tense, agonized stream of consciousness in which John's boyish desires and sensations counterpoint spiritual exhortations – put thy faith in the Lord and set thy house in order. If there is one element missing from the narrative above all else, it is perhaps the oddness, the tenderness, of childlike observation. But since John's childhood is itself lacking in gentler influences, their absence from the authorial voice is not surprising.

Man's highest devotion must be pledged to the Lord, but earthly love plays a central part in the novel. It is focused on the seventeen-year-old Brother Elisha: 'John stared at Elisha during the lesson, admiring the timbre of Elisha's voice, much deeper and manlier than his own, admiring the leanness, and grace, and strength, and darkness of Elisha in his Sunday suit.' In the final part, while John lies on the floor before the altar, he experiences 'in his heart yearning tenderness for holy Elisha; desire, sharp and awful as a reflecting knife, to usurp the body of Elisha, and lie where Elisha lay.'

The homosexual theme in Baldwin's first novel has gone mostly unremarked. A shifting focus is being kept in play between flesh and spirit, but the language is arrestingly sensual. At the end, the two youths walk away from the church, Elisha with an arm around John; as they part, Elisha kisses his new 'brother' on the forehead:

The sun had come full awake. It was waking the streets and the houses, and crying at the windows. It fell over Elisha like a golden robe, and struck John's forehead, where Elisha had kissed him, like a seal ineffaceable forever.

At the same moment, John turns away from his watching, unsmiling father, for he realizes that his father will never forgive him for the 'sin' of not being his own son, and will never give him love like Elisha, the love on which he depends. It is the acceptance of this knowledge, together with Elisha's 'ineffaceable' seal and his holy salvation, that liberates John, on the morning after his fourteenth birthday, and sets him on his own path: 'I'm ready . . . I'm coming. I'm on my way.'*

By mid-March Baldwin's novel had passed through the hands of his agent in New York and reached the Madison Avenue offices of Alfred A. Knopf. The first person to read it there was William Rossa Cole, the publicity director. Cole was only occasionally involved in editing, but he already knew Baldwin's name from having read his essays and stories in magazines, and he responded enthusiastically to the novel which still went under two titles, 'Go Tell It on the Mountain' and 'Crying Holy'. In spite of some reservations about the last chapter, he was prepared to gamble: 'This is a book (and a novelist) I would like to see us publish. I suspect that this is the first of a series of books about Harlem . . . He's one of the few exciting young writers around.'

Cole was almost alone at Knopf in his high opinion of the novel, however, and were it not for his influence *Go Tell It on the Mountain* would probably not have been published by that firm. The second reader, Arthur Ogden, admitted he did not find Baldwin 'as exciting a talent as does Bill Cole . . . I do not consider his manuscript anywhere near publication.' From Ogden it went to Harold Strauss, the editor-in-chief: 'This is definitely not my kind of book', he wrote on the Manuscript Record form, in the box headed 'Final Decision'. 'It is embroidery rather than narrative.' But he left vacant the space for 'Rejected', and passed the manuscript along to yet another reader.

This time it was Philip Vaudrin, a senior editor at the firm. Vaudrin noted Baldwin's 'unmistakable talents', but agreed with Ogden that the novel in its present form was not publishable. However, he had enough faith in the book to authorize 'a small investment', on condition that Baldwin take back his manuscript and revise it again. The investment amounted to a 'binder fee' of $250, to be regarded as part of an advance of $1,000, payable in full only when the novel had been revised to the publisher's satisfaction.

To a budding novelist, this could not be considered bad news. Baldwin

---

* A little-known curiosity of the fictional life of John Grimes is that he made his début as an eighteen-year-old three years before the publication of *Go Tell It on the Mountain*, in a short story, 'The Death of the Prophet' (*Commentary*, March 1950). Baldwin omitted the story from his 1965 collection, *Going to Meet the Man*.

had returned from Switzerland to Paris, but the conditional acceptance of his novel prompted him to settle up at his hotel and take the first boat back to New York. Many of Baldwin's Paris friends had gone back to America in the four years that he had lived there; some had even gone home and returned to Paris again. But for him there was only one way back – with a contract in his hand. Pride and determination made it so. If he did not actually have his contract signed and sealed when he boarded the SS *Île de France* in April 1952, together with Themistocles Hoetis, he had at least an assurance from Knopf that they were seriously interested, which for the time being was good enough.

In fact, the money to pay his outstanding hotel bill had been found through what Hoetis calls 'a hustle', involving Marlon Brando and *Zero* magazine. 'He had met Brando a few times in the States', says Hoetis. 'But now Brando had made something big of himself, and it's a case of Jimmy going to see a famous person that he knew before he was famous. And I'm the crutch. I'm the little Greek who's doing the magazine, but who's got no money. The idea was that we're all poor and we're trying to get this thing going, and this is Brando's chance to do something "for the arts". So that's the excuse to hustle Brando.

'Jimmy picked me up at the Deux Magots and took me to the Hôtel des Beaux Arts, off the rue Dauphine. I didn't really know what was happening, but whatever line Jimmy's giving Brando, I'm just there to agree. So the concierge calls up. Brando comes down to the lobby. Hello. Hi. Then Jimmy starts his hustle ... He's helping me make a little magazine. We've got no money. We're trying to publish the good young poets and novelists, et cetera ... Money was shuffled. We thank him – and it's out into the road.'

The debt was repaid in friendship, as Baldwin and Brando remained close over many years. If it took Brando to get him on to the boat, it needed his brother David to get him off it. When the SS *Île de France* docked at New York seven days later, Baldwin – who had spent much of the passage at the bar with Dizzy Gillespie, to whom Hoetis introduced him – had nothing left for the obligatory courtesy of tipping the steward. It was left to David to provide it.

Book or no book, the Baldwin family, as the eldest son was painfully aware, was still living in Harlem, on the fifth floor of a squalid tenement on West 131st Street, and Mrs Baldwin was still cleaning houses. On a visit home at the turn of 1949–50, Otto Friedrich had telephoned Baldwin's mother and invited her for dinner, together with his fiancée, Priscilla. He suggested that they all meet at one of Jimmy's old hang-outs, the San Remo bar and restaurant, on MacDougall and Bleecker, in Greenwich Village.

At about seven I left the bar and went into the adjoining restaurant to see whether Mrs Baldwin had arrived, and whether I should reserve a table. Like the bar, it was a plain place, but it was already nearly full of people eating pasta. After looking around and finding no sign of Mrs Baldwin, I approached the headwaiter and said I was expecting to meet my fiancée and the mother of a friend, a middle-aged Negro lady, and would he please let me know when they arrived?
'Oh, I'm sorry, sir,' he said. 'We can't do that.'
'Can't do what? What do you mean?' I honestly didn't understand.
'We can't serve Negroes in here.'
'Why on earth not?'
'It's against the rules. In the bar, okay, but not here.'
'You're kidding,' I said.
'Come on, now, we don't want any trouble,' he said. 'You'll just have to go somewhere else.'

Baldwin was certainly going to find that nothing had changed once he landed in New York. The nightmarish forces that had chased him out of the country in 1948 were still free to pursue him now, and would make him leave America again before the summer was out.

But Mrs Baldwin could *not* leave, and her undemonstrative strength – in Friedrich's understated manner of storytelling – is more remarkable than the wicked rules that made it necessary:

Standing on the corner, looking nervously around her, was a small, dark figure. She looked at us, and at the restaurant, but she didn't seem to know what to do. Priscilla walked over to her and said, 'Mrs Baldwin?'
'Yes, I'm Mrs Baldwin. You Jimmy's friends?'
'Yes, I'm Priscilla Boughton, and this is Otto Friedrich, and they say they're all full inside, so let's go eat somewhere else.'
'That's all right, I don't mind,' Mrs Baldwin said. 'I understand.'

*

By the middle of July, Baldwin had reworked his manuscript and delivered it. Philip Vaudrin read it, and a new report was circulated:

Baldwin has not carried out all of the revisions we proposed to him (the book ends just as it did in the first version we saw) but he has done a good deal and it is a better book all round. He has cut some of the come-to-Jesus scenes to which we all objected, and he has improved the opening section greatly . . . I find this a very powerful and a very moving book . . . I think we should take up our option on this book now.

It remained only for William Cole to add his endorsement – 'Baldwin has done a fine job of revision', he wrote – and the contract was drawn up and signed.

Baldwin was not in the mood to tarry in New York. He waited just long enough to act as best man at his youngest brother David's wedding and then returned to Paris in September. What additional monies he received in advance from Knopf he spent on the family, on his ocean voyage, and on settling in again on the Left Bank. He was doing his best to make sure he would not starve during the winter, he told Bill Cole, who was to remain his closest contact at Knopf. And, alluding to future literary projects, he added that he hoped things would not be as 'rough' with the next book as they had been the first time.

When a bound proof copy of the novel reached him at the beginning of the year, elation had subsided enough for him to express to Cole a few pent-up complaints about his editor Philip Vaudrin: he had resolved to fight harder next time over changes. He now regretted not having objected to the suppression of passages deemed by his editor to be obscene. Vaudrin had made some doubtful alterations, such as rewriting Baldwin's 'and his heart rise up like a hammer' to *pound* like a hammer. These and other changes and errors in the text made him suspect that Vaudrin might not be the right editor for him. Cole himself would have been his choice, he told his loyal friend, but Cole was not an editor.

Baldwin had been searching for a job in Paris, but with no success, and was now 'rather despairingly' considering the possibility of a loan from his agent, Helen Strauss of the William Morris Agency, or from Knopf. 'I don't imagine that either organization will be delighted by such a proposition.' His agent sent a little money; Bill Cole lent him $250; but early in 1953 Cole received another letter with a host of lamentations all on the subject of cash: he has been unable to pay his hotel bill; he wishes to go to Switzerland again to work but lacks the funds; it is hopeless trying to earn money by writing for French magazines, etc. Finally, an unexpected cheque turned up and he was able to pay his hotel bill – but when the rent was paid he didn't have any money to get out of town.

When at last he got to Loeche-les-Bains and Lucien's chalet once more, it was without Lucien himself – he by now was married. Themistocles Hoetis joined him for a week, and Baldwin was able to work on his play, *The Amen Corner*, drink absinthe, and 'throw the bull' in the evenings. Then Hoetis went back to Paris, and Baldwin followed in early spring. *Go Tell It on the Mountain* was published on 11 May.

It was something of a success. Many critics welcomed its author – as Bill Cole had predicted – as an unusually promising addition to the literary scene, and not only the 'Negro literary scene'. This was exactly how Baldwin wanted it, of course. 'He was very insistent', says David Ross, an English friend of the time, who saw him in Paris in the days immediately before and after publication, 'that he was not a black writer but an American one – indeed an English-language writer.'

Only the most blinkered of commentators would have had to put this accomplished novel in a sub-category before offering it praise, and few felt the need to do so. 'It is a cliché to say that a first novel shows promise,' wrote the reviewer in the New York *Herald-Tribune*. 'But what does one say when a first novel is fulfilment?' The *Saturday Review of Literature* declared that Baldwin's first novel was 'as skilfully written as many a man's fifth essay in fiction', while the critic in the *New Leader*, his old stamping-ground, wrote that 'there is no danger that it will be pigeonholed a novel of protest'.

Baldwin had made his point, and on the whole one finds little of the 'be-kind-to-niggers, be-kind-to-Jews' patronizing hospitality which, looking back, he would sometimes claim had greeted him at the outset of his career. The *New York Times* placed him alongside the black novelist Ralph Ellison, but since Ellison had won the National Book Award the previous year for *Invisible Man*, the comparison was nothing but complimentary.

In a modest but genuine way he was entitled to feel he had 'made it'. His talent had been noted; his name would be mentioned in future discussions of the younger generation of novelists; and whatever he chose to do now, over the next four or five years, he could count on the critics' attention.

Yet no amount of worldly success – and this was nothing compared with what was to come – could bridge the gap between him and those people among whom he was residing in Europe, or between him and the people in New York, blood relations of the Europeans, now so enthusiastically ushering him into their studies and their offices, and on to their invitation lists.

As if to remind himself of this 'mark' – as 'ineffaceable' as the seal placed on John Grimes's forehead by Brother Elisha – he wrote an essay, after finishing his novel, about his time in Loeche-les-Bains. He called it 'Stranger in the Village' (how often the word 'stranger' crops up in his prose in those days of early success) and used it to counter the idea of acceptance and of having 'made it' in any comfortable, final sense:

This village, even were it incomparably more remote and incredibly more primitive, is the West, the West on to which I have been so strangely grafted. These people cannot be, from the point of view of power, strangers anywhere in the world; they have made the modern world, in effect, even if they do not know it. The most illiterate among them is related, in a way that I am not, to Dante, Shakespeare, Michelangelo ... Go back a few centuries and they are in their full glory – but I am in Africa, watching the conquerors arrive.

Chapter Eight

From now on he would be moving around more or less constantly, abandoning one refuge for another, unwilling to pause long enough to feel like a stranger. The year following the publication of *Go Tell It on the Mountain* saw him in Gallardon, near Chartres; in Grasse; on the Côte d'Azur; in Italy; in Spain, and finally back in Paris. There was talk of going to Mexico with Hoetis and there was talk of returning home again to New York by Christmas (he did neither). He never seemed to be in one place long enough to settle down to work – and if he was, his bags were somewhere else.

He made one of his brief excursions into extravagance, renting an apartment with Hoetis in rue Nollet on the north side of Paris – 'No more hotel rooms for me' he chirped to Bill Cole – which temporarily raised his morale. 'Jimmy is around, looking gracious, almost regal', David Ross wrote to Mary Keen in London from Paris; Ross, a journalist and part of the crowd from the Hôtel de Verneuil, had known Baldwin when he was utterly down and out:

People apparently expect Jimmy to repay past kindnesses and he just can't. At one stage, he went to Spain, reputedly to escape creditors! He is not, of course, in anything like the condition he was in but he is by no means well off yet. He is planning to buy his mother a house and to help bring up his 275 brothers and sisters. Gidske's stories about how he is taking to fame vary with her mood: sometimes he is a sucker, lapping up praise from the lowest elements for whom she has only contempt; other times he is quite unspoilt by it all. I have had only a few words with him and I feel rather uncomfortably patronized.

The same two obsessions dominated Baldwin throughout every period, in every place: his love life and his writing life. Both tended towards a state of anarchy. Hoetis recalls a stream of unlikely visitors to the rue Nollet apartment, including a high-ranking police officer, while Baldwin's correspondence bears witness to a multitude of unconsummated literary projects.

Ideas came to him without difficulty – only to disappear with equal ease. Since finishing *Go Tell It on the Mountain*, he told his publisher, he had worked on two short stories, but had scrapped both the novels he thought he might write. 'Studies for a New Morality', of which the *Zero* essay 'Preservation of Innocence' was supposed to constitute the opening chapters, had also been abandoned. In another letter to Cole he outlined a critical study of Negro letters from the time of the Abolitionists to Richard Wright, but nothing more is heard of it; nor did anything come of a book about Harlem, which was Cole's idea.

Somehow, from the heat of this disarray, emerged *The Amen Corner*, a play set in the living-room and storefront church of Sister Margaret, a preacher. She is bringing up her son to worship the Lord and to be a church pianist, but their lives are unsettled by the return to the fold of Margaret's errant jazz musician husband, Luke.

Baldwin's dissatisfaction with Philip Vaudrin, his editor at Knopf, developed into contrariness when aggravated. His publishers were set to build him up into the next 'Negro novelist' and what they wanted from him was a second novel. A non-fiction book about Harlem might also be welcomed, and even short stories were acceptable – they could be sold to magazines and could be regarded as throat-clearing for a longer work of fiction. Any of these projects would have seemed a natural step forward – but not a play.

When Vaudrin discouraged him, however, it only made him more determined to finish it and to do something with it, even if it meant returning to New York and peddling it himself. (He did, and *The Amen Corner* was produced on Broadway, but not for another twelve years.) Vaudrin was being short-sighted, for in writing *The Amen Corner*, Baldwin, without apparently being conscious of it, had completed a trilogy of works about black life in Harlem and the black church, one in each of the genres in which he chose to write: first the unpublished non-fiction book in collaboration with the photographer Pelatowski; next his novel; and now a play. To these could be appended 'The Harlem Ghetto', the essay which first brought his name to Cole's attention.

His black consciousness was, so to speak, folk-based rather than politically based. Baldwin did not write in the service of a social or political idea

– as both Wright and Ellison, in different ways, had done – but out of the experience of one young black man growing up in a white world. Like Wright, he recognized that his pain was but a fragment of a nation-wide silent black agony, but he steered clear of the literature of protest and kept his bearings by following the advice of another of his early mentors, Hemingway: write about what you know. Baldwin's concern was with the specialness of his community, and, within it, of himself. He wrote about families and churches and fathers and sons. While the white world does not actually enter this community, the community would not exist in its particular form were it not for the white world surrounding and controlling it.

At the same time he brought to his pages an elegant introspection and a luminosity quite unlike Wright's often clumsy prose, revealing facets of the black man's burden – and the white man's – never seen or talked about before. A complicated social irony was involved here, for most of Baldwin's friends were white. Lucien was white, Hoetis, and his close female friends, Mary Painter, Gidske Anderson, Bosley Brotman and others, were white; all the Hôtel de Verneuil crowd were white, as was another group of literary Americans he had recently become acquainted with, centring on the rue de Verneuil apartment of Eileen and Stanley Geist. His editors on the New York magazines and his publishers and agents too were white. Richard Wright and the writers who hung around the Café Tournon were mostly black, but Baldwin had fallen out with Wright and didn't go to the Tournon anyway. There was Beauford Delaney, who had arrived in Paris during the past year, and the actor and folk singer Gordon Heath; but few others among his closest friends were black.

This was the way with him, then and always: to insist, as he had written in one of his first published book reviews, that there is one race and that we are all part of it; which meant, as far as possible, ignoring colour. And the principle would be carried over into his writing in the normal course of things. Whatever was *black* about him – his culture, more than his skin – would find its way into his art, as with the paintings of Beauford Delaney, as with singers and jazz musicians, without contrivance. If he wanted to write about whites, he would.

Therefore, Knopf's promising young black author was not simply being awkward when he wrote to Bill Cole on 13 January 1954, with the idea for yet another novel. It was a great departure for him, and he admitted that he had doubts about it – 'It's not about Negroes'. In fact, it was peopled entirely by whites. He disclosed its working title – 'One for My Baby', after the song written by Harold Arlen and Johnny Mercer, and sung by Billie Holiday – and the fact that it was set in the American colony in Paris. He wanted to convey something of the intensity of a particularly American insecurity and loneliness, and for that he had to use 'the good, white Protestant'. All he knew about this type he knew through pain and personal involvement. It's a love story, he continued, and – 'wouldn't you know it – tragic'.

There is a change of tone in his letters from previous years. Modesty and self-effacement had been prominent characteristics in the past. 'You might even, when you have the time, answer this letter', he unassumingly told William Phillips. When sending the requested 'Autobiographical Notes' to Bill Cole to use as publicity for *Go Tell It on the Mountain* (they later served as a preface to *Notes of a Native Son*), he added in a postscript that he didn't think 'for a moment' that they'd be able to use it. Despatching 'Many Thousands Gone' to Philip Rahv, he nervously asked him to look on it as 'the draft' of an essay.

Now there is greater self-assurance, often manifesting itself as cocksureness. Hadn't he made himself into a novelist, after all? And yet this new confidence had to wrestle with the old lack of self-confidence: his new book might not *sound* very exciting, he admitted to his agent Helen Strauss, but it was going to be, nonetheless, 'because it excites me'. To Bill Cole he excused himself for having rehearsed a long account of the project, but now someone at Knopf would know that he had not forsaken the novel form – he was just getting the hang of it, in fact.

He probably talked too much about his plans for work, tripping over his own typewriter in a race to keep up with the novelist he had suddenly become. He was always given to this habit. Some years earlier, Otto Friedrich had confided to his journal his wonder that Baldwin got anything finished at all:

The Richard Wright article, which was going to be in the mail to *Commentary** on Monday or Tuesday (it being now Friday) has only gotten as far as a first draft, which he doesn't like. And the new novel is only on page 19, which doesn't look very promising, although he still talks about getting it finished by Christmas. I was

* Probably 'Many Thousands Gone'; it was published in *Partisan Review*, Nov–Dec. 1951.

in his room this afternoon, and read what was in the typewriter, and it sounds just like *Crying Holy* all over again – has a character called Gabriel who discovers the Lord, and whose mother was slave. I said, 'Is this new novel just a version of *Crying Holy*?' He said, 'Well, yes and no.'

Changes of title and false starts were a part of his creative method. Within a month, the working title for 'One for My Baby' had changed to 'A Fable for Our Children'. It was also, at one stage, called 'Ignorant Armies'; eventually, it became *Giovanni's Room.*

He gave his agent a lengthy summary of the action, but at this point did not mention that the love affair at the centre of the novel was of a homosexual nature – not because he wished to hide the fact; simply because he did not yet know it himself. The love at the heart of this version – which, like the finished *Giovanni's Room*, was to involve blackmail and the guillotine – was between a woman and a man, a thirty-ish American divorcée, and a younger, unstable actor. By way of comparison, Baldwin mentions Hemingway's novel *The Sun Also Rises*, but he sees his heroine as being closer to Isabel Archer in James's *Portrait of a Lady* than to Hemingway's Brett Ashley.

Helen Strauss dutifully passed on the letter to Philip Vaudrin, saying 'I'm sure this news will please you'. It did; but her confidence, and Baldwin's optimistic boast that he was over his 'attack of second novel jitters', were premature.

I'm tired of Paris but I can't cope with New York – that was Baldwin's repeated SOS during 1953–4. Ever since returning to his place of refuge following the sale of *Go Tell It on the Mountain*, he had been talking, with a mixture of anticipation and procrastination, of coming home again. First it was going to be for the publication of *Mountain*, then it was going to be for autumn, then for New Year, then for the spring. He booked a passage on the SS *Flandre* for 4 May 1954, only to be held up again, by a panic-induced collapse. At last, he took the *Île de France* – the ship he had sailed on last time – on the first day of June. His suitcase held sketches for his tragic Parisian novel and the completed text of *The Amen Corner*.

Baldwin's arrival in New York on 7 June took place against the background of one of the most significant events in the history of the struggle for equal rights for black people in the United States: the outlawing of racial segregation in the nation's schools, which reversed the earlier doctrine of 'separate but equal'. The decision was reached by the Supreme Court on 17 May, just a fortnight before Baldwin stepped aboard the SS *Île de France* at Le Havre.

There is, however, a total absence of mention of this event in Baldwin's writing, both in his essays and his letters. This may seem surprising at first, but we ought to remember that the 'Negro problem' or the 'Negro question' was thought about and spoken of in a different way then – different, even, from how it would be spoken of in two or three years' time – especially by a Northerner, like Baldwin. There was not yet a popular front in the civil rights movement, even though that movement had long been in existence. It is quite likely, of course, that Baldwin talked of the historic decision and related matters with Gordon Heath and other friends in Paris, and with his family once he was home; but it had yet to capture him emotionally. Had it already done so, there would be evidence on the page, for whatever was prominent in Baldwin's feelings he quickly transmitted in his writing. The two were one.

Within two years he would be politically 'awakened', as blacks in the South realized how ineffective the Court's ruling was, and the struggle gathered momentum. But for the time being he was temperamentally disinclined to favour any kind of movement – literary, political or otherwise – with his membership.

In New York, Baldwin stayed with Bill Cole and his wife for a short time at their apartment on West 54th Street, with other friends in the Village, and he frequently went to visit his family in Harlem. Early one morning, he and Hoetis (who had returned from Mexico and joined Baldwin once again in New York) were walking down Third Avenue towards the subway station at 52nd Street when they were caught up in a police swoop on a gang of youngsters. Baldwin and Hoetis were carted off with the others to the notorious underground prison known as the Tombs and kept there overnight. They had stopped at bar on 53rd Street, and as they were leaving it, a group of young men came alongside them, holding a lamp which they had apparently taken from another bar or restaurant nearby. 'And just as they showed it to us,' recalls Hoetis, 'the whole lot of us were surrounded by cops, and we were all arrested. They put him in a cell next to me. And he just *screamed*. All night long. I said, Cool it, Jimmy, in the morning someone'll come for us and get us out – because they had allowed us one phone call. For me it was my editor, and for him it was Bill Cole. I was annoyed about it, but quite sure that we would get out in the morning.

But Jimmy – "*I'm a nigger*, they picked me up because I'm black", and so on. What a freak-out – all through the night, a raving maniac. And in the morning he was very indignant.'

It was not surprising. He had no doubt had to share his cell with ghosts of his previous incarceration in Paris, which had affected him deeply, according to Hoetis, and with older, crueller ghosts – 'We don't serve Negroes here', 'Why don't you niggers go back uptown where you belong', 'I don't let rooms to coloured people', and many, many more.

The next morning, Baldwin was arraigned before a judge on a charge of disorderly conduct, for a refusal to move on order of a policeman. He received a suspended sentence and walked free.

In August, he was settled at the peaceful MacDowell Colony for writers in the New Hampshire countryside, working hard: he had a studio in the middle of the woods, where no-one could see him without permission. Lunch was delivered punctually at twelve. The evenings, he told Bill Cole, were slightly painful because the studios were without electric light. 'Drawback: damn near impossible to get a drink.'

The year and more which Baldwin spent in America on this occasion was a productive period. Although he worked on his novel whenever he could, he did not finish it, but he wrote several important essays, including 'Equal in Paris' and 'Gide as Husband and Homosexual' (republished as 'The Male Prison'). He completed 'Notes of a Native Son', and used it as the title essay for his first collection, which was accepted by the Beacon Press, a small but venerable publisher situated in Boston. At the same time, he met many of the emerging New York writers, including William Styron, James Jones – both of whom would later become firm friends – Jack Kerouac and the poet John Ashbery.

Efforts to have his play performed on the professional stage were in vain. The part of the jazz musician, Luke, had been written with the commanding figure of Gordon Heath in mind, but since Heath was in Paris Baldwin asked his agent to try someone else – Louis Armstrong. That came to nothing, and he told Heath that the play was getting 'glowing rejections' from almost everybody, mentioning the name of Elia Kazan, among others.

However, between 10 May and 19 May 1955, a student production of *The Amen Corner* was mounted in Washington DC at Howard University, directed by Owen Dodson, himself a poet and playwright. Baldwin revelled in the occasion. Lucien, still his most trusted friend though they were no longer lovers, had arrived in New York the previous year, and he rented a car and drove some members of the Baldwin family down to Howard to be at the première.

The play had been revised and revised again, but when Baldwin saw the first rehearsals, and heard actors speaking his lines, he was horrified. It was like being 'bombarded with my own literature'. The exposition took far too long and some of the speeches were prolix and portentous. 'I had to begin cutting because I realized that actors could do many things in silence or make one word, one gesture, count more than two or three pages of talk.'*

The Howard University Players was an accomplished and respected group which had toured Europe, and, within its own terms, the production was a success. Baldwin was pleased – 'a fantastic and wonderful experience' was how he described it to Gordon Heath. But disappointment with Broadway was turning into disillusionment, and, suspecting that London might prove more receptive, he asked Heath to take his copy of the script across the Channel to try to sell it there. Heath did as requested, but to no avail, and *The Amen Corner* was not produced in either London or New York until much later, when Baldwin had made his name with other works, including a different play.

He was far less excited by the prospect of the publication of a book of his essays than he was about a student production of his play. His articles were 'magazine work'; they grew out of assignments; at their most basic they were simply a way of keeping the bread buttered. Baldwin didn't think of himself as an essayist, but as a novelist and playwright, and he seems to have made little or no conscious effort to refine his essay technique after his reviewing days at the *New Leader* had ended. But that is just the point: the form, and the style, came to him as he spoke, that is to say naturally.

His essays seldom started as discussions of race relations, getting around to the topic only after beginning as something else: literary criticism, or an account of a week in prison, or a boy's tempestuous relationship with his father, or a postcard from a snowy mountain village, or a

---

* It is not certain what version of the play was finally performed at Howard, but there is scarcely any resemblance at all between the original version, Act One of which was published in *Zero* No. 6, July 1954, and the text as it was performed on the professional stage in 1965. The text of the latter performance was published in 1968.

review of *Porgy and Bess* or of the black musical *Carmen Jones*. On reaching the by now characteristic rhetorical finale, they would exhibit a common theme: how to survive this pain – the pain of hatred and self-hatred – which threatens to wreck the structure of the self more violently than anything white people individually can do.

He did have lessons: from Henry James in punctuation and vocabulary; from Hemingway in conciseness; from Frederick Douglass and all the storefront preachers he had ever heard in the effective use of anecdote and cadence; and he never lost the sardonic edge of black speech, 'something ironic and perpetually understated'.

But his preoccupation with literary form – a deep and absorbing preoccupation – centres almost totally on the novel, the play and the short story. In his letters to Cole, Rahv and others in the mid-1950s he discussed his aesthetic problems at length; of his essays – apart from mentioning the fact that he is writing one or expecting payment for one – there is scarcely a word. When Baldwin discloses his sense of himself as a writer, it is always as a writer of fiction.

Yet it is the essay and not the novel – especially not the social-realist type of novel that Baldwin was writing – that provides space for the play of the intellect, and the intellect, not the imagination, was Baldwin's strong suit. (Here he differs most from his idol Henry James, who exemplifies what T. S. Eliot calls 'thinking with our feelings'.) Baldwin's quicksilver intelligence was the quality about him that most impressed his friends in Paris. 'He could assimilate everything you said,' remarks Gordon Heath, 'and synthesize it with such speed and eloquence, that you ended up being flattered by his version of your ideas.' The essay form enabled Baldwin to write as he spoke, to unfold his experience by discursive methods, until he came upon the meaning at the core.

Notes of a Native Son unharnesses his gift for autobiographical rumination, his willingness to force his way into new and awkward challenges. The greatest challenge of all was to be free to set his own terms for the course his life was going to follow in American society, where, in spite of all his disappearances, he knew he belonged. In order to achieve this, to slough off the old 'nigger' identity he had inherited, he had to invent another way of thinking about himself. The essay was the place to do it, and the didactic process is laid out in the pages of *Notes of a Native Son*.

The book appeared late in 1955, by which time Baldwin had returned to Paris. The title contains an obvious echo of Richard Wright's novel – an impertinent one to Wright's ears, no doubt – and also of Henry James's *Notes of a Son and Brother*. The small audience was mostly enthusiastic. One critic could only damn with faint praise, however, and from Baldwin's point of view he was probably the reviewer who mattered most: Langston Hughes.

Hughes had reacted peculiarly to the publication of *Go Tell It on the Mountain* two-and-a-half years earlier. To his friend Arna Bontemps he had said that Baldwin 'over-writes and over-poeticizes in images way over the heads of the people supposedly thinking them'. An '"art" book', he called it, 'about folks who aren't "art" folks'. *Mountain* was 'a low-down story in a velvet bag'.

All this was written before Baldwin's novel had actually been published, for William Cole at Knopf had sent Hughes an advance copy in the hope of eliciting a useful quotation. Once the book was released, however, and Baldwin had been tipped as the coming man, Hughes took off his hat to him. He went to the trouble of seeking him out in Paris, by letter, telling him he was 'very happy your book has been getting such good write-ups', singling out one section for particular praise, and even sending Baldwin extra copies of the reviews, 'to give away or something'.

When it came to reviewing *Notes of a Native Son* in the *New York Times*, Hughes, looking back, retreated to his original position on the novel, and was able only to offer a backhanded compliment on the new book of essays. He liked it better than he had liked *Go Tell It on the Mountain*, he confessed, but the 'American native son who signs his name James Baldwin' was some way off yet from being 'a great artist in writing'. When Baldwin could 'look at life purely as himself and for himself' and surrender his obsession with colour problems, then 'America and the world might well have a major contemporary commentator'.

As was often the way, Baldwin's mood rose and fell perilously during his stay in the United States. He had returned to New York from Paris high on a wave of success; Lucien, his 'buddy', had joined him in his native city; his play had had its première; another book was being made ready for the publishers; and he was in the preliminary stages of a new love affair. Yet two months after the 'fantastic' week of *The Amen Corner*, while still in Washington, he wrote to Edward Parone, a friend who had also attended the première, and who was an editor at Dell Books in New York, that things continued to go badly. The best he could say was that everything was so awful that his bad luck surely could not last long. A suspected illness is mentioned, but what really hurt was that Lucien had gone back to Europe without him. Baldwin followed, after the usual series of postponements, and his spirits sank even further. He was obsessed with the idea of a happy, settled domestic life with Lucien. Even if Lucien had been available and agreeable – and he was neither: he was married and as domesticated as he ever wanted to be – Baldwin would most likely have grown restless anyway before long. But loneliness and unhappiness cry out for the balm of security, and the greatest security is love. Baldwin was great at *talking* about love – he was capable of talking for hours of nothing else – but he was not always good at keeping it when it came to him. His wit and charm were irrepressible; they drew people to him easily, and he was never short of admirers – the sort who would buy him a drink at the Café de Flore – or of partners; and when he said some years later that nothing is more meaningless than an endless round of conquests, he spoke from first-hand experience.

When depressed, he moaned habitually of ill-health and a haunted psyche. Various disorders are listed in letters of the weeks following his return to Paris in the autumn of 1955. He left New York with a note to Edward Parone complaining of 'nerves', and updated it from the other side of the ocean with the news that he had been sick since he got back. To Gordon Heath he sent a message saying that something had gone wrong with his stomach, and his exclamatory 'Happy New Year!' to Bill Cole at the beginning of 1956 came with the accompanying news that he had had the 'minor crackup' he knew was coming – safely, over there, in the dark, alone.

Other letters of the time speak of 'phantomes and terrors', and 'rage and tears'. To Carl van Vechten he wrote that he had been attacked by a strange microbe, which led to visits to doctors and a paralysing gloom.

He confided to Parone his heartbreak over Lucien, which was at the root of it all. The most compelling reason he had got on the boat was that he simply could not stand not knowing how things were back in Europe with 'L'. Nothing can ever be recaptured, Baldwin says, but by the same token there are some things that never go away. How long the current situation would last he was unsure – how often had he tried to take flight only to discover that his feet refused to leave the ground? He was on the verge of accepting a crucial fact of life: that no condition could be escaped. But it could be transcended – and transcended, perhaps, with the very same energy that was spilled so 'fruitlessly' in tears and in rage.

Throughout it all there was the unremitting shortage of money. He told Lionel Trilling, who was endorsing his application for a grant, that he was always expecting that after the *next* book he would walk in a glow of confidence, interior and financial. Meanwhile the old pleas for help continued: he asked Parone to please send him five or ten dollars, and to 'thank Van' for the cheque. His French agent had received a request for 10,000 francs before he sailed for America, and, once he was back in Paris, he asked Bill Cole if he could raise his debt to him by two hundred dollars.

This displays an ingenuousness bordering on impudence – not only did Baldwin have little immediate prospect of paying the money back, but he adds that he is asking Cole rather than someone on his own side of the ocean, because one of the reasons he found himself in trouble was that he was liquidating all his Paris debts.

Cole, liking Baldwin immensely and regarding him as a personal friend as much as a professional investment, paid up. The money was never returned. Before long, Baldwin was forced to start looking for another publisher anyway. His tragic love story, which had originally involved a divorcée and an actor, was now called *Giovanni's Room* and while it was still tragic, still not about Negroes, the love affair at its centre had turned out to be between two men.

His editors at Knopf, already irritated at not receiving a second novel set in Harlem, feared legal action over the homosexual content of the novel and decided they wouldn't publish it. Indeed, they warned Baldwin (Cole was not among them), no one would touch it unless he toned it down.

Baldwin received this not unexpected news with a shrug of despair: toning down the book, he wrote to Parone, would mean, in effect, no book.

Chapter Nine

One of the first things he did on returning to Paris was to despatch a revised copy of *The Amen Corner* to Gordon Heath, whom he still wanted for the part of Luke. He sent it by messenger to the Villa Racine, where Heath was living, and scrawled a postscript at the foot of the accompanying note: 'Give bearer your phone number. Bearer's name is Arnold, musician, nice boy.'

Baldwin had met Arnold in the Village. They had been introduced, somewhat ironically, by Lucien. Arnold had travelled down to Howard for the production of *The Amen Corner*, and now was with Baldwin in Paris, while Lucien had returned to Switzerland to attend to his wife and children.

Arnold's life so far had led him through the ghetto triangle of Harlem, the army and drugs. He was younger than Baldwin, and the traps he had fallen into were the same traps as Baldwin feared might await his own younger brothers. Arnold was now seeking relief from the needle in music; his instrument was the vibraphone, and Baldwin tried to help him get on his feet by introducing him to some of the jazz musicians he knew. After Lucien, it was to be the most serious affair of Baldwin's time in Paris.

They stayed together throughout the winter, and no doubt the growing attachment contributed to Baldwin's change of mood, which, by the spring of 1956, was complete. In fact, a wholesale reversal of fortunes was taking place. For one thing, money came his way – a grant of $1,000 from the National Institute of Arts and Letters, and at the same time a fellowship worth three times that amount from *Partisan Review*. Better still, he had taken *Giovanni's Room* to London at the end of 1955, where Michael Joseph had read it, bought it, and promised to publish it no matter what the lawyers said. Contemptuous of the pusillanimity of his American counterparts, Baldwin's English publisher gave him $400 and told him he would take anything else he ever wrote (the promise was kept).

By the end of April, the troubles which had weighed so heavily on him during the previous year – illness, the continuing moral burden of his family, hardships of love and money – seemed to have evaporated. He was so 'heady with triumph' over the prestigious NIAL award that he almost forgot to tell Bill Cole about the much larger *Partisan Review* fellowship: it also began in May, the 'merry, merry, merry, merry month of'.

Partisan Review's sponsorship was to result in the forty-page story 'Sonny's Blues', which appeared in the issue for summer 1957; but the first thing the magazine published by Baldwin after the announcement was an essay – an argument, in fact. The argument was with one of the country's leading writers: William Faulkner.

The row which Faulkner had inadvertently sparked off, and which he was now desperately trying to stamp out, did not involve only Baldwin: it was taking place across the nation. In an interview with the English journalist Russell Howe, printed in the *Reporter* (March 1956), Faulkner had discussed the recent troubles in the South, which stemmed from the decision of the Supreme Court in 1954 to outlaw segregation in schools. A black girl, Autherine Lucy, acting in accordance with her new constitutional rights, had enrolled in and been admitted to the University of Alabama. However, whites throughout the state were protesting about the admission, and threatening violence to prevent her from entering the building. The National Association for the Advancement of Colored People (NAACP) supported her, of course, but the State of Alabama was now threatening to outlaw the NAACP, which would have the effect of removing the black campaigners' organizational focus.

Faulkner maintained a position of general sympathy with the Negro cause in discussing the problem with Howe, but at the same time he affirmed immovable solidarity with his own state, Mississippi, one of the most hard-line segregationist areas in the South. The only practical support he could muster for the black population was the by-now tired advice to 'go slow'. The consequence of ignoring this advice, he warned, would be riots in the streets, and

if it came to fighting I'd fight for Mississippi against the United States even if it meant going out into the street and shooting Negroes. After all, I'm not going to shoot Mississippians.

Attempting to clarify this last sentence (weren't Negroes also Mississippians?), Howe asked Faulkner if he meant 'white Mississippians'. The reply, hardly less confusing, was, 'No, I said Mississippians – in Mississippi the problem isn't racial.'

Faulkner's standing was not further enhanced by comments such as: 'My Negro boys down on the plantation would fight against the North [meaning white liberal supporters of equal rights] with me. If I say to them, "Go get your shotguns, boys", they'll come.' Nor by his repeated insistence that, left alone with time for reflection and time to see 'that the world is looking on and laughing at them', white Southerners would come to their senses and permit a rise in social status for the Negro quite willingly.

This type of reasoning was scarcely likely to persuade impatient blacks throughout the South to stop their (mainly peaceful) campaign of protest and go home to await the natural emergence of freedom and rights. They felt they had waited quite long enough. Fourteen-year-old Emmett Till had been lynched a few months before for having made a pass at a white woman; the two men who killed him had been acquitted in court – only to sell the story of how they did it to a national magazine. Martin Luther King's house had been bombed, so had the homes of his colleagues, and they had every reason to expect that they would be bombed again. White men and women of the so-called respectable middle classes exhibited a sudden propensity for mob rule and showed every willingness to use violent tactics, from spitting to lynching, to prevent a young girl from receiving tuition at her state university. Faulkner's view that it was only stubborn pride that was making white Southerners react so badly – an ancient antipathy to being pushed around by the North – was hardly what enlightened sections of the American public expected to hear from a famous writer and Nobel Prize winner.

Responding in the pages of *Partisan Review* at the request of Philip Rahv, Baldwin talked back boldly to the rambling 'Squire of Oxford': Faulkner's 'middle of the road' position, he declared in 'Faulkner and Desegregation', was no position at all. His oft-repeated claims of being on the side of the Negro were bogus.

Where is the evidence of the struggle he has been carrying on there on behalf of the Negro? Why, if he and his enlightened confrères in the South have been boring from within to destroy segregation, do they react with such panic when the walls show any sign of falling? Why – and how – does one move from the middle of the road where one was aiding Negroes into the street – to shoot them?

Faulkner – by all accounts more than a little drunk at the time of the interview – had since disavowed the inflammatory remarks attributed to him by Russell Howe, and the *Reporter* had published a denial. Underneath, however, was printed a further rebuttal from Howe: if Faulkner's remarks misconstrued his thoughts, Howe said, then 'I, as an admirer . . . am glad to know it. But what I set down is what he said.'

This confrontation increased the bitterness which Baldwin already felt concerning the South and whites who could affirm 'Negroes are right', yet were willing at the same time to take extreme measures to protect the status quo. It was the beginning of his political involvement, and his first public sign of impatience; but so far frustration was still held in check, and made to yield to a literary style whose essence was restraint.

At the same time, the debate marks a change in Baldwin's opinion of Faulkner's work. When he had published *Notes of a Native Son* the previous year, he had held the Mississippi novelist in high esteem. In the 'Autobiographical Notes' which preface the volume, he complained that there was a tendency to speak of the 'Negro problem' in the US as if it were a thing apart and not part of the general social fabric. But he praised the work of Faulkner (and Robert Penn Warren and Ralph Ellison), in which one saw 'the beginnings – at least – of a more genuinely penetrating search'.

After this, his remarks about Faulkner and his black creations were mainly uncomplimentary, though he cannot be said to have qualified his objections beyond a pithy assault on Faulkner's *Requiem for a Nun* in the pages of *No Name in the Street* (1972). Faulkner's portraits of Negroes, Baldwin said, 'lack a system of nuances which, perhaps, only a black writer can see in black life – for Faulkner could see Negroes only as they related to him, not as they related to each other.' This is at once a truism and not wholly accurate, but Baldwin does not stop to argue the case; instead he issues a supreme backhanded compliment of his own: while they lack subtlety, Faulkner's portraits of Negroes are nevertheless 'made vivid by the torment of their creator'.

'Faulkner and Desegregation' drew attention to Baldwin as a black spokesman, and heralded his entry into the debate about the Southern crisis. Yet the piece was written from Paris, and published while Baldwin continued to live there. He had never visited that 'South' about which he spoke so passionately. 'Still love Paris', he told the Harlem Renaissance veteran Harold Jackman at the same time as his essay was published. In America he felt that he always walked in the shadow of a kind of terror, which had not lightened since the time of his youth.

After his last trip home, Paris – which had not changed either – seemed to welcome him back. Yet something *had* changed: himself; and his return to Europe this time led him to the discovery that he was not part of this great, liberating city or its culture, and never would be. He acknowledged a large debt to Europe, but the most important thing Europe could give him was his own identity. That identity was not European, nor was it African, nor was it even principally Negro – it was American. Baldwin now accepted this emotionally – the only way he truly could accept things – and his acceptance was final.

It is out of this faith, in fact, that *Giovanni's Room* emerges, a book without the presence of a single black. The setting is Paris, and the cast includes a number of Parisians, together with Giovanni, the Italian of the title. Yet the most important character here is not Giovanni but David, a young middle-class American of the clean, upstanding type – blond, 'rather like an arrow' – loyal to his parents, keen to marry, start a family and launch a career which will, no doubt, be much like his father's. It is in this figure, and not the impetuous, vivacious Latin, that the novelist has invested his exploratory energy.

As Baldwin explained to Philip Rahv, he wrote the novel from a need to work all the 'Davids' he had ever known out of his system: whatever divided them, more united them. David was a composite of several different boys *and* girls he had known – and knowing them 'cost me a great deal'. He could save his life, Baldwin writes, only by figuring out from 'what they were trying to reveal' what they were attempting to conceal.

Giovanni's Room is a short novel with many flaws, yet it has commanded a regular following from its first publication in the autumn of 1956 to the present day. One germ of the novel lies in a New York murder case dating from 1943–4, involving a man named Lucien Carr and an older, wealthy figure who developed an obsession with him, David Kammerer. One night Carr and Kammerer were walking beside the Hudson River and Kammerer made a pass. A fight ensued, in which Carr stabbed his would-be suitor and dumped his body into the river.

The case also involved Jack Kerouac, who went with Carr to the cinema after Carr had confessed to him, and William Burroughs, who advised Carr to give himself up and get a good lawyer. But this went beyond

Baldwin's point of interest. What fascinated and repelled him was the readiness of a man to kill when confronted with another man's touch. When Kammerer's advances were turned down, he allegedly told the object of his desire, 'If you don't love me, then kill me.'

Baldwin does not quite succeed in getting this kind of drama into his story, though Giovanni is sent to the guillotine at the end – a fate that was also inspired by an actual event (according to Baldwin in a later interview). Baldwin's real concern lies elsewhere: for one thing, in producing a counter to the tough-guy novels of James M. Cain and Raymond Chandler, which he had criticized in 'Preservation of Innocence', novels wherein the homosexual, when he appears, is the excuse for an expression of disgust.

Giovanni's Room was among the first American novels to treat the subject of homosexuality with the same frankness permitted for discussions of heterosexual love. (Perhaps the all-white cast was the author's way of distancing himself from his own controversiality.) But there is virtually no graphic erotic description. Indeed, there is little in the book which would raise an eyebrow today in all but the most prurient circles. More likely causes of its continuing popularity are its neat, fable-like structure, and congruously neat moral warnings.

The plot of the novel is simple: David is in Paris while his fiancée Hella sojourns in Spain. In a bar he is introduced to Giovanni, and later the two go out on the town together, ending up in Giovanni's tiny room in bed. Giovanni is of a mainly homosexual inclination, but he has lived with a woman in Italy and had a child, and finally his response to love transcends consciousness of gender. The experience is confusing, though not entirely new, for David, who is inhibited by the social unacceptability of the love of one man for another.

In order to affirm his manhood, he seduces a pathetically willing female acquaintance, and then, when his fiancée returns from Spain, he shuns Giovanni, who takes to prostituting himself, commits a murder, and is eventually guillotined. David, meanwhile, is prowling around bars trying to pick up sailors, as much a victim as Giovanni – indeed, more so, for his death is a death of the soul. His punisher is not the inexorable legal machine of society, but his own inherited inability to face love when he finds it.

The theme is a traditional and typically American one: *Giovanni's Room* sets up a clash of puritanism and restraint with daring and adventure, and chronicles the loss of innocence that results. The action is formed into a quasi-allegory common to the nineteenth-century novel, which boils down, in this case, to a choice facing David: commitment to the one he loves, irrespective of caste, wealth or social standing; or compromise with the person he has been groomed to wed, his fiancée Hella. How would Dad react if he brought home Giovanni? How will *he* feel if he goes home with Hella?

Baldwin stretches his material somewhat to bring out the tragic implications of David's failure to strike the correct moral bargain, and his aesthetic compromises include a strong dose of melodrama, spurts of purple prose, and some mismanaged characterization. Giovanni is the first of those intensely human, yet idealized, characters, with a touch of the saint about them, who were later to dominate Baldwin's fiction. Their vulnerability – usually when forced to deal with others' 'inauthentic' values and behaviour – is the very measure of their moral intactness. In a choice between safety and honour, they choose the latter. After Giovanni, they were mostly black.

In a letter to Philip Rahv, Baldwin worried that an ignorance of details of David's life would falsify his portrait, but in such respects David is quite convincing; the main threat to his fictional integrity comes, rather, directly from his creator, and it was to prove a recurring flaw in Baldwin's fiction after *Go Tell It on the Mountain*. It is the author's inability to keep his own opinions and tone of voice out of his characters' mouths. This hardly crops up at all in *Mountain* or in the short stories which Baldwin wrote in the late 1940s. In *Giovanni's Room*, it first seeps in at the end of the opening chapter, and after that pollutes the fictional atmosphere.

It is paradoxical that the flaw in Baldwin's fiction should stem from the same root that strengthens and distinguishes his essays. The forthright opinions, the clarity of exposition, which breathe life into 'Notes of a Native Son' and 'Equal in Paris', corrode the fictionality of David, and to a lesser extent Giovanni. Baldwin's worry ought not to have been that he made his leading characters white, but that he had withheld the voices which would have enabled them to speak their own minds.

At the end of the first chapter, David describes himself as 'one of those people who pride themselves on their willpower', and then embarks on a self-examination, delivered not in his own voice but that of his creator: 'This virtue, like most virtues, is ambiguity itself. People who believe they are strong-willed and the masters of their own destiny can only continue to believe this by becoming specialists in self-deception.' This does not sound like a man who is condemning himself through lack of self-knowledge. Later on, David reflects, in an unmistakeably Baldwinian phrase, that 'home is not a place but simply an irrevocable condition'; and later still, 'the end of innocence is also the end of guilt'.

Equally disruptive are the frequent descents into poetic prose. The novel starts strongly with a scene in the south of France, in which David ruminates on the events which are about to be related to us in detail. But the bright prose which had made vivid the sphere of Harlem worship turns to soupy lyricism when transposed to cafés in the Paris dawn, where overtures are passed between David and Giovanni. Sitting in an all-night place in Les Halles, David looks towards a boy standing at the bar – 'he blushed, which made him, in the light of the pale, rising sun, resemble a freshly fallen angel'. One page on, he describes Giovanni's eyes as 'unbelievably, like morning stars', and, just a few lines later, Giovanni as 'like a kid about five years old waking up on Christmas morning'.

Incidental matters of style and structure apart, it took courage to write and to publish *Giovanni's Room* at a time when homosexuality was illegal on both sides of the Atlantic. The warning issued by his editor at Knopf, and by his agent Helen Strauss (who had told him to 'burn it') proved to be groundless. After its acceptance in England, it was read by the head of Dial Press, George Joel, who handed it over to a young editor, Jim Silberman. Silberman's initial reservations were cancelled out by the recognition of talent at work. He suggested moving the disclosure of Giovanni's tragic fate from the beginning of the novel – where it had been – to the end, and offered Baldwin a contract, worth $2,000, for this novel and his next.

'Your obsession with people half queer, half man, is very interesting indeed,' an American friend wrote to Baldwin after receiving a copy of the novel. Leslie Schenk, a would-be novelist himself enjoying Paris on the GI Bill, instanced Lucien and Arnold – and David. And he was curious to know 'how much of it is autobiographical'.

Others have wondered the same thing since, catching a whiff of a scent in the epigraph from Walt Whitman, 'I am the man, I suffered, I was there', and coupling this with the dedication, 'To Lucien'. But the story of Giovanni and David in no way reflects that of Baldwin and Happersberger, and the answer to the autobiography question, as with most such novels (including *Go Tell It on the Mountain*), is: a little bit here and a little bit there; something of atmosphere and feeling, but not much specific detail. Baldwin said that Giovanni was 'a composite of about four people', as was David, according to the letter he wrote about the novel to Philip Rahv. The 'room', Lucien and another friend, Mary Painter, agree, was inspired by that of a friend near the Porte de Vincennes where Baldwin often stayed. There was no important Latin lover in Baldwin's life in the early 1950s, although no particular conclusion should be drawn from that, for a novelist needs only one brief meeting with a living person to be inspired to give him or her a full life in fiction.

Most critics welcomed Baldwin's second novel, admiring his assured and sensitive treatment of a delicate subject, and many applauded his bold decision to produce a book without a black character. (It took the ingenious Harold Isaacs, writing in the magazine *Phylon* four years later, to discern an 'African thread' running through the story, in Baldwin's decision to take the first name of his 'very black' father and give it to his WASP protagonist.) Contrary to the assumption of the Knopf editorial team, which had advised him to come up with another 'Negro' novel, the better critics saw his latest move as a desire to step beyond the black writer's usual obsession with his situation: an obsession, remarked Leslie Fiedler in the *New Leader*, in what is surely a silent reference to Richard Wright, 'which keeps him forever writing a first book'.

Baldwin was aware of such a danger. He displayed artistic maturity in not giving in to his publishers' wishes. If his all-white novel with a taboo subject, set not in New York but in Paris, turned out to be a failure, then at least it wouldn't be a failure because he had made the mistake of trying to do the same thing twice.

Baldwin's friend Leslie Schenk was in general agreement with the critics over the novel's quality but in one department he found it seriously lacking:

it is inexcusable of you not to have had a French person check your French. Jimmie, of all the many times you lapse into French there is hardly once when there are not serious errors, and elementary errors at that . . . Page 46: 'Ma cheri' must be either 'ma chérie' or 'mon chéri' but not what it is. 59: 'Va te faire foutre' should be 'Vas te . . .' just as on the next page 'T'aura' should be 'T'auras'. P71, 'quelle boulot' should of course be 'quel boulot'. Page 77, since it is a woman speaking, she should say 'Je suis ravie' rather than 'Je suis ravi'. 79, nouveau riche should be nouveaux riches. 95, il faut beau bien should be il faut bien beau . . . and well this could go on forever.

The English edition appeared a year later than the American – despite the book having been accepted in England first – by which time the errors had been corrected, either by Baldwin himself or by someone else.*

Just as William Cole had been instrumental in having *Go Tell It on the Mountain* accepted at Knopf, the person who persuaded Dial Press to take *Giovanni's Room* was Philip Rahv, whose connections with the firm dated back more than a decade. He did not regard it as a great novel, but he persuaded George Joel that the author had great potential.

Dial Press remained Baldwin's publishers for over twenty years, although relations were often strained. 'They picked it up,' he said in 1984 about *Giovanni's Room*, 'because they had nothing to lose. And they published it – without my photograph.'

Here again we catch him in the act of rewriting his story. We should not read too much into an off-the-cuff remark, but Dial had plenty to lose by publishing a novel about homosexuality by a little-known author, black or white, in 1956. If they published it without his photograph, he would quite likely have approved, for he had taken an honourable gamble in writing a novel without black characters. This gamble, his agent had warned, could block his way forward as 'the next Negro novelist'. But in 1956, to be simply the next *Negro* novelist was not what he wanted.

---

* Curiously, however, the errors have been replicated in some later paperback editions.

Chapter Ten

Paris in 1956 transmitted nightly news of the war in Algeria. 'Dreadful (but interesting)' was Baldwin's comment to Philip Rahv – one of his few comments then on the struggle. He seems never to have considered settling down to write something – a 'Letter from Paris' for *Partisan Review* for example – about the colonial eruption which, at first glance, it would seem should have inspired him.

Baldwin's understanding of foreign situations came out of his understanding of his own. It made Paris seem more like home, he quipped to Rahv. He saw the Algerians as France's 'niggers', and the physiognomy which had often shown him kindness he now judged capable of cruelty, the same species of cruelty which he had spent so long outflanking in New York.

In French eyes he was an American; therefore he was free from imperial scorn; his stay in Europe was a holiday in the sense that he felt entitled to ignore the politics surrounding him. But what he saw of French treatment of the Arabs shocked him, and put an end, for the time being, to his love affair with France. He began to feel, with the kind of emotional certainty which always preceded action, that although he had scant wish to go back to America, there was less reason for remaining in Europe, Lucien's presence notwithstanding. Indeed, the choice of a new lover from Harlem at this time characterizes the demise of his marriage to France.

There was also his career to consider. In America his reputation was increasing, whereas in Parisian circles he was unknown. The French publication of *Go Tell It on the Mountain* had been postponed repeatedly, and his appearances in the pages of journals such as *Le Preuve* were rare. The storm that raged over his own country, moreover, drew his attention from the currents flowing through his adopted home.

By now he could read and speak French well, but he had little inclination to engage with the literature. He had not shared Richard Wright's enthusiasm for the company of Sartre and de Beauvoir, and neither they nor the older writers still active – Cocteau, Montherlant, Céline – held much fascination for him now. Nor, more significantly, did the Africa-centred intellectual movement based in Paris, known as *'Négritude'*, led by two poets, Leopold Senghor from Senegal and Aimé Césaire from Martinique.

Négritude was a self-consciously modernist political and literary grouping, which sought to draw a multitude of influences – avant-garde as well as traditional, including as much surrealism as African dance and song – into a new 'African originality', which would be suited to the modern age. Baldwin first came into contact with its leaders in 1956, when he covered the Conference of Negro-African Writers and Artists in Paris for *Le Preuve* and *Encounter* (resulting in the article entitled 'Princes and Powers'). Although it would seem, on the face of it, to be a suitable point of entry into what was for him as much as anyone a dark continent, there was little in the concept of *Négritude* with which he felt at ease.

For one thing, it was francophone, like existentialism; for another, he had little time for artistic manifestoes and self-conscious modernism: the artist's role, as he saw it, was to be a witness and to tell his story as clearly as the facts permitted; most important of all, the literary efforts of Senghor, Césaire, Léon Damas and others did nothing to modify or subvert Baldwin's idea of himself as a Negro (there being, in a sense, no 'Negroes' in Africa). He was still, in a way that they were not, a 'bastard of the West'. *Négritude* remained to him little more than an idea. And Baldwin was as impatient with ideas, when they did not stem directly from his own experience, as he was with literary movements.

He must have been disappointed with his lack of social success with Africans, for he could scarcely have anticipated it. The foreknowledge that Paris contained many Africans would have raised the hope that he might obtain there a translation of that inscrutable chapter of his history which he carried with him everywhere. Any young American black tracing his lineage back in time found himself not in Europe but on the Gold Coast; not watching Shakespeare or Racine, but listening to the beat of the tom-tom; not on the *Mayflower* but manacled in the hold of a slave ship. The thought of coming into close contact with Africans could only have seemed exciting. Both Richard Wright and the novelist William Gardner Smith had travelled in Africa, and Smith had even settled there.

But Africans and American Negroes, Baldwin discovered in Paris, were total strangers, divided by a common colour, facing each other across a gulf of centuries. Like it or not, he was committed to Western culture in a way they never were, never could be, never wanted to be.

'They disgusted me, I think,' Baldwin told Harold Isaacs during a conversation in 1959, making specific reference to Senghor:

They hated America, were full of racial stories, held their attitudes largely on racial grounds. Politically, they knew very little about it. Whenever I was with an African, we would both be uneasy ... The terms of our life were so different, we almost needed a dictionary to talk.

Baldwin never came to a coherent or thought-out position on the Afro-American's predicament *vis-à-vis* his ancient African cousins. As in many areas, his thought vacillated dizzyingly, often deflected by emotion, and it is impossible to discern a meaningful pattern. A change in mood occurred in keeping with the more radical feeling of the 1960s, and after he had visited Africa himself in 1962 he would never have been caught out saying something as shockingly frank as 'They disgusted me'.

In his early life, however, Africa symbolized confusion, a confusion that had existed ever since, as a small boy, he pictured the people dancing in his father's church as African savages, and his father himself as an African chieftain. Images of Africa in his early writing are images of primitivism, and – set down in full awareness of the unwelcome fact – of degradation: the 'despised beat of the tom-tom', in 'Encounter on the Seine'; the spectre of the conquerors arriving, in 'Stranger in the Village', and the mental picture of his father standing 'naked, with war paint on ... among spears', in 'Notes of a Native Son'.

Meetings with real Africans in Paris – to whom the tom-tom and the jungle probably signified less than they did to him – helped dispel his confusion, but did nothing to affirm their ties. In fact, these encounters only bound him more closely to his American brothers and sisters, black and white.

If we ask the question, how did Baldwin feel about himself at the turn of 1956–7, we see at first glance a young black man, thirty-two years old, with three books under his belt, beginning to make a living as a writer. He was 'a success'. Yet his private life, as he put it slightly later, looking back, 'had failed – had failed, had failed'.

He was not at ease with his own character, and worked deliberately at achieving a 'genuine' vulnerability. Yet he was conscious that at the same time he employed a wide range of defensive tricks to protect himself from hurt: capable of charming others all too easily, he flirted, leapt into casual affairs, then got bruised and bruised others in turn; he never arrived for meetings on time; he broke appointments and forgot about debts; and he tried to make himself over into a dominating personality, as a way, he wrote to Schenk, of shielding himself from his own manipulative traits.

He was sensitive about being small and not terribly handsome; certain that people were going to leave him anyway, his instinct was to push and push, to see how much they would take before they did. He felt orphaned in Europe; he was depressed at his failure to create a stable, lasting relationship, and aware that even if he did succeed, it would be a union without children. He was afraid of failing in his chosen vocation, and feared the prospect of ending up alone and broke, or even – as had already happened to many of the young people he grew up with – going mad and dying young. When he looked in his mirror, he saw that the witty, loquacious, brilliant, fun-to-be-with, pub-crawling Jimmy – or 'Jim' or 'James' or 'Jamie' – was just a mask for a frightened, insecure, 'weird black boy who wants to write'.

This crisis of confidence – not the first, nor the last – was principal among the motors which drove him down to Corsica in September 1956, after the closing speeches of the Conference of Negro-African Writers and Artists at the Sorbonne. Arnold was with him, but their flight was not a carefree one, for they were breaking up – the trigger of his own disintegration.

The original plan had been to go to Ischia, off the coast of Naples, but they stopped instead in Île Rousse, Corsica, the home of Mme Dumont, *propriétaire* of the Hôtel de Verneuil. There they stayed in a house belonging to a friend of Lucien's just outside the town. Île Rousse, Baldwin wrote to Schenk, was no bigger than the Café de Flore, and was closed much earlier.

For his friends in Paris the departure had been dismayingly abrupt. But other matters besides goodbyes were occupying him. He wanted to untie the knot with Arnold away from Paris. Had they separated there, he told Schenk from Corsica – a month into his stony exile, on the very morning that Arnold left – with the bitterness they then felt, they would never have been able to face each other again.

Baldwin stayed in Corsica for six months, with just a dog for company. He was writing the first drafts of *Another Country*, but finding it difficult to work in the grip of heartache. For the moment his private difficulties overwhelmed his concern with the rapidly worsening situation in the American South. One love affair lay in a heap, and another had just crashed into the wreckage. He was full of self-analysis and self-reproach. He was suddenly thinking of Arnold, he confessed in a letter to Gordon Heath, and asking himself where he had gone wrong. Was there something the matter with *him*? Did he need Arnold only as an adjunct to himself?

He rehearsed the whole sad story and the reasons for it in another long letter, to Leslie Schenk. Poor Arnold. It must have been painful for him to have to watch someone trying to pull off a mask. The miracle was not that he left, but that he stayed so long. 'Ah. Poor Arnold.'

At the beginning of 1957 Baldwin travelled up to Paris to see Heath, Schenk, Beauford Delaney, Mary Painter and other friends, and to celebrate the French publication of *Go Tell It on the Mountain*;* it was the last time he was to visit that city in his status as resident. He returned to Île Rousse, and when next he left his island retreat it was for New York.

The atmosphere in the black expatriate community had taken a turn for the worse. A falling-out had occurred between the Africans and the Americans the previous summer, at the Conference of Negro-African Writers and Artists, following charges by Aimé Césaire that the American Negro delegation (which did not include Baldwin) was an élite and was therefore unrepresentative of the people. What's more, rumours were flying in the cafés the blacks frequented, the Monaco and the Tournon, about FBI and CIA informers. Even Richard Wright himself – the prime target of FBI surveillance – had come under suspicion.

Two incidents which had occurred during the Conference of Negro-African Writers and Artists had made a deep impression on Baldwin. At the opening, a message was read out to the audience and delegates from the venerable black writer and civil-rights campaigner W. E. B. DuBois: 'I am not present at your meeting because the US government will not give me a passport. Any American travelling abroad today must either not care about Negroes or say what the State Department wishes him to say.' If this incisive thrust were not enough to persuade Baldwin that he was

* *Les Elus du Seigneur*

in the wrong place at the wrong time, what he saw the next day on leaving the Sorbonne finally convinced him. Strolling along the Boulevard St-Germain at lunchtime in the company of, among other people, Richard Wright, he was confronted on every newstand by a picture of a fifteen-year-old girl in Charlotte, North Carolina, trying to gain admission to the local school. Around her, white people, men and women, young and old, formed a jeering, violent mob, a human barricade to prevent her reaching the door.

The news was emanating not only from North Carolina but from all over the South, and in DuBois's view all American blacks – all Americans, in fact – were implicated.

Where, then, they might justifiably ask, was high-minded, fine-speaking Mr Baldwin? While distant cousins, some no more than children, stood at the front line of the most important event in black history since Emancipation, he was in the Brasserie Lipp.

It took almost a year for him to act, but it was on that bright September afternoon in 1956 that the image of a young girl being jeered and spat at had implanted in his conscience the knowledge that, whether he wanted to or not, he must go home.

'I would like to go wherever you go,' Giovanni tells David. 'I do not feel so strongly about Paris as you do. I have never liked Paris very much.' One hears behind this speech – a mixture of plea and declaration, an admission of vulnerability and an assertion of humanity – the sceptical voice of Giovanni's creator. But Giovanni *is* Paris, for David; Giovanni's life-giving freedom of spirit – which might liberate David for ever, or merely for a season, depending on how he chooses – is inseparable from the freedom David has found in the cafés and boulevards of Paris. Whereas Giovanni was prepared for love, David was only capable of romance.

Baldwin realized that the same dilemma, in another form, confronted him: if he remained in Europe, where he felt most at home, he risked falling into the trap of the expatriate, the refuge-seeker, the man who reads the news a day or two late and at a distance of a thousand miles. On the other hand, if he returned to the United States, he would have to face again the things that had forced him to flee in the first place.

In the end, it was just this reasoning that drew him back: he did not wish to return to America, he was afraid to, but if only fear was preventing him, then fear was the very reason he should go.

Europe was where the talk, the sunshine, the friends, the beauty, the fun were; but America was where the action was. And the action which most concerned him, at that moment, was in the Southern states, where the system of racial segregation was being broken down.

As a man, a black man, he should be standing shoulder to shoulder with other blacks; as a writer, he was duty-bound to observe a subject. He might have felt that he was under a moral obligation to go to North Carolina to witness the movement for himself, but he was also enough of a journalist to know a good story when he saw one. Here was a gift to the writer: an event which could raise his remarkable talents to the plane of genius.

Yet, as he recrossed the ocean to be close to the heat of this event, he sailed into a contradiction: never again would he be as free from the daily ravages of America's deep colour complex, or from the politics now assailing it, as he had been in Paris. Paris was his heyday as an artist.

Go Tell It on the Mountain, Baldwin's first novel, comes out of the rural South and the urban black church; but *Giovanni's Room* comes from the streets of Paris and the discovery of Henry James. Baldwin had studied James's anatomization of society, his use of dramatic contrast between Old World and New. He borrowed something of James's grandeur to refine the biblical grandeur of his own. In James, more than any other American writer, he found an attention to that 'intensest thing' – one's essential self – that was truly his own subject. He came to quote James regularly, and he admired the mind 'so fine that no idea could violate it'.

T. S. Eliot's famous remark might have stood as a warning to him. In the South the black leadership had felt their hearts light up with the fire of an idea – the idea of justice. Baldwin, too, longed to see justice done, and would have to strive, from now on, to ensure that the writer in him was not shouted down, or violated, by the idealogue.

PART III
A Severe Cross

BALDWIN: But it's not my life, and if I pretend it is, I'll die. I am *not* a public speaker. I *am* an artist.

INTERVIEWER: You are stealing from the artist to pay for the Negro?

BALDWIN: Yes. It's one of the prices of my success.

Interview in *Mademoiselle*, May 1963

Chapter Eleven

'I will always consider myself among the greatly privileged', he declared many years after his first trip to the American South, 'because, however inadequately, I was there.'

I was there – a political struggle, the nation in turmoil, and his own people at the eye of the storm. From having been white America's inside-eye on the closed families and locked churches of Harlem, the discreet observer of homosexual scenes in Paris, above all the sensitive recorder of the human heart in conflict with itself, Baldwin suddenly became committed to politics – not the politics of right and left, but the politics of right and wrong. He recognized straight away the significance of the revolution which was starting to move forward in the South, and like the authors he had left behind in France he was made into a writer *engagé*.

His full weight would not be added to the fight until later. Baldwin's presence at the first attempts to desegregate Southern schools was not especially significant, though nor was it in the least 'inadequate'; he simply did what he was there to do, an honest job of reporting.

On his return to New York from France in July 1957, he dallied in the city for a few weeks, just long enough to see his family and close friends. He had always wanted to visit the land, blood-stained in his imagination, where his parents had been raised and their parents and grandparents had been slaves, which in some ways he regarded as his home. Another home! And now it seemed a matter of urgency. He had crossed the seas to get there. Every day, in Little Rock, Arkansas, in Birmingham, Alabama, in Atlanta, Georgia, in Charlotte, North Carolina, black people – including schoolchildren – were being beaten and abused and threatened with death, over nothing more than the right to attend the same schools as their white counterparts. It was one battle in a great campaign aimed at ending the institution of segregation, which translated easily into institutionalized racism. Blacks had been the South's slaves (for a handful of people it was still within living memory), but an unofficial condition of their emancipation had been that they remain underfoot, living within the bounds of a system which deemed them inferior. Now, *en masse*, they were coming out from underneath the heel.

'Sitting in the house . . . / . . . With everything on my mind' was the split epigraph to the two parts of Baldwin's book-in-the-making, *Nobody Knows My Name*. During this interval in New York he was stuck fast 'in the house', in one of his moods – a brooding, self-absorbed frame of mind which overwhelmed his customary good spirit and appeared to whoever was in his company to be a sudden, unwarranted reclusiveness. In this humour, he would shut out everyone and everything, responding slowly even to the most simple enquiries, preoccupied with his own silent disturbances.

He was reflecting on the nine years he had just spent in Europe, on the America he had left behind and the America he had come back to. He accepted that the country had changed but wondered if it had got better. Things literally unimaginable had happened to Negroes in the Old South, and one reason for Baldwin's wanting to go there was his recognition that, for better or worse, it was never going to be the same again. If it was an opportunity to witness the formation of a new South, it was also a last chance to see the old. Only his usual state of penury delayed him from heading down immediately; it was first necessary to fix up an assignment.

Although segregation in schools had been ruled unlawful by the Supreme Court in 1954, most Southern states were purposefully slow in putting the Court's decision into practice. When, in the spring of 1957, it was further ordered that the ruling be implemented with 'all deliberate speed', desegregation began in selected districts of most states, accompanied by violent protests by organizations with titles such as the White Citizens' Council, not to mention the Ku-Klux-Klan.

The crisis reached a well-publicized climax in the town of Little Rock, Arkansas. After much disagreement among members of the all-white school committee over what should be done about the Supreme Court's ruling, and expressions of disgust not only at the prospect of mixed schools but also at federal government interference in Southern 'state sovereignty', it was finally decided that nine black children should be enrolled at Little Rock Central High when classes recommenced after the summer recess on 3 September 1957. The nine would join 2,500 other students, every one of them white.

Undeterred, publicly if not privately, by the death threats and the bricks hurled through the windows of their houses, the Little Rock nine turned out for their first day at school, only to find that the building was surrounded by armed members of the National Guard. The governor of the state had called them out in answer to the threat of rioting. The children went home, but the next day made their way to school again. The National Guard was still there, and now thousands of white protestors swarmed around the building, carrying anti-black placards and chanting slogans. When one of the black girls, Elizabeth Eckford, became separated from her group and tried to approach the military barricade for safety, she found a bayonet raised in front of her face and a mob at her back yelling, 'Lynch her! Drag her over to the tree! No nigger bitch is going to get in our school!'

Elizabeth Eckford later recalled that when she met the eyes of an elderly white woman, searching for a look or a word of assistance, 'she spat on me'.

This was the situation on which Baldwin touched down in late September. A commission had come through at last, from *Harper's* magazine. As the plane hovered over the tree-tops and 'the rust-red earth', he pressed his forehead to the window and tried to banish from his mind the thought that the ground 'had acquired its colour from the blood that had dripped down from these trees'. Family ghosts were on hand to welcome him: 'My father must have seen such sights . . . or heard of them, or had this danger touch him.'

Baldwin had returned from Paris voluntarily to submit to the storm, but he also conceived of his involvement as an event unavoidable, something dictated by fate – or, to put it more literally, without changing the premiss, forced by the will of his ancestors:

'You can take the child out of the country,' my elders were fond of saying, 'but you can't take the country out of the child.' They were speaking of their own antecedents, I supposed; it didn't, anyway, seem possible that they could be warning me; I took myself out of the country and went to Paris. It was there that I discovered that the old folks knew what they were talking about: I found myself, willy-nilly, alchemized into an American the moment I touched French soil.

Now, back again after nearly nine years, it was ironical to reflect that if I had not lived in France for so long I would never have found it necessary – or possible – to visit the American South.

His first stop was Charlotte, North Carolina, where integrated education was being enforced, as it was in Little Rock. (While Baldwin visited Little Rock, he never wrote about it.) The tactics employed by the white authorities were heartless: of 50,000 blacks in the town, four had been assigned to formerly all-white schools, each one to a separate establishment. It took tremendous courage to be one of these four black children, or one of the parents. If the experiment to integrate schools could be made to work, there was no saying where it might lead; certainly there was infinite scope for improvement. In this American state, in 1957, Baldwin discovered, Negroes were 'not even licensed to become electricians or plumbers. I was also told, several times, by white people, that "race relations" there were excellent. I failed to find a single Negro who agreed with this, which is the usual story of "race relations" in this country.'

In Charlotte, Baldwin gathered material for his essay 'A Fly in the Buttermilk', which *Harper's* published in October 1958.* He interviewed a fifteen-year-old schoolboy, Gus Roberts, and his mother. They were identified in the article only as 'G' and 'Mrs R' – so protective was the reporter that he shrank from naming the school, the town or even the state. Admiring of, almost entranced by, the unassuming courage of Gus Roberts, Baldwin described him to Bill Cole as 'ingrown, bitter, but beautifully so'. He had Knopf send Gus a copy of *Go Tell It on the Mountain*, with the bill posted to himself in New York.

From Charlotte, he flew to Atlanta, where he met Martin Luther King for the first time, albeit only briefly. From there he proceeded to Birmingham and Montgomery, in the heart of Alabama. The trip lasted longer than it had been meant to. Everything was a revelation, and every revelation confirmed him in his commitment.

The struggle was not about education. How could it be? Those leading the brutal assault on black children seeking entrance to the classroom included hordes of 'the eminently uneducated', as Baldwin put it. Rather, the battle had to do with political power; and it had to do with sex.

Baldwin's ancestors were Africans, who had become Southern Negroes. But like millions of other American black people, he had another set of ancestors, who were white. And this fact – literally, in the South, unspeakable – was, as he saw it, the crux of the so-called 'colour problem'. 'The Northern Negro in the South', Baldwin wrote, 'sees, whatever he or

* Published originally as 'The Hard Kind of Courage'.

anyone else may wish to believe, that his ancestors are both white and black. The white men, flesh of his flesh, hate him for that very reason.' Integration, a light-skinned man in Atlanta told him, 'has always worked very well in the South, after the sun goes down'.

The interracial strife of Georgia and North Carolina and Alabama was not a mere consequence of enforced integration, as the newspaper editorials and the television voice-overs supposed it to be. Here Baldwin first formulated the expression which he later often repeated, *we were integrated in the womb*. As this magnificent passage relates, Baldwin read Southern history as it was written in the faces of people in the street.

It was on the outskirts of Atlanta that I first felt how the Southern landscape – the trees, the silence, the liquid heat, and the fact that one always seems to be traveling great distances – seems designed for violence, seems, almost, to demand it. What passions cannot be unleashed on a dark road in a Southern night! Everything seems so sensual, so languid, and so private. Desire can be acted out here; over this fence, behind that tree, in the darkness, there; and no one will see, no one will ever know. Only the night is watching and the night was made for desire. Protestantism is the wrong religion for people in such climates; America is perhaps the last nation in which such a climate belongs. In the Southern night everything seems possible, the most private, unspeakable longings; but then arrives the Southern day, as hard and brazen as the night was soft and dark. It must have seemed something like this for those people who made the region what it is today. It must have caused them great pain. Perhaps the master who had coupled with his slave saw the guilt in his wife's pale eyes in the morning. And the wife saw his children in the slave quarters, saw the way his concubine, the sensual-looking black girl, looked at her – a woman, after all, and scarcely less sensual, but white. The youth, nursed and raised by the black Mammy whose arms had then held all that there was of warmth and love and desire, and still confounded by the dreadful taboos set up between himself and her progeny, must have wondered, after his first experiment with black flesh, where, under the blazing heavens, he could hide. And the white man must have seen his guilt written somewhere else, seen it all the time, even if his sin was merely lust, even if his sin lay in nothing but his power: in the eyes of the black man. He may not have stolen his woman, but he had certainly stolen his freedom – this black man, who had a body like his, and passions like his, and a ruder, more erotic beauty. How many times has the Southern day come up to find that black man, sexless, hanging from a tree!

*

The whites who surrounded Little Rock High School and spat at Elizabeth Eckford and her eight colleagues, shouting 'Lynch her!' and 'Drag her over to the tree!', were not making empty threats. It had been done before – by their fathers and grandfathers – and it would be done again.

'Niggers ain't gonna vote where I live', J. W. Millam told the journalist William Bradford Huie:

If they did they'd control the government. They ain't gonna go to school with my kids. And when a nigger even gets close to mentioning sex with a white woman, he's tired o' livin'. I'm likely to kill him.

Millam, in fact, had already killed – one Emmett Till, a fourteen-year-old boy, in Mississippi in August 1955 – and he was being paid $4,000 for telling Huie all about it. Accepting a dare from some friends, Emmett Till had gone into a store and asked the young woman behind the counter for a date. He called her 'baby'. She told her husband Roy Bryant about it, and he and Millam went to the house where Till was staying and drove him away in a car. After torturing him for several hours, they murdered him and threw the body into the river.

In court, they were acquitted for lack of evidence, whereupon their stories were immediately bought by *Look* magazine. The article, by William Bradford Huie, appeared in the issue for January 1956 (with a warning from the editors about its appalling contents), four months after Millam and his co-accused walked free. 'As long as I live and can do anything about it', Millam told the readers of *Look*, 'niggers are gonna stay in their place.'

The Emmett Till killing was not by any means an isolated incident. Apart from other lynchings, and the common occurrence of black bodies turning up in rivers, there was now an organized campaign of violence against the people at the forefront of the civil rights movement. Their houses were bombed, their children were threatened, bricks came crashing through their windows at night with death warnings attached. But two features of the Till case made it stand out from other, equally atrocious murders. For one thing, Till was from Chicago, the North. This captured the attention of the media and focused Northern eyes on backward Southern states. For another, the transparent injustice of Millam and Bryant's acquittal, and their subsequent well-paid confession, disgusted many whites as well as blacks, and helped to make Till a martyr.

Millam told William Bradford Huie that he had held a .45 to the boy's head after repeated pistol-whipping and asked him: 'You still as good as I am?' The answer was 'Yeah,' and Millam shot him through the ear.

Baldwin would one day use the Emmett Till case as the basis for a play, but for the time being it lay dormant in his imagination. He did not need this particular lynching to convince him of the willingness of a certain breed of white person to make a bloody example of blacks who stepped out of line. He had already included references to lynching in *Go Tell It on the Mountain*. He had learned about it from his Southern forebears, from *Uncle Tom's Cabin*, from rumour and legend, from old blues songs, and new ones such as Billie Holiday's 'Strange Fruit'.

This 'folk knowledge', compounded by a reading of the daily news, instilled an intense fear in him when he crossed the Mason-Dixon line for the first time – fear that was converted into feverish excitement when he got there, made his contacts, and witnessed at first hand things previously only read or heard about. The place was ready to 'blow apart', he wrote to Bill Cole from the office of the *Carolina Israelite* newspaper; there was no way to exaggerate the danger of the situation.

In spite of his excitement, Baldwin's on-the-spot reporting from the South is, from one point of view, a little tame. It is not action-packed, but reflective. He did not attempt to capture the heat and fear of a mob, of a riot or protest. Freedom, to Baldwin, was 'complex, difficult – and private'. True to himself, therefore, he wrote about the internal effects of the violence he saw happening all around him. Leaving the mass media to report the broken noses, he set about investigating broken hearts. When an old man in Atlanta directed him to his first segregated bus, Baldwin wondered how people like him had borne their indignities for so long:

He seemed to know what I was feeling. His eyes seemed to say that what I was feeling he had been feeling, at much higher pressure, all his life. But my eyes had never seen the hell his eyes had seen. And this hell was, simply, that he had never in his life owned anything, not his wife, not his house, not his child, which could not, at any instant, be taken from him by the power of white people. This is what paternalism means. And for the rest of the time that I was in the South, I watched the eyes of old black men.

At this stage in his career, Baldwin was a diligent, self-disciplined reporter, willing to sacrifice his own intimate, acute feelings, if necessary, to the objectivity of the report, even when he seemed to be at his most personal. A decade and a half later, however, in his memoir *No Name in the Street*, he recalled his first visit to Alabama, including subjective details and a sense of dreadful excitement which he had omitted when reporting for *Harper's* or *Partisan Review*.

My first night in Montgomery, I, like a good reporter, decided to investigate the town a little. I had been warned to be very careful how I moved about in the South after dark – indeed, I had been told not to move at all; but it was a pleasant evening, night just beginning to fall: suppertime . . . On the corner about a block away there was a restaurant. When I reached the corner, I entered the restaurant.

I will never forget it. I don't know if I can describe it. Everything abruptly froze into what, even at that moment, struck me as a kind of Marx Brothers parody of horror. Every white face turned to stone: the arrival of the messenger of death could not have had a more devastating effect than the appearance in the restaurant doorway of a small, unarmed, utterly astounded black man. I had realized my error as soon as I opened the door: but the absolute terror on all these white faces – I swear that not a soul moved – paralyzed me. They stared at me, I stared at them.

The spell was broken by one of those women, produced, I hope, only in the South, with a face like a rusty hatchet, and eyes like two rusty nails – nails left from the crucifixion. She rushed at me as though to club me down, and she barked – for it was not a human sound: 'What you want, boy? What you want in here?' And then, a de-contaminating gesture, 'Right around there, boy. Right around there.'

I had no idea what she was talking about. I backed out of the door.

'Right around there, boy,' said a voice behind me.

A white man had appeared out of nowhere, on the side-walk which had been empty not more than a second before. I stared at him blankly. He watched me steadily, with a kind of suspended menace . . .

I found myself in a small cubicle, with one electric light, and a counter with, perhaps, four or five stools. On one side of the cubicle was a window. This window more closely resembled a cage-wire mesh, and an opening in the mesh. I was, now, in the back of the restaurant, though no one in the restaurant could see me. I was behind the restaurant counter, behind the hatchet-faced woman, who had her back to me, serving the white customers at the counter. I was nearly close enough to touch them, certainly close enough to touch her, close enough to kill them all, but they couldn't see me, either.

Hatchet-Face now turned to me, and said, 'What you want?' This time, she did not say, 'boy': it was no longer necessary.

As much as it was a magazine assignment, this first journey to the South was a voyage of discovery and a rite of initiation. 'I realized what tremendous things were happening', Baldwin told Harold Isaacs of *Phylon* a year later, 'and that I did have a role to play.' And he added, 'I can't be happy here' – meaning the United States – 'but I can work here.'

What a change from Europe. What a different atmosphere from Corsica, Loeche-les-Bains, Aix, Chartres, if not Paris itself – 'tremendous things', 'a role'; to Bill Cole he had written as if from a war zone that there was no way to exaggerate the complexity and danger of the situation. And in the restless conscience of his remark, 'I can't be happy here, but I can work here', we read the conviction of a man who has found a cause.

By his 'role' he means working for the movement, writing reports, getting the story past the editor's desk – the editor of any one of the highest-circulation newspapers and magazines in the land: the *New York Times*, *Harper's*, *Esquire*, the *New Yorker*. It was a unique duty, for no other black writer was in a position to fulfil it. Richard Wright's star was in decline, and anyway he was still in France and had more interest in the decolonization of Africa than in the crisis in his own country. Ralph Ellison would take no active part in the civil rights movement, now or later. Langston Hughes was not that way inclined.

Baldwin, however, while still regarding himself primarily as an artist, recognized in his people's struggle a personal cause. He had said he could not bear to sit in Paris, 'polishing my fingernails', trying to explain Little Rock to the French, while children daily ran a vicious gauntlet in order to get to school. Well, now he had seen Little Rock, in addition to several other battlegrounds, and had surveyed the terrain for himself. By making the journey, he had forced his way into an area of darkness which it fell to him to illuminate. The role in which he could best operate was still that of a writer; for the moment, it seemed the only feasible commitment he could be asked to make.

As a way of balancing his new political involvement, he began to develop his artistic activity, taking an increased interest in the theatre. Returning from the South, he retired once more to the New Hampshire woods and the MacDowell Colony, where he started work on a dramatization of *Giovanni's Room*. The project was initiated by the Actors Studio, which had commissioned a treatment of Baldwin's novel for workshop presentation. The idea behind the workshop was that dramatic themes could be explored and developed, as actors played their parts in front of other actors; if successful, the play might then be staged at the Studio's Bijou Theatre in a full production.

When Baldwin saw the Studio-approved version of his novel, however, he was disappointed, and he undertook to write a new one himself. He had found the perfect Giovanni in a stocky young Turkish actor of sensual looks, Engin Cezzar, who had dropped out of Yale to join the Actors Studio, and he wrote to Cezzar from MacDowell on 9 December 1957 to say that he had finished the first act. The dramatization was to be, to some extent, a collaborative effort (to 'work together' was always Baldwin's desire); Cezzar offered technical advice on stagecraft and made suggestions concerning the script.

Baldwin grew excited about the play, and wrote frequently to his 'Giovanni' from wherever he happened to be, to inform him as to the state of conception of his 'David'. Paul Newman is mentioned, as is Montgomery Clift, and also Marlon Brando, all actors associated with the Studio. Baldwin aimed high; he was hopeful but realistic. 'One good thing,' he quipped to Cezzar, they were unlikely to get a rejection from Brando, 'because he never answers anybody'.

The Actors Studio presented *Giovanni's Room* as a workshop production in the spring of 1958, with Cezzar and Mark Richman in the leading roles, directed by Eli Rill. It did not materialize into the full-scale production for the Bijou Theatre that Baldwin had hoped for, however.

Baldwin continued planning for a stage or film production of *Giovanni's Room* until, literally, his final days. His collaboration with Cezzar was still alive in 1962, five years after its genesis. Baldwin claimed that the play could have made Broadway – his dream – if the Studio had been able to persuade an actor with box-office appeal to play the part of David, the all-American boy with homosexual secrets. 'But,' said Baldwin, 'we couldn't.' Brando was willing but too busy (he *did* reply), and no other actor whom they approached would take the part for fear of being tainted by the subject.

As at Howard University, where *The Amen Corner* had played to enthusiastic audiences yet failed to transfer to the professional stage, Baldwin emerged from the theatre with enlarged experience but little else. And once again he attributed his lack of success to pusillanimity on the part of theatre producers, who were put off by the fact that the subject of the play was of 'minority interest': Harlem life, in the case of *The Amen Corner*, homosexuality in *Giovanni's Room*.

Still, the Actors Studio was the place for experimentation in the theatre, and it excited him to be a part of it. In October 1958, following a three-month summer sojourn in Paris, where he stayed with Beauford Delaney, Baldwin flew back to New York to take up a post at the side of Elia Kazan. He was to be the director's assistant on Actors Studio productions of *JB* by Archibald MacLeish and *Sweet Bird of Youth* by Tennessee Williams.

Kazan's hope was that Baldwin would mature into a resident Studio playwright: by serving an apprenticeship he could gain all-round knowledge of the theatre. Kazan had been offered *The Amen Corner* and rejected it, but something in the work must have impressed him. He invited Baldwin to join a new group then in the process of being set up, the Playwrights Unit, which embraced some of the best talents in the new generation of American writers. Norman Mailer's adaptation of his own novel, *The Deer Park*, was presented by the Unit, as were two of Edward Albee's plays, *Zoo Story* and *The Death of Bessie Smith*. Kazan suggested to Baldwin that he write a full-length play based on the murder of Emmett Till, once he had completed the novel he was writing.

But the experience of assisting Kazan did nothing to convince Baldwin that theatre in America was in a healthy condition. He had enjoyed working on the Williams play, but was uncomplimentary about the Mac-Leish (the producer of *JB*, Alfred de Liagre, recalled Baldwin's 'unnecessary' derogatory remarks). His dislike was part of the contempt in which he claimed to hold the American theatre in general: 'They get all those people involved,' he said. 'All this energy, you know, for weeks and weeks and weeks . . . And what have you got on the stage, after all that effort and money? A *crock*.'

Part of the failure of the theatre – its main failure, as far as he was concerned – was its inability to deal properly with the lives of black people (he was not impressed by *The Death of Bessie Smith*). This was nothing less than a moral failure. If the theatre could not deal with the lives of blacks – Baldwin's dialectic was being pared down to a beautiful simplicity – then it was scarcely equipped to deal with the lives of whites.

Chapter Twelve

In late 1950s New York the talk was of hip and square, of modern jazz, of getting kicks, of cool and hot, the Miles Davis Quintet and the fractured soul of Billie Holiday. There was method acting and action painting; there was the *Village Voice* and Norman Mailer's weekly column; and there was Ginsberg's *Howl*, the Paris edition of *Naked Lunch*, the meaning of 'Beat' – beatitude or just beat up? – and going on the road.

American culture was energetic and optimistic. The writers – Mailer, Styron, Capote, Vidal, Baldwin and others – individualist though each one was, showed every sign of coming together in the reading public's mind to form a 'generation'.

Much though he might claim to dislike New York, for the meantime Baldwin was staying put. At the turn of 1957–8 he took a small apartment at 81 Horatio Street, at the westernmost boundary of Greenwich Village, in view of the Hudson River. As soon as he could clear his desk of magazine assignments, which was becoming less easy to do, there was other work in hand: *Another Country*, for example. It had already occupied him for three years when he wrote to Bill Cole at four a.m. one morning, groggy and frustrated, that it was turning him into a mental and physical wreck. He was beginning to feel, he said rather dramatically, that this was the novel he was destined not to survive.

Baldwin did most of his writing after midnight, often working until dawn and then sleeping past noon. Frequent ailments, complaints of strain and stress, must be counted as hangovers from an extraordinary dynamism. He was possessed of a boundless capacity for socializing – which involved more drinking and talking than eating – and he sought multifarious ways of imprinting his energy on paper. The novel he was engaged in writing would eventually be handed in at close to 450 pages; between 1957 and 1960 he also wrote two long stories – 'Sonny's Blues' and 'This Morning, This Evening, So Soon' – which come to about half the length of an average novel; during the same period he wrote most of the essays included in *Nobody Knows My Name*, plus extra articles which could have extended the book by half its length again. At the same time he was working with Kazan and the Actors Studio, and produced the dramatic treatment of *Giovanni's Room*.

One of his freelance assignments in the early spring of 1959 was to review the *Selected Poems* of Langston Hughes for the *New York Times Book Review*. The resulting article, and the ripples it spread, illustrate the way in which, as the decade reached an end, Baldwin set himself apart from the school of 'Negro writing' which came before him, and aligned himself with mainstream American literature.

Born in 1902, Hughes was a central character in the Harlem Renaissance and one of the first professional black writers. In addition to his poetry, he produced novels, short stories, plays, libretti and two autobiographies. While Richard Wright was the world's best-known black novelist throughout the 1930s and 1940s, Hughes was its poet. He was a Harlem man from head to toe; once, when asked why he didn't move to the suburbs, now that he had found success, he replied that he preferred the company of wild men to wild animals. When confronted with the poverty and squalor of his habitat, Hughes veered away from Baldwin's insistence on Harlem's degrading aspects, stressing its vitality and warmth. Asked on television if Harlem was not congested, Hughes answered: 'It is. Congested with people. All kinds. And I'm lucky enough to call a great many of them my friends.'

But 'the bard of Harlem' was scarcely less bitter than his young rival about his treatment as a black man in a white world. He claimed to have had a friendlier reception as a writer in the Soviet Union, supposedly an enemy state, than he was accustomed to receiving at home. Taking part in a radio discussion with Baldwin, among others, in 1962, Hughes told listeners that booking agencies would never find him engagements to speak or read his poems at women's clubs, because 'women's clubs have teas [and] they do not wish to mingle socially with their speaker' – if, that is, the speaker happened to be a coloured man.

Hughes suspected Baldwin of setting out on purpose to solicit the admiration of the white world, and of turning on his origins – suspicions which were confirmed in Hughes's mind, and grew bitter, as Baldwin became more and more famous, and was fêted by a white audience and white critics. Baldwin, for his part, continued to insist on seeing himself as an *American* writer; he saw no more reason to pay homage to Hughes than he had to Wright; considerably less, in fact, since nothing the poet had written had influenced him, or seemed to open windows for him, the way Wright's *Native Son* and *Black Boy* had done.

This atmosphere of distrust between the two led to some harsh words and double-dealing – more, it must be said, on Hughes's part than on Baldwin's. We have already seen his devious response to *Go Tell It on the Mountain* – praising it to Baldwin's face while damning it behind his back – and the grudging welcome he gave to *Notes of a Native Son*. Hughes had claimed to admire much of that collection, and had predicted that Baldwin might develop into a 'major contemporary commentator'; but within a few years he had cancelled this view, and was speaking out against Baldwin's first book of essays as 'the *Uncle Tom's Cabin* of today'.

Hughes's review of *Notes of a Native Son* had been published in the *New York Times Book Review*; when the same paper asked Baldwin to review Hughes's *Selected Poems*, it gave him an opportunity to tip his hat in kind. 'Every time I read Langston Hughes', he wrote, 'I am amazed all over again by his genuine gifts – and depressed that he has done so little with them.' The book under review contained 'a great deal which a more disciplined poet would have thrown into the waste-basket'.

According to Hughes's biographer, Arnold Rampersad, this review shocked Hughes 'to the core'. On the day that the piece appeared, he sent Baldwin a postcard containing the message

Hey Jimmy:
>Ain't you heard?
>*RACE and ART*
>*Are far apart.*

It was an allusion to his personal theory that Baldwin, in spite of appearances to the contrary, was more tightly bound by the constricting obsession with race than he, Hughes, was. Baldwin probably did not actually intend his review to be regarded as payback – it was not his style – and Hughes did not take it that way, as the settling of a debt. In the words of his assistant, Raoul Abdul, Hughes was 'downright angry' at the review, and now he wanted 'to get back'. His anger was restrained, however. He took his revenge by way of derogatory comments, such as comparing *Notes of a Native Son* to *Uncle Tom's Cabin*, and by sending missives like this one, posted in May 1962 after reading advance proofs of Baldwin's new collection of essays:

I fear you are becoming a 'NEGRO' writer – and a propaganda one, at that! What's happening?????? (Or am I reading wrong?)

Anyhow, NOBODY KNOWS MY NAME is fascinating reading, wonderful for many evenings of discussion for the talkative uptown and downtown – and surely makes you a sage – a culled sage – whose hair, once processed, seems to be reverting.

Hope it makes the best-seller list. You might as well suffer in comfort.

This may seem genial and harmless enough on first reading, but all its compliments are ironic, and between the lines it is packed with spite. Hughes's jokey tone isn't sufficient to sweeten his venomous barbs about 'becoming a "NEGRO" writer', about the book being fodder for 'the talkative uptown and downtown', about 'processed' hair now reverting, and so on.

Hughes and Baldwin might have been studying each other from a distance – the distance, far more than just a hundred blocks, separating uptown from downtown, Harlem from Greenwich Village, the American Negro Theatre from Broadway, and poetry readings, at women's clubs or anywhere else, from the bestseller list. Each could not help wondering what the other was doing there. To Baldwin, Hughes's 'people's poet' persona was uninteresting and limiting; as far back as 1943, when recommending poetry to a friend, it had been the modernist T. S. Eliot he had cited, not the folk troubadour of Harlem. To Hughes, surely at least a touch envious of Baldwin's success with white audiences, the younger writer seemed just what Hughes said he was – an Uncle Tom.

Their differences illustrate how black writers in New York in the post-war years, as their numbers increased, were not bound together by class or racial solidarity, but frequently had their views of one another muddied by suspicion, jealousy, fear of treachery, and fear of each other's success. The same was true of black writers in Paris, and Richard Wright would devote his last public appearance, in November 1960, to a discussion of the topic.

Baldwin, rapidly growing into the most successful black writer of all, on the whole kept himself free from petty squabbling. The quarrel between him and Wright had started as a literary disagreement, concerning the usefulness of protest literature, and the same was true of his falling-out with Hughes (although Hughes was blinded to the fact by hurt pride). It was really a disagreement over technique.

There can be little doubt that, had Baldwin been of the opinion that Hughes was a major poet, he would have been outspoken in his praise. He never hid his admiration for Ralph Ellison's novel *Invisible Man*, for example, although his personal relations with Ellison were similarly strained. But Baldwin could not find much to advertise in Hughes's work. The remark about the *Selected Poems* containing much that a 'more disciplined poet would have thrown into the waste-basket' has been quoted many times, usually presented as if it were the most nonchalant of dismissals. What Baldwin goes on to say is more specific and more interesting, however, though it is usually overlooked. 'Negro speech', he writes,

is vivid largely because it is private. It is a kind of emotional shorthand – or sleight-of-hand – by means of which Negroes express, not only their relationship to each other, but their judgment of the white world. And, as the white world takes over this vocabulary – without the faintest notion of what it really means – the vocabulary is forced to change. The same thing is true of Negro music, which has had to become more and more complex in order to continue to express any of the private or collective experience.

Hughes knows the bitter truth behind these hieroglyphics: what they are designed to protect, what they are designed to convey. But he has not forced them into the realm of art where their meaning would become clear and overwhelming. 'Hey, pop! / Re-bop! / Mop!' conveys much more on Lenox Avenue than it does in this book, which is not the way it ought to be.

Perhaps the difference, finally, was one of generation; Hughes was fascinated, and at the same time disgusted, by the young black writers who seemed to gain white approval in proportion to the extent that they castigated white society and chastised individual members. They fattened themselves on white guilt, they had become 'America's prophets of doom, black ravens cawing over carrion'. Hughes believed that black writers should express the unique and essential qualities of their race, which effort by itself would do away with the stereotypes he accused Baldwin and others of perpetuating. These qualities he defined as 'soul', the American *Négritude*, 'a synthesis of the essence of Negro folk art redistilled', which, when expressed in contemporary forms, was capable of revealing 'to the Negro people and the world the beauty within themselves'.

As far as success in writing was concerned, Hughes took an old-fashioned pride in craftsmanship, and regarded a poem or story well made as reward enough in itself. Baldwin, not in the least contemptuous of craft, was nevertheless driven by another sort of pride – ambition – which made him reach for the heights of the best-seller list, as much *his* right, as much within *his* grasp, as anyone else's.

It was all part of a changing climate, the same change as that which was currently altering the racial composition of Southern schools, buses and lunch counters. The momentum was so great and sudden that members of an older generation could easily be frightened and left behind. It happened, for example, with elderly Southern Negroes who saw the interference of young radical 'agitators' as dangerous, and in many cases resisted their pressure to have them register to vote. But as a result of this struggle, over many years and in many different forms, it had become possible, in a way barely countenanced before, for ambitious young men like Baldwin to straddle two worlds, standing with one foot uptown and the other downtown, walking out of Smalls Paradise in Harlem and into the White Horse Tavern in Greenwich Village, mixing black and white on equal terms.

It didn't mean turning your back on Harlem, but it meant not being stranded there, literally or figuratively. In the figurative sense, for example, Billie Holiday, famous the world over, had lived in a ghetto all her life. On tour with a white band, as their star singer, she was forced to use the service elevator in concert halls, and was taken off to 'blacks only' hotels at night.

No longer would black figures in public life put up with this sort of ordeal, or that suffered by Marian Anderson, who could sing for Eleanor Roosevelt, the First Lady in the 1940s, but could not sing at the Met; or, indeed, with the humiliating, embittering experience of Langston Hughes, forbidden to mix socially with white women, even as an entertainer at their 'teas'.

Baldwin's anti-establishment vehemence led him into some awkward compromises, which a writer with greater financial security might have been able to avoid. During his stay in Paris, Jean-Paul Sartre had turned down the Nobel Prize and its attendant tax-free fortune, declaring that a writer should not allow himself to be turned into an institution; Baldwin, in spite of a privately stated dislike of Sartre, surely admired the gesture.

He himself, however, had been living on institutional money for some time: launched by Saxton and Rosenwald, kept afloat by Guggenheim and NIAL; now, when his reputation was growing steadily but commercial success had yet to catch up, he accepted provision from the most American of all institutions: Ford.

Years of work on *Another Country* had brought him to the pass where all he could do was lament to Bill Cole that he might not live to complete it. But the letter from the Ford Foundation, in February 1959, notifying him that his application for a fellowship had been accepted, renewed his energies. He would be receiving $12,000 over a two-year period, to be paid in quarterly instalments.

If not exactly a first taste of wealth, this was at least enough to stop him worrying: $6,000 a year in the late 1950s, as a supplement to earned income, could provide a decent living by Greenwich Village standards.

More was to come: in the next few years he would write three best-selling books and a Broadway play. He had achieved part of what he set out to achieve – his mother need no longer clean other people's houses for a living (though she maddened her son by continuing to do so, 'to keep busy'); this brother could be given a hand up to fulfil his ambition of becoming an actor, that one of being a jazz musician, this sister of being a clothes designer. He could begin to believe that his ambition of buying his mother a house outside Harlem might be realized. His guilt about having left the family behind on a desperate flight to Europe was relieved, and where he could assist them now and in the future, he did.

In his application to the Ford Foundation, Baldwin stated that he was hammering into final shape (in fact, it was to take almost another three years) a 'very long' novel which comes out of his life in two cities, New York and Paris, and out of the 'wonder' which this life had caused in him as to what it means to be an American.

After listing the cast of *Another Country* (Rufus, the black jazz musician whose story takes up the first ninety pages but who was born last is, of course, not mentioned), he goes on to say that the novel is based on his assumption that the two 'most profound realities' that the American citizen has to deal with are 'colour and sex': Ida is a girl who is afraid to love black men – she has seen too many of them destroyed. But she cannot love white men either. Although she is deeply involved with Vivaldo, her 'real impulse' is to hurt him. Through his dealings with Ida, however, Vivaldo reaches a new station in his search for his own identity.

Baldwin then proceeds to outline the novel he intends writing once *Another Country* is completed – a slave novel, set on Emancipation Day, that he has had in mind since the early 1950s, provisionally entitled 'Talking at the Gates' or 'Talking at the Big Gate'. He proclaims himself here less concerned with race than with the relationships which have obtained in a 'very complex society', and with what happens to those relationships once the basis for the particular society crumbles. In this novel he meant to explore his belief that black and white in America were bound by strong ties, including blood ties, and that it was the pathological denial of these bonds, as opposed to actual differences, that fuelled the racial nightmare.

The idea sounds promising, but it existed only in his head. Given that the intention of writing the slave novel had been with him for at least six years (and he would still be talking about it in another six), it is somewhat surprising to find Baldwin admitting to the Ford people that he is ignorant of such details as how slaves dressed, what they ate, at what hour they rose, the condition of their living quarters, and so on. It was not his style to embark on detailed research for a book, and 'Talking at the Gates' – like other historical projects that at one time or another fired his imagination – remained unwritten.

The merest trace of it – the only trace among his published writings – can be found in the unlikely context of a profile of the Swedish film director Ingmar Bergman, written in 1960. Baldwin is inspired by his meeting with Bergman to project, in his imagination, a movie of his own. While it differs substantially from the outline he provided for the Ford Foundation, it contains a suggestion of how his mind might have developed the idea in writing:

My film would begin with slaves, boarding the good ship *Jesus*: a white ship, on a dark sea, with masters as white as the sails of their ships, and slaves as black as the ocean. There would be one intransigent slave, an eternal figure, destined to appear, and to be put to death, in every generation. In the hold of the slave-ship, he would be a witch-doctor or a chief or a prince or a singer; and he would die, be hurled into the ocean, for protecting a black woman. Who would bear his child, however, and this child would lead a slave insurrection; and be hanged. During the Reconstruction, he would be murdered upon leaving Congress. He would be a returning soldier during the First World War, and be buried alive; and then, during the Depression, he would become a jazz musician, and go mad. Which would bring him up to our own day – what would his fate be now? What would I title this grim and vengeful fantasy? What would be happening, during all this time, to the descendants of the masters?

Baldwin concluded his application to Ford with a plea – 'You can have no idea of how sincerely I pray' – that the Foundation would give him a grant to see him through his current work. They make an unlikely alliance, indeed – the monument to big business, the assembly line and the American Way, and the maverick writer who attempted, with every sentence, to subvert it. An optimistic view would have it that it says something for the open-endedness of American democracy and the ultimately democratic and open-handed nature of American enterprise. But Baldwin himself was not inclined to see things that way. His 'sincerely I pray' protests too much conciliation, respect, deference. Sincere he no doubt was in his desire to land some free money, but such solemn gratitude converts easily to cynicism, especially when the money came from an institution he would have regarded as racist, and to whose *raison d'être* he was profoundly unsympathetic.

Journalists did not fail to question him about his acceptance of these hand-outs and he did not hesitate to justify himself. In 1964, by which time the money was spent – Baldwin being as extravagant with his own cash as he was irresponsible with other people's – he answered an enquiry about his patronage so far – from the Eugene Saxton Foundation, from Rosenwald, from Guggenheim, from the National Institute of Arts and Letters, from *Partisan Review*, from Ford – with a lash of the tongue: 'I'd have to be a fool to think they were subsidizing me – they were not doing *that*; they were proving to themselves how liberal they were.'

Chapter Thirteen

A photograph of 26 January 1961 shows Baldwin in an apartment in Christopher Street, Greenwich Village, at a party being held to commemorate the 'death of the Beat Generation'. Others who appear in the picture are Seymour Krim, a 'beat' journalist on the *Village Voice* and other papers, Ted Joans, a poet, and Norman Mailer. Also present at the 'funeral' (organized by Robert Cordier, a Belgian theatre director whom Baldwin had met in Paris) were William Styron, Susan Sontag and Tuli Kupferberg, later of the rock group The Fugs. The none-too-solemn purpose, according to Cordier, was to inter the remnants of a movement, an idiom, a style, whose soul had been snatched by commerce and the media. There could be nothing beat, beaten, or even beatific, about a mode which was now only the latest fashion.

Mailer, though not a Beat Generation writer, was nevertheless the most formidable apologist for the psychology of 'hip', and of the hipster, on the present scene. In 1957 he had written an essay, 'The White Negro', in which he cast the hipster as the product of a marriage between white and black: 'and in this wedding', Mailer wrote, '. . . it was the Negro who brought the cultural dowry.' This referred not only to the way in which black speech was being rifled by 'hip' young whites for a vocabulary which approximated to their experience, and to black music finding favour with a large white audience; it pointed to what Mailer saw as the search by young whites for an alternative to 'the sophisticated inhibitions of civilizations'. The Negro, living with fear, existed 'for his Saturday night kicks', sacrificing the pleasures of the mind 'for the more obligatory pleasures of the body'. Now the young white man, reacting to the spectre of the concentration camp and the atomic bomb, to the 'stench of fear' pervading modern life, could be stitched into the same pathology. And in rejecting conventional behaviour, it was to the black man that he looked for an alternative:

So there was a new breed of adventurers, urban adventurers who drifted out at night looking for action with a black man's code to fit their facts. The hipster had absorbed the existentialist synapses of the Negro, and for practical purposes could be considered a white Negro.

What did Baldwin, the most talented black writer of his generation, make of this? He was uncompromising. He had expressed his views on the adoption of black speech and music by whites in his review of Langston Hughes's *Selected Poems* ('the white world takes over this vocabulary – without the faintest notion of what it really means'), and he told Mailer, with a large dose of calculated condescension – but with scarcely less affection – that although he had tried to read 'The White Negro', he couldn't understand it.

Baldwin did not share Mailer's fascination with the Beats and their 'psychopathology'. He had met Kerouac at parties during return visits from Paris in the mid-1950s, but took little interest in him. He was personally fond of Ginsberg, but was cautious of Burroughs and his liking for guns and drugs, and he differed from Mailer over *Naked Lunch*: 'It's not a book,' his later impromptu judgement on Burroughs's novel went, 'it's a convulsion!'

Baldwin's general view of beatniks was that their hipness and their cool were artificial. How, he reasoned, could it be otherwise? How could they know what 'hip' really meant? What did they know of what it cost to be 'cool'? When their ersatz bohemianism failed them, they would simply go home and 'take over the family business' (a deliberate hyperbole, probably inspired by the knowledge that Burroughs was in line to inherit his family's adding-machine business). The privileges which the young whites rejec-ted – voting rights, education rights – were the same things being fought for at that very moment, at a cost of lives, by Negroes in the South. Beatniks and hipsters who chattered on about 'the black man's code' and 'the existentialist synapses of the Negro' should have had the decency to sound embarrassed when reminded of it.

What Baldwin resented was what most beguiled Mailer: the way in which the hipsters appropriated and exploited the souls of black folk, without proper respect for the experience of the people in question; they wanted 'soul' without considering the history that distilled it. No beatnik had been denied a place to live in New York, or anywhere else in his native land, because of his race. If Allen Ginsberg was ejected from his home, or from his college, or from a cocktail party or a restaurant, or had to leave the country, it was because he had declined to accept society on its terms, not the other way round. From the point of view of Baldwin, or Richard Wright, or Langston Hughes – each of whom had found a peace of mind abroad that they could not expect at home – this was a luxury never to be experienced, and therefore contemptible. The black man's survival depended on gauging the temper of the status quo and co-existing with it, progressing down every path a step at a time, to see how far he could go and how much society would take. The drop-outs had drawn the mark of Cain on themselves; the black man had been born with it, in a society which repudiated him.

If it was the wish of the Beats, the beatniks, the hipsters, and so on, to reject and revolt, there was nothing Baldwin could do to stop them; but it was asking too much that he endorse their adoption of his 'code'.

Shortly after he attended his friend Cordier's Death of the Beat Generation party in New York, Baldwin began work on an essay about Mailer. In it he quoted a passage from Kerouac's novel *On the Road*:

At lilac evening I walked with every muscle aching among the lights of 27th and Welton in the Denver coloured section, wishing I were a Negro, feeling that the best the white world had offered was not enough ecstasy for me, not enough life, joy, kicks, darkness, music, not enough night. I wished I were a Denver Mexican, or even a poor overworked Jap, anything but what I so drearily was, a 'white man' disillusioned. All my life I'd had white ambitions ... I passed the dark porches of Mexican and Negro homes; soft voices were there, occasionally the dusky knee of some mysterious sensual gal; and dark faces of the men behind rose arbours. Little children sat like sages in ancient rocking chairs.

After repeating Kerouac's words, Baldwin followed through with the perfect counter-punch: 'This is absolute nonsense, of course, objectively considered, and offensive nonsense at that: I would hate to be in Kerouac's shoes if he should ever be mad enough to read this aloud from the stage of Harlem's Apollo Theatre.'

Although Baldwin spent little time thinking about the modish applications of 'hip', or indeed about the writers of the Beat Generation, he was greatly fond of Mailer. He was even somewhat in awe of him. Mailer was possessed of volcanic energy, he threw off endless showers of ideas – half the thoughts of a genius, half those of a fool. He was captivating, a writer with vision.

Like others, however, Baldwin had occasion to be bemused, if not offended, by Mailer's odd notion of friendship, which, as readily as it entailed great hospitality, wit and charm, might involve a challenge to a head-butting contest, or sudden, unnecessary barbs about one's work or one's physical features (Baldwin, for example, was 'little, ugly, and black as the ace of spades'). During the Death of the Beat Generation party, Baldwin said to Mailer, 'I'm a Greek, you're a Roman', meaning, presumably, that he was in closer alliance with the classical sensibility of Europe than with the fragmenting culture he found in America, where Mailer was hugely, creatively, at home. Even 'hip', in his view, was essentially a private affair, something a man like Mailer, with his fondness for public gestures, failed to understand.

Baldwin had met Mailer in Paris in 1956, at the Montparnasse apartment of Jean Malaquais, novelist and translator of Mailer's novel *The Naked and the Dead*. The two men liked each other instantly. 'Jimmy had an absolutely wonderful personality in those years,' says Mailer. 'I don't think there was anyone in the literary world who was more beloved than Jimmy. He had the loveliest manners. And he had these extraordinary moods: he walked around with a deep mahogany melancholy when he was unhappy, and when things amused him it was wonderful to watch him laugh, because it came out of this sorrow he had.'

Writing five years after their introduction, in 1961, Baldwin cast the nights which followed in the clubs and cafés of Paris, accompanied by Arnold and by Mailer's wife Adele, as he might characterize the happy dawn of a love affair which could never be recaptured. Mailer is 'exuberant and loving', striding through 'the soft Paris nights like a gladiator'. Beneath all his showing off, 'something very wonderful was happening. I was aware of a new and warm presence in my life.'

These remarks are taken from the essay, 'The Black Boy Looks at the White Boy', which appeared first in *Esquire* and then in *Nobody Knows My Name*; by the time they were written, the presence of Mailer in Baldwin's life, though it was yet 'warm', appeared more complex than it had on those first, happy Paris nights.

Baldwin styled his essay a 'love letter', a term which has drawn little comment in a relationship more often described in terms of a boxing match. 'Baldwin hated him with a passion,' said Frank Corsaro, a theatre director at the Actors Studio, to a journalist compiling material for a book on Mailer. 'When he and Norman were together it was like the two of

them were wrestling for position.' Later, in 1962, Baldwin and Mailer met
in Chicago when each was covering the first Sonny Liston–Floyd Patterson fight, and the title of Baldwin's essay on Mailer echoes the earlier
clash between Patterson and Ingemar Johanssen. There is even a book
with the subtitle 'Baldwin vs Mailer', which outlines, with no great
subtlety, the build-up to a showdown that never came – that never could
come, because the mutual hostility that could have fuelled it, in spite of
what Corsaro says, did not exist.

If Wright, Hughes and others fell under the shadow of Baldwin's father,
and were made into adversaries, Mailer was seen as a partner, an equal,
and therefore a lover, for partnership was usually equivalent to love in
Baldwin's prospectus. If there was, momentarily, passionate hatred, then it
surely stemmed from its opposite emotion.

What did exist, on both sides and in plentiful supply, was petulance,
ego, vanity, impatience with the other's direction and aspirations. There
was a considerable amount of mutual respect, but also a feeling on
Mailer's side that Baldwin had wasted his substance in Europe, and on
Baldwin's that Mailer's much-vaunted theories about Negroes' superior
sexuality and elegance amounted to nothing more than a portrait of the
noble savage re-drawn. They mirrored, after all, the kind of stereotypes he
had been fighting for years. 'Next thing you'll be telling me is that all
coloured folks have rhythm!' was one of his favourite rebuffs, borrowed
from Richard Wright.

The friendship which had begun so promisingly first turned sour with
the publication of Mailer's book *Advertisements for Myself* in 1959, a
collection of essays, articles, interviews and fragments, including 'Evaluations – Quick and Expensive Comments on Some Talent in the Room',
in which Mailer delivers his verdict on a score of what he calls 'com-
petitors'.

Baldwin was back in Paris, staying at the home of James Jones, when a
copy of the book found its way into their hands. William Styron was also
present. They read Mailer's comments on Saul Bellow: 'knows words, but
writes in a style I find self-willed . . . I cannot take him seriously as a major
novelist'; on Ralph Ellison: 'essentially a hateful writer'; on Gore Vidal: 'in
need of a wound which would turn the prides of his detachment into new
perception'.

Not all of the comments on these and other contemporaries were wide
of the mark, nor were they all intended to hurt. But that was undoubtedly

the effect they had on James Jones ('has sold out badly over the years'), on Styron ('has spent years oiling every literary lever and power that could help him on his way'), and on Baldwin himself, as they read aloud Mailer's words 'in a kind of drunken, masochistic fascination' in Jones's apartment. All three had considered themselves to be Mailer's friends.

Of Baldwin, Mailer said that he was 'too charming to be major . . . even the best of his paragraphs is sprayed with perfume'. *Giovanni's Room*, the novel Baldwin had published at the time of their first meeting in Paris three years before, was 'a bad book'. Overall, Baldwin seemed 'incapable of saying "F— you" to the reader'.

His first temptation, Baldwin rejoined in 'The Black Boy Looks at the White Boy', was to send a cablegram 'which would disabuse him of that notion, at least in so far as one reader was concerned.' The disabusing had to wait, however, until Baldwin's essay was published in 1961. There he administered an unanswerable put-down to the apostle of hip: the black musicians in Paris among whom they sometimes found themselves, Baldwin wrote, 'really liked Norman'. But they did not for a moment 'consider him as even remotely "hip" . . . They thought he was a real sweet, offay cat, but a little frantic.'

Good, stylish jousting, but Baldwin's purpose in 'The Black Boy Looks at the White Boy' is more serious, and more generous, than Mailer's taunting antics in 'Evaluations'. Baldwin was repelled by Mailer's division of life into winners and losers. He used his 'love letter' as the vehicle for a confession and a plea: to say that love is more important to him than power, while the opposite seems true for Mailer. It is, moreover, the kind of confession of which he knows Mailer to be incapable. In offering it, Baldwin is hoping to curtail the excesses of an important, visionary writer.

Instead, he succeeded only in wounding, as he had been wounded. 'There was a change after that,' Mailer says. 'I was hurt slightly by the piece. It was out of whack. He had me strong where I wasn't strong, and weak where I wasn't weak. These things are more annoying than maliciousness. He was condescending. It may have been payback for something I'd written about him.'

Most of the aggression, when this partnership turned into a contest, came from Mailer's corner, and it might have been his way of dealing with a difficult friendship. They had their worst argument at a boxing match, which seems appropriate, the Liston–Patterson fight which took place at the end of 1962. Mailer was covering it for *Esquire* and Baldwin for the

'Men's magazine' *Nugget*, and each refers to the squabble in his article. Baldwin:

I left for the fight full of a weird and violent depression, which I traced partly to fatigue – it had been a pretty gruelling time – partly to the fact that I had bet more money than I should have – on Patterson – and partly to the fact that I had had a pretty definitive fight with someone with whom I had hoped to be friends.

At first, Mailer, too, had hoped to be friends, and had welcomed Baldwin into his life; but then, seeing a competitor, he obeyed his natural impulse, which was to hit. Like Hemingway, his hero, he seems often to have had to hurt the people who cared for him most.

Baldwin was entering the big time. His agent told *Ebony* magazine that he could expect to earn $20,000 in 1961, a substantial sum. His diary was beginning to take on the shape of a star American writer's. At the end of 1959 he had sailed to Paris, left there after Christmas for Stockholm, then returned to New York to write the *Esquire* profile of Bergman. In May he went South again, with commissions from two glossy magazines. He spent some days trailing Martin Luther King and wrote a 12,000-word article on him, but – like much of his writing from the South – it lacks flair, and he did not reprint it in his forthcoming collection of essays. In the autumn he was in San Francisco for the third annual *Esquire* symposium on 'The role of the writer in America'.

It is the kind of schedule that begins to squeeze out the thing the fêted writer really needs – time and space for writing – and Baldwin thus adopted what became a lifelong habit, of stealing time to write. During March and April, before heading down South, he retreated once more to the MacDowell Colony in New Hampshire; early the following year, he crept away to William Styron's place in Connecticut; later on in 1961, still trying to reach the end of *Another Country*, he took refuge in a house belonging to the publisher of Dial Press, Richard Baron, in upper Westchester. 'He was always complaining that he was bothered by people in New York,' says Baron, 'but once he got somewhere, somehow the place would start filling up.' Later still that year, having discovered that New England just wasn't far enough away, he fled to Turkey.

His gregariousness kept pace with his new success. 'I am what you'd call a drinking man', he told the *Ebony* reporter who came to interview him at

Horatio Street ('a neatly-kept three-room apartment in a slightly shabby walk-up building . . . a stone's throw from the Hudson River'). People began to tell stories about his capacity for bourbon or Scotch, and he found robust drinking cronies among literary contemporaries, such as William Styron and James Jones. At a symposium organized by *Esquire* magazine in San Francisco in 1960, he met Philip Roth for the first time, and also struck up a rapport with John Cheever, whose short stories he admired. Cheever later returned the compliment: 'What a style!' he said. 'What intensity! What religious feeling!' The two writers shared a love not only of beautiful prose and of hard liquor but of other men, although the truth about Cheever was not then generally known.

While on the West Coast for the symposium, at which he delivered the lecture 'Notes for a Hypothetical Novel' (included in *Nobody Knows My Name*), Baldwin stayed with his old friend Theodore Pelatowski, with whom he had collaborated on the unpublished book about Harlem in 1946. Pelatowski was now more taken up with painting than photography, and he gave one of his pictures to Baldwin as a present, which was later hung in Horatio Street. 'Jimmy stayed with us from Monday till Friday,' Mrs Marjorie Pelatowski recalls, 'and I don't think I slept all week.'

There is a difference, both in tenor and content, between the writing Baldwin did during the period 1949–57 and what he wrote afterwards, when once again domiciled in New York. Of the two novels he released from Paris, one is set in the past and the other among white expatriates living in Paris; his major essays of the period are either literary criticism or memoirs. Once he had returned to his duties at home, however, his writing became more immediately responsive to the pulse of American life, and takes a committed stance which is largely absent from the earlier work. The turning point was his attack on Faulkner, and his new book *Nobody Knows My Name* is full of warnings, pleas and dark prophecies. But the range of subjects in the book is wider than is sometimes assumed: apart from Faulkner, Bergman and Mailer, there are essays on André Gide and Richard Wright, about the craft of novel writing and 'The Discovery of What it Means to Be an American'. Baldwin's talent is evident on every page, his prose supple and virtuosic, his intelligence bold, his prophetic wisdom in abundant supply.

The book was published in July 1961 and went straight on to the best-seller list, where it remained for six months – an unusual success for a collection of essays. It was the first book by Baldwin to be issued while he was actually living in America, and he was subjected for the first time to celebrity treatment. He appeared on television on several occasions, once being interviewed by Mike Wallace, who introduced him as 'one of the people other people are interested in'. In Chicago in July he did an extended radio interview with Studs Terkel, who used superlatives such as 'remarkable', 'beautiful', 'brilliant', 'astute', etc. to describe his guest and his new work.

Baldwin's performance on the air was likewise a commanding one. He outlined the black man's predicament in terms that a white person could understand. Terkel called him one of the few people in the world today who knows who he is. He asked Baldwin about the tendency of the black to accept the white man's stereotype of him, and Baldwin explained it in terms of the images the Negro saw all around him: 'none of it applies to you. You go to the movies and, like everybody else, you fall in love with Joan Crawford, and you root for the good guys who are killing off the Indians. It comes as a great surprise when you realize that all of these things are really metaphors for your oppression.'

His approach to questions about the troubles in the South was characteristically conciliatory – 'it is very difficult for a Negro really to hate white people: he is too involved with them' – and he made a dreadful prophecy concerning Birmingham, Alabama: 'There will be violence (and of this I am as convinced as I am that I am sitting in this chair) one day in Birmingham. And it won't be the fault of the Negroes.' Three years later, in the wake of extended rioting, four black children were killed by a bomb there while attending Sunday school.

The conversational tone of this half-hour-long interview exhibits an authority and a depth of conviction (and also an anger) which is new, which was not present in the letters home from Paris just five years before. There the 'Negro problem' is seldom mentioned, even in correspondence with close friends, and the host country's Algerian 'problem' is simply 'interesting'. To many of his letters Baldwin would typically add, 'I'm sure you won't want to use this', or 'I'm sure this won't interest you', as a self-protective postscript; or else he might humbly ask Philip Rahv's advice on the 'ethics' of publishing an article critical of Richard Wright, without first showing the piece to Wright himself.

Even-temperedness of that sort had gone from his typewriter, and with it went, not entirely coincidentally, Philip Rahv himself and the kind of solidly intellectual journal he represented.

The ties had been fraying for some time. He had not appeared in *Commentary* or the *Nation* since 1956, in the *New Leader* since 1954. *Partisan Review*, however, had published his 'Letter from the South' (later the title essay of *Nobody Knows My Name*) in 1959, and for his second trip south in the spring of 1960 he asked the magazine for an advance of $100 against a piece which they commissioned. This he received, and added to the advances from *Harper's* and *Mademoiselle*, magazines which were, as Philip Rahv and William Phillips were well aware, substantially more affluent than *Partisan Review*.

By the turn of the year, however, he had fulfilled his commissions for the former two journals ('The Dangerous Road before Martin Luther King' and 'They Can't Turn Back'), but had produced nothing for *Partisan Review*. He had something planned, but never finished it; nor, despite a string of enquiries from Phillips, did he explain why. Almost a year after the deadline had elapsed, Phillips was still left wondering, 'Where have you disappeared to? How about the piece for us?'

Baldwin was often a poor deliverer, but contributing to his failure on this occasion was a mild falling-out with *Partisan Review* that had taken place at the same time as his second trip south was being arranged. The tiff centred on a chapter from the work-in-progress *Another Country*, which the magazine wanted to publish in the issue for spring 1960, entitled 'Any Day Now'.*

From the MacDowell Colony in early April, Baldwin wrote to Phillips, a little impatiently, asking for the verdict on the excerpt from his novel. Phillips replied, assuring him that they were taking it, but, 'As you know, we're following Fitelson's advice about the dirty stuff.' Baldwin's response was snappy: so they were following Fitelson's advice 'and that's great' – but what *was* his advice?

William Fitelson was the attorney for the magazine and he had counselled the editors that it might be risking prosecution to print four-letter words. Phillips then had Fitelson write and explain to Baldwin that the printers had refused to set the words 'fuck', 'motherfucker', 'cocksuckers' and 'blow job'. The journal's second-class mailing rights were at stake, and possibly its tax-exemption status. In the resultant text, therefore, the words are rendered as 'f***', 'mother******', 'c***suckers' and 'b*** j**'.

---

* 'Any Day Now' is the title Baldwin gave to Book Two of the finished version of *Another Country*; curiously, however, the *Partisan Review* excerpt is taken from Book One.

MILTON J. ARONDS
"Moogy"   Rochester
Program Sq.
To know all the answers
Do unto others before they do
unto you.

RUSSELL HAMILTON ARONDS
"Russ"   Rutgers
Locker Sq.; Service L.; Lunchroom
Sq.; Biology Sq.; Lib. Sq.
Salesman
"I cash clothes."

ALAN B. ARONSOHN
"Al"   Dartmouth
Regents Book Sq.; Admit and Pro-
gram Comm.
To fly to Hawaii
What did Howard Hughes ever
do to deserve all that?

JOSEPH D. AZZNARA
"Azzi"   Fordham
Service L.; Locker Sq.
Science Teacher
To be or not to be this June, that
is the question.

JAMES A. BALDWIN
"Baldy"   C.C.N.Y.
Magpie Editorial Board; Student
Court.
Novelist-Playwright
Fame is the spur and—ouch!

JOHN F. BAME
"Jack"   Texas Christian
Engineer
I came, I slept, I graduated.

1. James Baldwin, aged seventeen, pictured in the DeWitt Clinton High
School graduation yearbook, 1941; 'Fame is the spur . . .'

2. David Baldwin, the writer's stepfather.
'He knew that he was black but did not
know that he was beautiful.'

THESE TWO

A Play in Six Scenes

JAMES BALDWIN

Illustrated by HAROLD ALTMAN

Scene 1.—A cold wet alley about five A.M. Day is just breaking. We hear the swish and patter of heavy rain. Drunkard stumbles into alley. He is completely intoxicated.

DRUNKARD—Gosh . . . shure ish dark . . . (*He stumbles over something and mutters inaudible curses.*) Wha'sh devil . . . deshent man can't even git home peashful. (*He stumbles again and falls.*) Well I'll be . . . ish two men . . . hey! wake up. Hey! . . . ish rainin' . . . (*He attempts to lift one body which is lying atop the other. Suddenly he lets it drop, recoils, yells.*) Hey! They're dead—dead. (*He stumbles to the mouth of the alley*). Moider! Moider! Help, police! (*We hear windows slammed up.*) Moider! Moider!

(*Now we hear voices from the windows.*) "Hey! What's all the racket down there? . . . What's wrong? . . . Shut up down there!"

DRUNKARD—Ish two dead men down here! Moider! (*And he is off again.*)

(*We hear the voices from the window.*) "He said it's a murder . . . murder? . . . Yep . . . Aw, he's stewed. He's probably seein' things . . . He said they're dead. . . . Call the police, somebody . . ." (*Two policemen enter the alley.*)

1ST POLICEMAN—What's the matter here? What's wrong?

DRUNKARD—(*Points to bodies.*) They're dead, offisher.

1ST POLICEMAN—You know anything about this?

3. A page from the school magazine, the *Magpie*, 1941, with the opening of Baldwin's play 'These Two' and an illustration by Harold Altman.

4. West 130th Street, New York, from east of Lenox to west of Fifth Avenue, 1932 – 'We never lived beyond those boundaries; this is where we grew up.' (Courtesy of New York Public Library)

5. Baldwin on the Left Bank, shortly after arriving in Paris, 1949. (Gidske Anderson)

6. (above) Baldwin in Aix-en-Provence in the autumn of 1949 with two unknown friends; he fell ill and was soon to be hospitalized. (Gidske Anderson)

7. (top right) At the window of the Hôtel Mirabeau in Aix. (Gidske Anderson)

8. (right) The Hôtel de Verneuil, where Baldwin first stayed in Paris in the late 1940s; managed by the same family, the hotel is virtually unchanged today. (Ceridwen Loxley)

9. (left) Themistocles Hoetis, the editor of *Zero* magazine and one of Baldwin's best friends in Paris, photographed in Tangier, 1951. (Paul Bowles)

10. (right) Gordon Heath at the folk club he ran on the Left Bank, L'Abbaye, *c.* 1950; Baldwin created the role of Luke in *The Amen Corner* for him. (Courtesy of Gordon Heath)

11. (left) William Rossa Cole, Baldwin's ally at his first publishers, the house of Knopf. (Elliot Erwitt)

12. (right) Lucien Happersberger, Baldwin's lifelong friend, whom he met in Paris in 1949. (Courtesy of Lucien Happersberger)

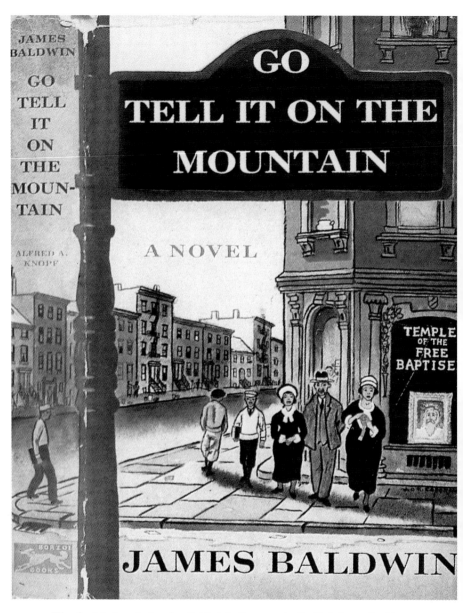

13. The final jacket design for Baldwin's first novel, *Go Tell It on the Mountain*. An earlier version was rejected, but not before several bound proofs bearing it had been sent out to reviewers. These copies are now very rare collector's items. In this version, 'Temple of the Free Baptised', the name of the church, should in fact be 'of the Fire Baptised'. (Courtesy Alfred A. Knopf)

14. (left) Langston Hughes in the 1930s.

15. (right) Richard Wright: 'Richard accused me of trying to destroy his reputation . . .' (Courtesy Michel Fabre)

16. Istanbul, 1966: in the foreground sits the painter Beauford Delaney, 'the man who helped me grow up'; in the background, centre, can be seen a detail of one of his portraits of Baldwin. (Sedat Pakay)

UNITED STATES GOVERNMENT

Memorandum

TO : DIRECTOR, FBI

FROM : SAC, WFO (145-0)

DATE: 9/19/62

ATTENTION: FBI LABORATORY

SUBJECT: JAMES BALDWIN; THE DIAL PRESS
NEW YORK, NEW YORK
ITOM

403878

Enclosed is a book entitled "Another Country"
written by JAMES BALDWIN. This book was published in 1962
by the Dial Press, New York, New York.
In many aspects it is
similar to the "Tropic" books by MILLER. It need not be
returned.

3 - Bureau (Enc.1)
1 - WFO
(4)

17. A memorandum from Baldwin's 1,750-page FBI file, addressed to the Director,
J. Edgar Hoover, concerning the novel *Another Country*.

18 (left) Norman Mailer: 'Norman is my very good friend, but perhaps I do not really
understand him at all . . .' (News Photo)

19. (right) Baldwin at a press conference in London on the day after the assassination of
Malcolm X in February 1965. Baldwin told reporters: 'What happened to him will
probably happen to all of us.' (*Times* Picture Library)

20. The first Freedom Bus, whose passengers were attempting to integrate Southern waiting-rooms, after it was set alight outside Anniston, Alabama, on 14 May 1961. (Archive Collection, Birmingham Public Library, Birmingham, Alabama)

21. A fireman helps a woman escape the blaze at the height of the Birmingham riots. (Archive Collection, Birmingham Public Library, Birmingham, Alabama)

A CORGI BOOK

GIOVANNI'S ROOM

James Baldwin's second novel has been widely praised by the critics.

"The story of a young American involved with both a woman and with another man. Mr. Baldwin writes of these matters with an unusual degree of candour and yet with such dignity and intensity that he is saved from sensationalism." N.Y.HERALD-TRIBUNE

"Remarkable for its challenging assumption that it is as valid for the author to describe the processes of homosexual as of a heterosexual affair." SUNDAY TIMES

"Possibly the best and certainly the frankest novel about homosexuality for many years... cleanly and capably written." EVENING STANDARD

JAMES BALDWIN

is recognised as one of the most accomplished writers of our day. He is the author of GO TELL IT ON THE MOUNTAIN and the current bestsellers ANOTHER COUNTRY and THE FIRE NEXT TIME.

PHOTOGRAPH BY WALTER DARAN

22. The back jacket of an early paperback edition of *Giovanni's Room*.

23. (left) Advertisement announcing the opening of *Blues for Mr Charlie* in April 1964; note the 'unusually reasonable prices' requested by the author.

24. (below) At Urcan, at a restaurant on the Bosphorus, in the mid-1960s; left to right, David Baldwin, Engin Cezzar, Marlon Brando, James Baldwin, David Leeming. (Courtesy Engin Cezzar)

25. Baldwin with new friends on the steps of Yeni Cami
(New Mosque), Istanbul, 1966. (Sedat Pakay)

26. In Istanbul, 1966, with the singer Bertice Reading and her daughter.

27. Baldwin with the playwright Arthur Miller, on an official visit to the Soviet Union in October 1986. (Courtesy Yashar Kemal)

28. Baldwin the theatre director, supervising rehearsals of John Herbert's play *Fortune and Men's Eyes*, performed with Engin Cezzar (standing, left) in the leading role, at the Cezzars' Milky Way Theatre, Istanbul 1969–70. (Courtesy Engin Cezzar)

29. Baldwin with his friend the Turkish novelist Yashar Kemal, in the café La Palette, Paris 1976; reflected in the mirror is the photographer Ara Guler.

30. Baldwin with Beauford Delaney during the painter's final hospitalization in the late 1970s.

31. Baldwin with the author, at Baldwin's home in St-Paul de Vence, July 1984. (Fanny Dubes)

32. Baldwin, aged sixty. (Fanny Dubes)

33. The funeral at the Cathedral of St John the Devine, 8 December 1987. In the centre is Baldwin's mother.

Baldwin was annoyed and Phillips's attempts to cajole him – 'The dashes are creating more excitement than if the words were printed normally' – made no impression. He replied sardonically that he was distressed to learn from Fitelson that the printer led such a 'blameless life'. Had he known, he would probably have withdrawn the piece. There was consolation, though, he added sardonically, in having implanted two new dirty words into the language – 'blow' and 'job'.*

Baldwin was writing from Tallahassee, Florida, where he was staying in the Negroes-only hotel in the 'disreputable' Negro section of town, confused by talk of progress and evidence of backwardness. He had come to report on student activism for *Mademoiselle*, but he mentioned to Phillips that he was at work on a piece for *Partisan* entitled 'The Book of Revelations', and snarled that if the printer didn't like it, 'you'd damn well better fire the printer'.

But since the piece did not arrive, Phillips never had the chance.

---

* Apparently he had some second thoughts by the time he handed in the finished book, for in a number of places, the 'dirty stuff' is omitted altogether.

Chapter Fourteen

At the end of 'A Fly in the Buttermilk', Baldwin predicted that 'what is happening in the South today will be happening in the North tomorrow'. He had long contended that segregation existed in the North as much as in the South, only in an unofficial form. The North had not so far developed the crises which were splitting the South, but one of the questions which Studs Terkel asked Baldwin during their radio interview touched on the emergence of the Black Muslims, a new force in the civil rights struggle. The Islamic movement had lately captured the eye of the press and television, with talk of a separate black nation and the eschewal of non-violence; and it was a movement peculiar to the North.

Martin Luther King was regarded by the nation at large as the principal black leader. But King's homeland was the South, his religion Christianity. It was out of this background that his policy and his strategy emerged, that all men were created equal, and that black people should pursue their right to equality via the path of non-violent resistance. It was beginning to be recognized, by Baldwin among others, that those policies had outlasted their effectiveness, and that they seemed out of context when transferred to Northern cities with burgeoning, often violent, black ghettos, such as Detroit, Chicago, Philadelphia and New York, where poverty was rife, and its partners, drug addiction and crime, ruled the streets. It was in such cities, particularly Chicago, where he had his base, that the Black Muslim leader Elijah Muhammed found support.

The 'Nation of Islam' was populated by young blacks, mainly from the cities, who changed their names and began to live according to Islamic teachings. Black Muslims were not permitted the use of narcotics, alcohol or tobacco, but, paradoxically, this gave the movement its appeal in the ghettos – abstinence and devotion to the Lord being traditional ways of transcending a slum existence. The main difference from past times was that the Lord was now Allah, and the teaching had donned an

Islamic garb in place of the old Christian one.

Many of the movement's followers, such as Malcolm X, were recruited while serving time in prison; others, such as the poet and playwright Amiri Baraka (Leroi Jones) and the boxer Muhammed Ali, changed their names along with their creed after having achieved success in areas administered mainly by whites. In their view, King's 'dream' of a world in which peoples of all colours could live on equal terms was merely an aid to the white man to keep his hold on power. 'You *are* an American citizen', Malcolm X would tell the crowds who gathered, in ever-increasing numbers, at Muslim rallies, 'so why have you got to fight for your rights as a citizen?' Malcolm spread the message that it was time for black people to stop turning the other cheek and to seize their rights themselves, 'by any means necessary'.

In place of King's desire for integration, the Black Muslims possessed an exclusive faith based on a scheme which postulated a complete reversal of the world-view which had enslaved blacks ever since the first white man set foot in Africa. The Muslims preached that the black man, far from being inferior, was in fact superior; although whites now held power over blacks, that was but a stage in the working out of a properly ordered universe, in which the present hierarchy would finally be overturned. They believed that the first humans, Original Man, were black people, and that they founded the holy city of Mecca. In Mecca lived twenty-four scientists, and the creation there of a bleached-out race was the mischief of an embittered member of their team. Mankind's strongest strain – that to which black people belonged – was diluted by this scientist, 'Mr Yacub', to produce a brown race, then further diluted to develop a red, then a yellow, and at last a race of cold-blue-eyed, pale-skinned savages, nude and shameless – white devils.

It was furthermore 'written' (in the lost Book of Moses) that the white race would rule the earth for an allotted span of 6,000 years. That era was ending now, in the mid-twentieth century, as Elijah Muhammed, the Messenger of Allah, came to the fore. Elijah had inherited Allah's message and had the divine guidance to save the Lost-Found Nation of Islam; and he taught that faith would be rewarded with the 'life' which would put blacks 'on the same level with all other civilized and independent nations and peoples on this earth'.

Even Baldwin, a committed integrationist and a devoted admirer of King's, conceded that King commanded scant following in the North, and he admitted that he himself might be wavering on the efficacy of King's policies. It was an intellectual ambivalence, however; emotionally, he was solidly behind King.

He did not expand on the subject of the Black Muslims, in response to questioning by Studs Terkel in Chicago, but the next month, August 1961, he was back in the city, this time to meet the leader of the Nation of Islam, Elijah Muhammed. The visit provided the spark for the essay that made him internationally famous, and which is probably his masterpiece, 'Down at the Cross'.*

Baldwin had not come to Chicago expecting to meet the Honourable Elijah – he was there on other business but was invited to the 'Temple' for dinner after being seen on television with Malcolm X, the Nation's second-in-command. When he arrived, he was shown into a dining-room where the men sat at one table and the women sat at another, and was introduced to the prophet. When Elijah Muhammed spoke,

a kind of chorus arose from the table, saying 'Yes, that's right.' This began to set my teeth on edge. And Elijah himself had a further, unnerving habit, which was to ricochet his questions and comments off someone else on their way to you. Now, turning to the man on his right, he began to speak of the white devils with whom I had last appeared on TV: What had they made *him* (me) feel?

Many things about Elijah impressed Baldwin, however: his courtesy, his authority, his sincerity, the way in which he managed his responsibilities: 'I felt that I knew something of his pain, and his fury and yes, even his beauty.' He would have liked to be able to honour him, as 'an ally'.

On re-reading, the account of the meeting in 'Down at the Cross' seems soft-centred, a foretaste of that sentimentality which was later to flow from Baldwin's pen whenever he wrote about other blacks, especially those placed in a position of leadership, or martyrdom. Within a year or so, he had adjusted his position on the Nation of Islam and the faith it offered to young blacks, telling an interviewer that the Muslims 'frightened' him, and that he considered them irresponsible –

irresponsible in terms of what I consider to be their obligations to the Negro community, as all racists are irresponsible. They batten on the despair of black men.

* 'Down at the Cross' was published in book form, with one other short piece, and given the title *The Fire Next Time*. It is now generally known by that name.

Elijah's later exposure as a hypocrite and a fraud, who embezzled movement funds and molested the female faithful – Malcolm X, at one time his heir-apparent, described him in 1964 as 'a faker' – could not have been foreseen by Baldwin. Yet he did not seriously challenge the Messenger of Allah's crackpot theories about the creation, white devils, and so on, nor did he allow them to deter his filial admiration. He needed to seek out father-figures who would at once receive his admiration and, reciprocally, bless him with approval. Not only as 'an ally' would he have liked to have honoured Elijah, he wrote, but as 'a father' too.

But although he could not condemn Elijah, he could not tolerate a selective view of humanity. He himself had left the church on discovering that the 'love' preached from the pulpit applied only 'to those who believed as we did, and did not apply to white people at all'. He would try to give Elijah Muhammed and the Nation of Islam a fair press, but when the time came for him to leave the Temple, he made it quite plain that the way along which the Messenger would like to guide him was not the route he was taking:

Elijah and I shook hands, and he asked me where I was going. Wherever it was, I would be driven there – 'because, when we invite someone here,' he said, 'we take the responsibility of protecting him from the white devils until he gets wherever it is he's going.'

Baldwin took a deep breath, then admitted that, as a matter of fact, he was going to have a drink with some white devils right now, on the other side of town.

Back in New York, Baldwin met Norman Podhoretz, the new editor of *Commentary*, and Podhoretz suggested that he write an article for the magazine on the subject of the Nation of Islam and its importance in the lives of Northern blacks. Baldwin agreed, and began work almost immediately.

The following month, weary of life in Greenwich Village, he reverted to what had by now become a lifetime's lonely habit: packing a trunk. He simply had to get out, he wrote to the critic Alfred Kazin, in the course of thanking him for a thoughtful review of *Nobody Knows My Name*. Notes for the essay he had agreed to write for Podhoretz were among his luggage. By that time, September 1961, he was well overdue with *Another Country*. But instead of postponing the trip in order to finish his book, as most writers would have done, he packed that too – a manuscript by now running to several hundred pages.

When he had returned home to New York from Paris in 1957, it was with the idea of staying; but his periodic absences from the city were becoming more and more frequent. He did not wish to expatriate himself again, yet the 'strain and terror' of living in New York would, he wrote to his agent Robert Mills, 'prove, finally, to be more than I can stand'. In the same letter, he said he was reconciling himself to being 'a transatlantic commuter', and lamented the fact 'that I am a stranger everywhere.'

He gave up the keys to his Horatio Street apartment, planning to allow himself at least six months' relief from New York. First stop was Paris. Lucien had been in the US during the year, and the plan was that he would meet Baldwin in Paris, bringing Baldwin's nineteen-year-old sister Paula Maria with him. Baldwin wished to show her something of Europe. But the major impetus behind this voyage was another magazine assignment, this time to write about Africa, for the *New Yorker*.

According to William Shawn, then editor, Baldwin approached the magazine sometime late in 1959 or early 1960 with the idea of writing a series of articles based on a trip to Africa. 'We gave him an advance,' says Shawn, 'and then we didn't hear from him again. For years.' (If it was Baldwin's style of working, it was also the *New Yorker*'s: staff writers have been known to take years to complete a piece, only to wait more years to see it published.)

In addition to his work – the novel, the essay, the series of articles, and a play he had promised to write for Elia Kazan, based on the Emmett Till murder – there was a burgeoning crop of invitations to manage: official ones, such as that from the Israeli government to be their guest in October, and another to participate in the judging of the Prix International des Editeurs in Majorca in April; and unofficial ones, like the invitation to visit Turkey from Engin Cezzar, the young actor who in 1958 had seemed to fit perfectly the title role in the Actors Studio version of *Giovanni's Room*. His plan was eventually to write a book about Africa, and he intended to include his Israeli observations too, as a 'prologue'. 'One cannot but respect the energy and courage of this handful of people', he wrote to Robert Mills about Israel; 'but one can't but suspect that a vast amount of political cynicism, on the part of the English and the Americans, went into the creation of this state.'

Baldwin's head fairly bubbled with projects during his travels, and he saw ways of involving not only Israel and the Arab question but even Algeria in his African book. 'I intend, before I leave . . . to get at least the Israeli section out to you, so that you can send it to Shawn', he wrote to his agent. There was also a Turkish essay in the offing. But none of it came to anything.

Baldwin went here when he wasn't expected, didn't go there when he was. His favoured principle when travelling was free-fall. For every plan there was a change of plan, for every date kept in a foreign city, a date broken in another. He went to London when he didn't intend to, but failed to meet Kazan in Athens to discuss the play, as promised. 'Bear with me,' he pleaded to Mills during the winter, as far from Africa as ever (and therefore from fulfilling his lucrative *New Yorker* commission, in which Mills had an interest); 'I make my journeys by radar . . . I know it's hard on everybody's nerves.'

It was hard on his nerves, as well. In Paris for Christmas, his body took its traditional refuge: illness and a collapse. 'Collapse' had become a way of coping with pressure, and 'going to pieces' one of his favourite phrases. A doctor advised against going to Africa in a state of such exhaustion, and Baldwin allowed himself to be shunted over the Alps to Switzerland and Loeche-les-Bains, where he had finished *Go Tell It on the Mountain* exactly a decade before. Lucien came with him, to help him settle and relax.

There was relief in all of this: Africa ought to be a pilgrimage, not a grim duty. In his letters to Mills, he admits to being frightened of what to expect there: 'it would be nice to be able to dream about Africa, but once I have been there, I will not be able to dream anymore'. Africa spelt *conundrum*, and Baldwin, constantly troubled by riddles of colour, had a 'gloomy feeling' that in Africa he would not find any answers, 'only more questions'.

It was restful, therefore, to be with Lucien, who took time off from his job as a salesman and from his family, in the place where he had happy memories of packing up his first novel. Such innocent pleasure, it must have seemed now.

Somehow, during those six months of shuttling across borders and seas, making drafts of books and essays he would never finish, he managed not only to write a portion of 'Down at the Cross', keenly awaited by Podhoretz at *Commentary*, but to complete *Another Country* and mail it to Jim Silberman, his editor at Dial Press. Not before time – the novel had been with him since before the publication of *Giovanni's Room*. The final full-stop was put down in Turkey, where he stayed with the family of Engin Cezzar, and he solemnized the occasion by pinning 'Istanbul, Dec 10, 1961' on to the last page.

Then came his visit to Switzerland, and then home. There had been much travelling and much talk about Africa (at one stage he actually told Mills: 'I am going, now, Saturday, from Paris to Dakar'), but the trip itself was put off. The delays had accumulated to the extent where they naturally formed a postponement. The land of his ancestors, which he was so desperate to recognize, but was desperately afraid would not recognize him, would have to wait.

'In most of the novels written by Negroes until today,' Baldwin wrote in 'Alas, Poor Richard', '. . . there is a great space where sex ought to be; and what usually fills this space is violence.'

Not only does this remark implicitly criticize Richard Wright (once again), it announces the imminent publication of *Another Country*. There is a measure of violence in Baldwin's novel, most of it felt in the heart rather than on the flesh, but there is a good deal more sex – heterosexual, homosexual, interracial, extra-marital, onanistic, and possibly more; heady stuff for 1962, when Henry Miller's *Tropic* books, Burroughs's *Naked Lunch*, and the words 'fuck' and 'cunt', among others, were banned on the grounds of obscenity. While he might admit to wanting to shock, Baldwin never meant to be obscene. The themes of *Giovanni's Room* – expatriation, the healing force of love and the difficulty of accepting it – are amplified in *Another Country*. In addition, it seeks to investigate the complex racial grief buried in the American soul.

There is, as usual, little plot; the true drama of life was in the human personality, and *Another Country* proceeds by spotlighting the artistic careers and interrelationships of seven characters in New York City. Two are black: Rufus, a jazz drummer, and Ida, his sister, a singer. The others are white: Richard, a cheap novelist; Cass, his wife; Vivaldo, a would-be writer and Ida's lover; Yves, a young Frenchman, and Eric, an actor, lover of Yves and almost everyone else.

Another Country is ambitious in length and scope; it attempts to show black and white characters sharing an equal footing, and explores the reasons for their failure to do so. It is set in the mid-1950s, when it was begun, and is redolent of the period. One of its successes is its rendering of the actuality of New York City – apartments, bars and streets – and the kind of people found there. Deeply rooted in the social-realist tradition, its concern is to examine the lives of a group of Americans at a specific moment in history. If a comparison is to be made, it is with Balzac. Baldwin said that he discovered Paris and Parisians in advance of arriving in the city by reading the *Comédie humaine*, and Balzac would have learned much about the daily comedy of New York City in the mid-twentieth century, had he had the opportunity to read *Another Country*.

Rufus Scott is probably Baldwin's most fully realized black character after Peter in 'Previous Condition', for the plain reason that, like Peter, he is less sentimentalized than most of the others (in this he compares favourably with his sister Ida). The story of Rufus's brief, brutal life and death, which occupies the first fifth of *Another Country*, is one of the best pieces of extended writing his creator achieved. Based on Baldwin's friend Eugene Worth, Rufus hurls himself to his death from the George Washington Bridge – 'built to honour the father of his country'.

Another Country went through many drafts – and some alternative titles, such as 'The Only Pretty Ring Time' – and Rufus was created last. Baldwin later said that he had to install the story of Rufus at the beginning in order to 'make sense of the rest of the novel'. Once he had invented Rufus, he re-wrote the story so that it centred on him and his suicide. And Rufus undoubtedly dominates the novel. Yet the effect of his death is to flatten the remaining four-fifths of the book into an extended anti-climax, for his disappearance leaves an absence which is never satisfactorily filled or explained.

Rufus's abrupt departure from the scene is not the only problem to which readers of Baldwin's third novel must reconcile themselves. The prose of *Another Country* is, in places, startlingly clumsy. It was exhausting, Baldwin told his French agent in June 1957, to realize how badly one writes almost all of the time, joking that this was a secret he was at great pains to keep back from the public. Much excellent writing there is in the novel, but for every passage of vivid realization there is a corresponding one of purple prose; for every precise image an inflated one; for every taut exchange of dialogue a conversation which is allowed to run on far beyond the extent of its contribution to the action.

In spite of the protests which arose from the moment of publication, there is comparatively little specific sexual description in *Another Country*. In *Giovanni's Room*, Baldwin gave only discreet accounts of sexual activity, if he did not leave the room altogether; in *Another Country* he remains present, but instead of reporting graphically (the b*** j** to which *Partisan Review*'s printer took exception occurs in conversation only), he serves up helpings of creamy prose.

Sometimes it is hard to see that the pen which crafted the sentences of 'Notes of a Native Son', 'Alas, Poor Richard' and 'The Black Boy Looks at the White Boy' – a pen which gives the impression that its versatility is unlimited – is responsible for *Another Country*. And the effusiveness shows up worst in the sex scenes. When Vivaldo makes love to Ida, he travels 'up a savage jungle river, looking for the source which remained hidden just beyond the black, dangerous, dripping foliage'. Afterwards, Ida looks 'very much like a woman and very much like a shy little girl'. Bodies 'strain together', 'thrash and throb', while orgasms happen to the sound of 'the far-off pounding of the sea'. Elsewhere, a train rushes 'into the blackness with a phallic abandon', a woman wears 'all her beauty as a great queen wears her robes'; a lover's eyes light up 'the grave darkness' like 'the searchlight of the Eiffel Tower or the sweep of a lighthouse light'. The compact, jewelled prose of *Go Tell It on the Mountain* here turns to paste.

A writer of Baldwin's calibre should have adjusted these mannered phrases, or, better, erased them. That he let them pass, in a novel he had worked on for seven years, must be put down, in part, to the lack of continuity in his creative life. A long novel requires the discipline of concentrated work; since its inception, *Another Country* had had to compete with *Giovanni's Room*, 'Notes of a Native Son', some short stories, all of the essays in *Nobody Knows My Name*, his work for the Actors Studio, trips around the world, 'Down at the Cross', and more besides. A hectic life like this was kinder to shorter work, such as the well-crafted stories 'Sonny's Blues' and 'This Morning, This Evening, So Soon'.

Another problem with *Another Country* is that here the occasionally breathless novelist has to share the page with his cool rival, the essayist. The essayist had barged into *Giovanni's Room*, where he had prompted David to say things only his creator could have thought of, but his presence is even more noticeable in *Another Country*. Already Baldwin was conscious of an encroaching duty as a 'Negro leader': he had used the phrase in a letter to Mills of February 1962, and stated that he would decline the role. For he knew then that while a leader or spokesman's intention is to explain, a novelist wants to portray.

This matter was raised by Lionel Trilling, in his review of the novel in the *Mid-Century*, and the venerable critic proffered a mild warning to the writer whom he had known since the mid-1950s, and had once recommended for a Rockefeller grant: 'How, in the extravagant publicness in which Mr Baldwin lives, is he to find the inwardness which we take to be the condition of truth in the writer?' While critical of the sloppy writing in *Another Country*, Trilling nevertheless appreciated its 'power', comparing Baldwin to Theodore Dreiser, a writer whose greatness did not depend on 'fineness and delicacy of art'.

Other critics were less generous: 'degrading ... pornography ... ', spat Stanley Edgar Hyman in the *New Leader*, but that was not his only objection – 'the writing is bad by any standard and exceptionally bad by Baldwin's own high standard'. A deeper cut was made by Norman Mailer, scenting an opportunity to hit back after Baldwin's elegant dismissal of him in 'The Black Boy Looks at the White Boy': 'abominably written ... sluggish ... lifeless ... stilted ... Baldwin commits every *gaffe* in the art of novel writing'. And yet, Mailer conceded, he had written 'a powerful book'.

'Powerful' seems to have been the word which came most easily to the critics' minds. Even Langston Hughes, who could scarcely have been expected to enjoy this novel of 'tormented love ... between men and women, homosexuals, whites and Negroes', ended his anonymous notice for the *Kirkus* reviews service with a tribute to 'a certain emotional power' in the book.

If Baldwin was wounded by these thrusts, immediate and lasting bestsellerdom helped soothe the pain. Mainstream critical acclaim was important to him, so were money and fame, and *Another Country* brought plenty of all three. When it was reissued in paperback in 1963, it was the second-largest-selling book of the year (after William Golding's *Lord of the Flies*). Baldwin seemed to have written a novel which could appeal to everyone. He already had a following among the intelligentsia, and to it he now added a less demanding readership, thrilled by his offer of the password that admitted them to taboo worlds. If his essays, subtle and discriminating, were his 'cool mode', *Another Country* showed Baldwin playing, as jazz musicians say, on top of the beat.

Another Country caught the attention not only of the public and the critics, but also of the FBI. Because of its similarity 'in many aspects ... to the "Tropic" books by MILLER', Baldwin's novel was subject to personal scrutiny by the FBI's director, J. Edgar Hoover, who, on 19 September

1962, forwarded it to the FBI Laboratory for 'examination'. While legal action was thought to be unnecessary, the book prompted several memoranda, added to a file which, by the time it was closed in 1974, comprised 1,750 pages.

Whenever *Another Country* made the news for extra-literary reasons, the FBI took note – for example when a New Orleans bookseller was arrested for stocking copies, thus violating 'city ordinances pertaining to the sale of obscene literature' (the District Attorney decided against pressing charges). In January 1965, a citizen of Fort Worth, Texas, wrote to Hoover complaining that *Another Country* was available in city drugstores, and pleading for action to prevent the further sale of this example of 'sex perversion at its vilest'. Wasn't there a federal law that could be used against its author?

Hoover replied that an investigation had concluded that the author had not so far broken any law, but he appreciated the letter-writer's concern. To show solidarity, he enclosed some publications which expressed his own views 'on the widespread accessibility of obscene and pornographic literature': *Combating Merchants of Filth: The role of the FBI, Let's Wipe Out the Schoolyard Sex Racket!* and *The Fight Against Filth*.

Neither Baldwin nor his publishers were yet aware of the FBI's interest. Their problem, for the time being, was how to cope with success. Dial Press organized a party for the celebrity author at Big Wilt's Smalls Paradise in Harlem, with a guest list numbering hundreds. A particular memory of the evening sticks in the mind of Baldwin's editor, Jim Silberman: 'I looked at all those people having a wonderful time, and I turned to my wife and said: "This is it. It can't get any better than this." And I was right.'

Chapter Fifteen

Baldwin reached Africa eventually, a year after first setting out. Accompanied by his sister Gloria, he travelled through Senegal, Ghana and Sierra Leone. Little things occurred which pleased him, such as being mistaken for a native of Dahomey, but there was no revelation, no discovery; the hidden ancestor was not suddenly made visible, the darkness of his homeland was unilluminated.

In the 1950s he had spoken with utter candour of his lack of communication with the Africans he had met in Paris ('They disgusted me, I think,' he had told the magazine *Phylon*), but 'Africa' was a different concept now. Africa was 'in' with American blacks, was hip. And Baldwin, nothing if not alert to changes in nuance, was aware of the shift in the terms of reference. 'I think of the poor Negroes of the US who identify themselves with Africa – and on what basis?' he wrote in a letter of 1962. 'American Negroes did not identify themselves with Africa until Africa became identified with power.'

Baldwin felt the poignancy of his failure to connect, but he was unembarrassed by it. He was an American, and no one in Senegal was going to think more of him for dressing up in a dashiki, as some American blacks were doing, and looking for his tribe. 'My bones know, somehow, something of what waits for me in Africa', he had written to Mills the previous year; what he discovered was a familiar feeling of homelessness. Nothing forcible enough took place, finally, to commit him to print.

Succour was sought in travel, the homeliness of other people, and he rounded off his African trip with another visit to Turkey, where the Cezzars had previously welcomed him. There he completed 'Down at the Cross'. It had swollen far beyond the dimensions of the original idea, which was to comment on the recent rise of Islam in the Northern cities. He was pleased with the essay, but he had a practical problem. Since the bottom had fallen out of his projected series of articles on Africa, he had nothing on his desk to give the *New Yorker*, and it was now about three years since the date of the commission.

Podhoretz, for his part, was becoming impatient, having also waited a long time. He had been trying to contact Baldwin for months. Finally, once Baldwin was back from Africa, Podhoretz reached him by telephone and asked about the essay he was supposed to be writing for *Commentary* on the Black Muslims. As a matter of fact, Baldwin told him, his essay was finished. Excellent, said Podhoretz, he would send someone over right away to pick it up. Well, actually, Baldwin replied, his agent had it . . . In fact, he thought his agent was probably showing it to Shawn at the *New Yorker*, since he owed them a piece. But not to worry – he was sure it would be unsuitable, and as soon as they rejected it he would pass it on to *Commentary*.

Podhoretz tells the story without giving the impression that time has softened his fury – the *New Yorker*, of course, took 'Down at the Cross' or *The Fire Next Time*, as it was to be called, and *Commentary* ended up with nothing – and he had every right to be angry. Baldwin had acted unprofessionally, and dishonourably, in failing to deliver on his promise to Podhoretz and going after the money. For the 20,000 words of 'Down at the Cross', he was paid $6,500 by the *New Yorker*, roughly twice the annual income of the average Harlem family in 1962, and a fee that *Commentary* could not hope to match. He never wrote again for the magazine in which he had had his original success.

William Shawn, meanwhile, was delighted with the article which landed on his desk in place of the expected stuff on Africa. He retitled it 'Letter from a Region in My Mind', to fit in with the *New Yorker*'s strict system of classification (it had to be a 'Letter from . . .'; it was after that that the category 'Reflections' was instituted), and published it in the issue of 17 November, during the week of Thanksgiving.

'I would say that it was one of only two or three things that really caused a sensation during my time at the magazine', says Shawn. 'The *New Yorker* came out week after week, and normally there was a consistent excellence about the writing. But Baldwin's piece had a political content. It was exciting. It was unexpected. If you read it now, the ideas might seem like generally assumed ideas – but then he was saying things that hadn't been said before. And everybody was talking about it.'

The content of *The Fire Next Time* does not seem as commonplace today as Shawn fears. Besides containing a report of his visit to Elijah

Muhammed's 'Temple', and giving his views on the Nation of Islam, the essay is also a personal memoir. Baldwin incorporates his childhood, puberty, his changing perception, his need to anchor himself to a rock in the ghetto wilderness, his brief glory in the pulpit, the competition with his father, and his ultimate defection to humanism. It is the essay which comes closest to representing his ideas *in toto* – not in a schematic way, but in the form of a mature and exemplary world-view. Baldwin's essay reads like the conversation of a genius; his critique of American society ranges over the poor state of American bread as a reflection of the national soul, the importance in life of the acceptance of death, the illusion of the 'Russian menace', the reality of the Negro's past – 'rope, fire, torture' – and the healing force of love and reconciliation:

If we – and now I mean the relatively conscious whites and the relatively conscious blacks, who must, like lovers, insist on, or create, the consciousness of others – do not falter in our duty now, we may be able, handful that we are, to end the racial nightmare, and achieve our country . . .

It was a visionary sermon; Baldwin had taken on the role of confessor to the American people, or at least the 'relatively conscious' part of it. The timing was also perfect, for the essay was published on the eve of the 100th anniversary of the Emancipation of the slaves.

Meanwhile, the situation in the South was running out of control, and forcing its way north. A young black man, James Meredith, had attempted to enrol at university – he was only now legally entitled to do so – and had created an emergency in the state of Mississippi. The issue was headline news. The Kennedy brothers had for some time been faltering and making clumsy attempts to tackle the problem, but their hesitant speeches had little impact. When the President made a tactical address to the State of Mississippi over the Meredith crisis, Baldwin called his speech 'shameful', and accused him of speaking to Mississippi 'as if there were no Negroes there'.

Baldwin was not a politician: he had no need to count votes and consider tactics, and *he* had made a great speech. His vision and optimism inspired others to rally to the cause – 'we may be able, handful that we are . . .' – and made him seem, at that moment, to be the spiritual leader the country needed.

The national press thought so. On 10 May 1963, the cover of *Time* magazine showed the face of Abraham Lincoln, in celebration of the anniversary of Emancipation. One week later – in a sequence which the publisher of *Time* considered 'appropriate' – the face on the cover was that of James Baldwin.

In *The Fire Next Time*, Baldwin's work on behalf of the black struggle and his creative work merge. All the disquisitions he had written on the subject of black–white relations might have been practice for the writing of this one. A private torment had been elevated to a public drama. His essay included everything he had to say on the subject.

As with two of his previous book titles, this one was taken from a Negro spiritual. One of the verses of 'I Got a Home in Dat Rock' runs:

> God gave Noah the rainbow sign, don't you see?
> God gave Noah the rainbow sign, don't you see?
> God gave Noah the rainbow sign, no more water, the fire next time.
> Better get a home in dat rock, don't you see?

Not everyone was persuaded of its greatness as a work of art, however, nor even as a polemic. Once the rhetorical finery had faded, what was left seemed to some rather thin and, where actual ideas were concerned, poverty-stricken. Writing in the *New York Review of Books*, F. W. Dupee criticized the lack of 'homework' in Baldwin's study of the Black Muslim movement's aims and finances, and disliked the overall randomness of the ideas. Robert Coles, in *Partisan Review*, placed a large question mark over his panacea, love. Another critic, Marcus Klein, concluded that Baldwin's essays were 'evasive' and lacking in 'ideational development', indulging instead 'Edenic fantasies'.

A more friendly attempt to point out a flaw in the philosophy came in a personal letter from the social philosopher Hannah Arendt: what 'frightened' her, she wrote, was the gospel of love which Baldwin began to preach at the end of the essay. 'In politics, love is a stranger,' she told him,

and when it intrudes upon it nothing is being achieved except hypocrisy. All the characteristics you stress in the Negro people: their beauty, their capacity for joy, their warmth, and their humanity, are well-known characteristics of all oppressed people. They grow out of suffering and they are the proudest possession of all pariahs. Unfortunately, they have never survived the hour of liberation by even five minutes.

A week after his face appeared on the cover of *Time*, Baldwin kept an appointment with the Attorney General, Robert Kennedy, at his Virginia home, Hickory Hill. The breakfast meeting was arranged to discuss problems related to the current crisis, but Baldwin turned up late and there was time for little more than a suggestion from the Attorney General that they get together again the following day in New York, this time with a group of leading blacks, to be assembled by Baldwin.

In the next twenty-four hours, a mixed dozen of blacks *and* whites (to Kennedy's consternation) was rounded up. It included such figures as Lena Horne and Harry Belafonte, the white actor Rip Torn, the black playwright Lorraine Hansberry, Edwin C. Berry, director of the Chicago Urban League, the sociologist Kenneth Clark, Martin Luther King's lawyer Clarence Jones, Baldwin's agent Robert Mills, Baldwin's brother David, a young man who bore brutal scars of mob beatings in the South, and one or two others.

This delegation represented the leading blacks in one sense – they were mostly successful in their chosen fields. A few of them – Clark, Berry, Jones – had the experience necessary to engage in the kind of dialogue envisaged by Kennedy and his civil rights chief Burke Marshall, who was also present, but from the start of the discussion they were drowned out by the emotional outbursts of the others.

Baldwin's aim was to make the Attorney General see and feel what it was like to be a Negro in America, how you had constant difficulties with the police, and difficulty getting an apartment, even if you were Lena Horne. Kennedy, for his part, wanted to discuss the developing crisis in the deprived urban centres of big Northern cities, and the rise of the Black Muslims. It was a case of Mr Inner Man facing Mr Outer Man, and both talking at once. Consequently, as a political event, the meeting was disastrous, though as a publicity exercise for Baldwin and the black spokesmen, who claimed that a 'sympathetic' Kennedy administration lacked the imagination needed to understand the scope of their problems, and the will to solve them, it was something of a triumph. Later on, the Kennedy–Baldwin meeting was apt to be represented as a confrontation between Robin Hood and the Sheriff of Nottingham, as the man of the people obstructed in his good mission by the agent of the government. That was how Baldwin himself saw it.

Kennedy was regarded by Martin Luther King and others as a liberal and an ally. He recognized the need for desegregation in the Southern states, and a better deal for black people nationwide. But he was necessarily also a pragmatist, one who calculated every decision as part of a larger strategy – the ultimate end of the strategy perhaps being to retain office. His authority in the conservative South had already been eroded as a result of the part he played in defending the so-called 'Mother's Day' Freedom Riders in May 1961, when their attempt to implement new desegregation rulings on Greyhound and Trailways buses throughout the Southern states had led to violence and rioting on a mass scale. The Freedom Riders, black and white, male and female, had been savagely beaten at several stages in their two-week long journey, as they tried, within the law, to use what were now only nominally 'whites only' waiting-rooms and lunch counters. The Kennedy brothers had then been forced into some awkward positions by stubbornly segregationist Southern governors, such as John Patterson of Alabama, who told Robert Kennedy's administrative assistant, John Seigenthaler, 'There's nobody in the whole country that's got the spine to stand up to the goddamned niggers except me.' 'Standing up' to the Freedom Riders entailed ensuring a total absence of police protection when the steadfastly non-violent crusaders were set upon by a mob of Ku Klux Klansmen wielding lead pipes and baseball bats. The first Freedom Riders reached New Orleans, their destination, bloodied and broken, less through the intervention of the government than through their own courage and determination.

One of the people whom Baldwin had brought along to the meeting at Kennedy's New York office was Jerome Smith, who had been on the 'Mother's Day' Freedom Ride. He had been beaten, jailed and beaten again, while attempting to integrate bus facilities in McComb, Mississippi. As a result, he was scarred and walked with a limp. Until now a dedicatee of non-violence, Smith warned Kennedy that he was 'close to the moment' when he would pick up a gun.

'It makes me nauseous to have to be here,' Smith declared, to open the meeting with the Attorney General, meaning that it should not have been necessary for American citizens to plead with their own government for protection while they sat at a lunch counter or rode on a bus, quite within their rights. Ten thousand US soldiers had been needed the previous September to guarantee the safe passage of James Meredith to his class at the University of Mississippi.

However, the Attorney General took offence at Jerome Smith's language and tone of voice – 'When I pull the trigger,' Smith told him, 'kiss it goodbye' – and the meeting never recovered. When Kennedy tried to ignore Smith's remarks and address himself to the others, Baldwin turned back to Smith to ask if he could imagine himself going overseas to fight for his country. 'Never! Never!' Smith shouted. How could he risk his life to defend a country that could not protect him in the state where he was born? Kennedy was shocked by this lack of patriotism. 'Oh, I can't believe that,' he retorted sharply. But Smith meant it; he knew, and so did the others, that tens of thousands of blacks felt the same way. Kennedy's surprise only proved what they had suspected all along, that he was out of touch with how blacks really thought and felt.

Kennedy's current concern – how to tackle the developing crisis in the 'urban centres of the North' – was never aired. The others would have called those urban centres ghettos; the two sides approached each other with different moral weaponry, and spoke in different tongues.

In the ensuing babble of argument and disagreement, David Baldwin shook a fist in the Attorney General's face, while James Baldwin impugned the neutrality of the FBI. Lena Horne suggested that Kennedy's understanding of the problems in the South was naïve, and Lorraine Hansberry cursed the 'specimens of white manhood' – Alabama policemen – who had been shown in a recent *Time* photograph pinning a black woman to the ground, one with a knee on her throat.

The convention broke up, leaving both parties more frustrated and distrustful than before. The meeting's failure to achieve anything significant is perhaps indicated by the way in which each side claimed that the other had been responsible for arranging it. *Newsweek* presented the story, based on an interview with Baldwin (3 June), as if he and Kennedy were on confidential terms and were out to solve a little local difficulty: 'Kennedy himself had instigated the talks ... "Look, Jim," he said, "get some of your best people together in New York and I'll come up and we'll talk this whole thing over".' Fern Eckman, on the other hand, in the book she wrote on Baldwin in the mid-1960s, gives the sequence of communication as follows: a cablegram from Baldwin to Kennedy on 12 May calling for action on the race rioting then taking place on the streets of Birmingham, then a response from Burke Marshall on 22 May, leading to an invitation to take breakfast at Hickory Hill on 23 May, with the larger meeting the next day. As for Kennedy himself, in this test of one-upmanship, he later put it on record that Baldwin had pestered him into giving an audience: 'I don't know who wanted me to see him – Arthur Schlesinger or Dick

Goodwin. I kept getting messages that he wanted to see me.'

In the same record – a sequence of interviews conducted in 1967 in which Kennedy gave his version of significant events of his time – he and Marshall were off-hand about the meeting with Baldwin and his 'people':

He came out ... Lorraine Hansberry said that they were going to go down and get guns, and they were going to give the guns to the people on the street, and they were going to start to kill white people ... But it obtained a lot of publicity for him, see. So he played it – James Baldwin – put him in the centre of things and gave him a position of leadership.

In saying, 'Look, Jim, get some of your best people together,' Kennedy, whether he instigated the talks or not, had not paused to consider the man he was dealing with. Baldwin's approach to socio-economic problems was emotional, not theoretical. He could no more have engaged in the type of practical dialogue that Kennedy had in mind than he could banish the horrors of racism by appealing to people's better natures.

Something similar happened early the following year when he was asked by Podhoretz to take part in a round-table discussion entitled 'Liberalism and the Negro', with Sydney Hook, Nathan Glazer and Gunner Myrdal, all well-versed in the social sciences and the theoretical dimensions of the 'Negro problem'. Before the seminar got underway, Baldwin, ill at ease in such company, asked a cohort what the hell he was supposed to say to them in there about all this 'sociology and economics jazz'. Baldwin's 'best people' were sincere in their desire to arrest the crisis in the South, and in the streets of Harlem, but of sociology and economics jazz most of them – the ones who did the talking – knew next to nothing.

Baldwin never saw Robert Kennedy again, although he continued to criticize the Attorney General and the Kennedys as a team. When John F. Kennedy was killed in Dallas six months later, instead of mourning, Baldwin made a speech expressing indignation at the fact that for 'many generations ... black men's heads have been blown off – and nobody cared. Because it wasn't happening to a person, it was happening to a "nigger".'

Possibly as a result of such remarks, and the violent outbursts he had heard at their meeting, Robert Kennedy was eager to keep in touch with Baldwin – in a special way. It was after the New York get-together that the

FBI began to take a serious interest in Baldwin, his concerns and his movements. In the days following the Kennedy meeting, top officials in the FBI's Washington headquarters began exchanging snippets from the press about it. At the foot of one set of clippings, Hoover's highest associate and bachelor housemate, Clyde Tolson, scribbled the question: 'What do our files show about James Baldwin?' This was only four days after the date of the meeting with Robert Kennedy. The next day, 29 May, a memorandum headed 'JAMES ARTHUR BALDWIN/INFORMATION CONCERNING' was addressed to Assistant Director Alan Rosen and circulated to six top Bureau offices.

Mr Tolson enquired as to information concerning James Baldwin who recently met with the Attorney General.

Bureau files reveal that Baldwin, a Negro author, was born in New York City and has lived and travelled in Europe. He has become rather well-known due to his writings dealing with the relationship of whites and Negroes. In 1960 he sponsored an advertisement of the Fair Play for Cuba Committee and was identified as one of its prominent members. This group is a pro-Castro organization in the United States ... Baldwin has supported organizations supporting integration and in 1961 reportedly stated a period of revolution confronted the world and only in revolution could the problems of the United States be solved. He has advocated the abolition of capital punishment and criticized the Director stating that Mr Hoover 'is not a lawgiver, nor is there any reason to suppose him a particularly profound student of human nature ...'

Information on the 'other individuals who participated in the recent conference with the Attorney General' was also gathered and incorporated into 'informative memoranda for dissemination to the Attorney General'. On the same day as Alan Rosen received his memo, it was being requested in New York that the FBI's New York office indices be searched for any information concerning Baldwin, 'particularly of a derogatory nature'. All they came up with was the brouhaha in 1954 in which he and Themistocles Hoetis were arrested and spent the night in prison.

Baldwin's name had first come to the attention of the FBI in 1960, as a result of the briefest of flirtations with the Fair Play for Cuba Committee (FPCC). According to Richard Gibson, a Paris associate from the 1950s and an organizer of the FPCC, Baldwin had little interest in the aims of the organization. 'I tried to get him more deeply involved,' says Gibson, 'but he always avoided aligning himself politically.' Baldwin was, however, briefly a sponsor of the FPCC; he added his signature to an advertisement stating the organization's aims which appeared in the *New York Times* in April 1960. During the decade and more in which the FBI took a serious interest in Baldwin's activities (roughly 1963–74) the fact that his name had appeared once in association with a group sympathetic to Communist Cuba was likely to be given prominent mention whenever a memo passed between one FBI official and another.

It was doubtless the same advertisement that prompted the FBI to mark Baldwin's card 'Communist', confirming its now infamous inability to distinguish between communist, radical and liberal, and to consider him a full-blown revolutionary. By the middle of 1961, the FBI had taken note of Baldwin's Horatio Street telephone number, WA–9 5921 and also of his 'influence' with the 'intellectuals' in New York City.

In addition to his explosive performance in Kennedy's office, another thing made Baldwin seem a proper target for FBI surveillance: his intention, stated *circa* mid-1963, of writing a book about the Bureau itself. This news caused considerable excitement in Hoover's office in Washington. Sales figures for *The Fire Next Time* were even circulated, with the implication that Baldwin on the FBI would be a certain best-seller. Agents were urged to make 'discreet' inquiries at Dial Press, using 'established sources' (a further memo noted, however, that the FBI had no such contacts at Dial), and if possible to obtain a set of galleys or an early copy of the book. A memo of 17 July 1964, sent to Hoover's political guardian, Assistant Director Cartha 'Deke' DeLoach, reads in part:

the book section of 'The Washington Post' for 6–21–64, announced captioned individual was contemplating at least four future books. Among these will be one about 'the FBI in the South'. Our New York Office was advised and requested to make discreet checks among its publication sources in an attempt to verify this information . . .

The 7–14–64 edition of the 'New York Herald Tribune' contained additional information concerning this matter. According to it, Baldwin's book will be published next spring; however, it will be featured in 'The New Yorker' magazine prior to its publication in book form . . .

'The New Yorker' over the years has been irresponsible and unreliable with respect to references concerning the Director and the FBI. It has published articles of a satirical nature concerning FBI tours, 'The FBI Story' (both the book and the movie) and crime statistics. Baldwin's book 'The Fire Next Time', appeared in the magazine before it was released in book form.

William Shawn, ex-editor of the *New Yorker*, has no memory of an arrangement whereby an article or articles by Baldwin on the FBI were planned for the magazine. The FBI also noted that, in a newspaper interview, Baldwin had 'urged the removal of the Director', J. Edgar Hoover. Hoover, Baldwin said, had used 'his enormous power and prestige to corroborate the blindest and basest instincts of the retaliatory mob'. This inspired Hoover to prepare a statement 'which can be made in the event Baldwin should make false charges against the Bureau', which would be issued 'if the circumstances warrant'. No doubt the information 'of a derogatory nature', had they discovered any, would have come in useful there.

What the FBI did not know was that, typically, while Baldwin had a title for his book – 'The Blood Counters' – he had little else. But FBI interest in the project remained high. The Bureau picked up a conversation between Martin Luther King and some of his associates, in which Baldwin's name was mentioned. A person whose name is blacked out on the FBI document told the assembled company that Baldwin was preparing a 'statement' about the FBI. This person claimed to have seen it, and told the company, 'I have seen some statements on the FBI but I have never seen one like this. He [Baldwin] is going to nail them to the wall.'

That phrase 'nail them to the wall' stuck in the throats of Hoover and his assistant directors, and was frequently repeated in memos concerning Baldwin. But the 'statement', if it ever existed beyond the idea, was never published.

Following the row with Kennedy, Baldwin's name was added to the FBI's Reserve Index, which consisted of that category of people who, in the event of an emergency, 'will receive priority consideration with respect to investigation and/or other action following apprehension of Security Index subjects'. By December 1963, however, Baldwin's status within the Bureau had risen, and he was placed on the Security Index itself. In a memo dated 18 December 1964, Hoover informed the New York office that information on Baldwin collected by Special Agent (name censored), 'clearly depicts the subject as a dangerous individual who could be expected to commit acts inimical to the national defense and public safety of the United States in time of an emergency. Consequently, his name is being included in the Security Index.' Robert Kennedy, it was noted, considered Baldwin 'a nut'.

Baldwin became aware of the sudden FBI interest in his life as stories about the Kennedy–Baldwin palaver were running in the press. Enquiring telephone calls were made to his home (the FBI's 'pretext phone calls', by which they established a 'subject's' place of residence, whether he was in or out of the country, etc.); Lucien Happersberger, invited from Switzerland to New York, was detained at customs on arrival, for no apparent reason, and then released with a warning actually mentioning the name Baldwin; two FBI men turned up at Baldwin's apartment on East Third Street shortly after the Kennedy meeting and tried to gain entry, only to be refused by the superintendent; Happersberger, who came to live in New York at about this time, tells of the constant presence in Baldwin's life of threats, assassination fears, and the certain knowledge that some of Baldwin's closest associates, including a secretary and a lawyer, were acting, or had acted, as paid informers.

Baldwin complained to the FBI about harassment. He also told Fern Eckman, who was researching his past and present life, about it, and Eckman dutifully asked Burke Marshall. In her book *The Furious Passage of James Baldwin*, she quoted Marshall's reply:

'It was not true that the FBI was persecuting Baldwin. But in true bureaucratic fashion' – he cannot quite suppress a smile – 'the FBI insisted upon seeing Baldwin and telling him so. Which, of course, only convinced him all the more that they *were* persecuting him.'

This might account for the unannounced visit of the two men to Baldwin's place on East Third Street. But since it can now be established that the Attorney General had requested and received information concerning Baldwin within days of their conference, and as Baldwin was even then on the FBI's high-priority Reserve Index, it is natural to conclude that the Assistant Attorney General was being less than frank with his interviewer.

Unless, of course – and it is quite possible – Marshall himself was ill-informed as to the extent of FBI interest in Baldwin. If we assume that Marshall believes what he told Fern Eckman – 'It was not true that the FBI was persecuting Baldwin' – then the very existence of the FBI file goes to show that, at the height of the civil-rights crisis, Baldwin knew more about what the FBI was doing than did Burke Marshall, the Assistant Attorney General for the Justice Department's Civil Rights Division.

It was certainly the case that Baldwin, whose intelligence was as intuitive as it was penetrating, realized the true role of the FBI in the civil rights movement before most people did, including Martin Luther King. At this time, King saw the Kennedys as friends and the FBI as an ally, and he favoured active intervention by the FBI in the South.

In fact, there was more FBI activity than King was aware of – much of it directed against *him*. In October 1962, an article had appeared in the New Orleans *Times-Picayune*, which alleged that King's Southern Christian Leadership Conference (SCLC) was infiltrated by Communists at its highest levels. It named Jack O'Dell, a senior member of the SCLC. King did not know that the FBI had planted the article. And in November 1962, the home of one his most trusted lieutenants, Stanley Levinson, was bugged, so that the FBI could listen in on conversations at a house which King believed to be safe. This made a total of four wire-taps on Levinson. It was considered at that particular time too risky an enterprise to wire-tap King himself, but within a year this mood of caution had blown over. Eventually King was being listened to by the FBI almost everywhere he went, through a total of fifteen hidden microphones.

Because of the large number of pages withheld by the FBI from Baldwin's file,* and the extent of the censorship on those pages which have been released under the Freedom of Information Act, it is not yet possible to say for certain whether Baldwin himself was ever wire-tapped. He believed firmly that he was, and both David Baldwin and Lucien Happersberger, two of the people closest to him at this time, remain convinced of it. However, in the files which have so far been made available, there is no concrete evidence to corroborate the suspicion.

After Baldwin's name was added to the Security Index (along with 10,000 other Americans, including 1,500 blacks), frequent checks were made on his home to confirm that he was continuing to reside at the

---

* The number of pages in Baldwin's file, gathered together from several FBI offices, totals 1,750; however, once duplications are allowed for, this is reduced to 1,302. Of this, to date, the FBI has declassified and released roughly 1,000 pages, which in turn are heavily censored.

Baldwin's file was large compared to that of other American writers. The Nobel Prize winner Sinclair Lewis, for example, who, like Baldwin had loose ties with left-wing organizations, accumulated only 150 pages. The file on Pearl Buck was 280 pages, that on John Dos Passos (who later cooperated with the FBI, 'naming names'), a mere eighty-two. Nelson Algren's file was 546 pages thick, William Faulkner's only eighteen.

For more information on the subject, see Herbert Mitgang's article in the *New Yorker*, 5 October 1987, 'Investigating Writers'.

address given on his file. This was usually done by means of a 'pretext phone call' or a 'pretext interview', or else by spying on his entrances and exits. On the face of it, such methods of verification would have been unnecessary had the FBI been eavesdropping on his telephone calls. (It is, of course, possible that Baldwin's telephone was being tapped by a separate government intelligence agency, such as the CIA.) Even neighbours in the apartment building where Baldwin lived, 470 West End Avenue, were unknowingly recruited as spies by the FBI. A 'Verification of Information' memorandum of 2 June 1964 states that, on a suitable pretext, '[name censored], 470 West End Avenue, was interviewed concerning this individual and volunteered info re subject'.

In October 1963, having heard the allegations made by Baldwin that two suspicious-seeming men had appeared on his doorstep, the FBI took the trouble to deny categorically that Baldwin had been harassed to John F. Kennedy's Special Assistant, P. Kenneth O'Donnell (although this was contradicted by Burke Marshall, who conceded that a visit *had* taken place, albeit only to clear the air). The Bureau 'had not conducted any investigation of Baldwin', the memo said.

This claim does not mean quite what it seems to. Clearly, the FBI was gathering information on Baldwin: that was the purpose of the memo to the White House, to inform it of their progress. It was even thought worthwhile to compile collections of his 'dangerous' sayings and to circulate them around top Bureau offices (for example, 'Baldwin says: "I have never been afraid of Russia, China or Cuba but I am terrified of this country"'). That he had not been 'investigated' means simply that the FBI had not yet used its heavy machinery to try and crush him. Not that they withheld fire out of a love of liberty – the simple fact is that they were afraid of his gift for publicity. Any attempt by the FBI to interview Baldwin, it was repeatedly stated in memoranda, would be likely to be turned by Baldwin to his own advantage, and 'could prove highly embarrassing to the Bureau'.

Baldwin was considered a fit subject for FBI surveillance not only because he was a 'dangerous individual' with an attachment to 'subversive causes', and because he was given to such statements as, 'We must make the establishment afraid of us', but also because of his homosexuality. A memo dated 17 July 1964 was returned to its sender with a scribbled note from Hoover asking, 'Isn't Baldwin a well-known pervert?' A further memo was then prepared which shows that this remark, which might otherwise have been disregarded as a trivial rhetorical question, was taken seriously.

The memo 'JAMES ARTHUR BALDWIN/INFORMATION CONCERNING' of 20 July solemnly states: 'It is not a matter of official record that he is a pervert; however, the theme of homosexuality has figured prominently in two of his three published novels.' The memo-writer then proceeds to list certain remarks made by Baldwin on the subject of homosexuality – for example, 'In Italy . . . no one ends up going to a psychiatrist or turning into a junkie because he's afraid of being touched' – and concludes with impeccable objectivity: 'While it is not possible to state that he is a pervert, he has expressed a sympathetic viewpoint about homosexuality on several occasions, and a very definite hostility toward the revulsion of the American public regarding it.'

Bureaucracy moves in mysterious ways: by 1966, in spite of a lifelong refusal by Baldwin to make a secret of his sexual proclivities, the Bureau preferred to leave the question open. A memo of 29 March 1966, reads:

Nothing is known about the current location of JAMES BALDWIN, the Negro Aughor and Playwright. BALDWIN was at an affair held for PAUL ROBINSON in 1965 at the Americana Hotel. It has been heard that BALDWIN may be a homosexual and he appeared as if he may be one.

The memo is composed in classic Bureau house-style: mis-spellings (Paul Robeson was one of the most famous Americans alive at the time, and was himself the subject of a vast FBI investigation), misuse of capital letters and subjunctives, cluttered sentences – and no information at the end of it.

The FBI had Baldwin marked down as a Communist when he was politically independent; they had him married when he wasn't (one snooper claimed to have had a conversation with Mrs Baldwin, 'subject's wife'); they had him coming from Boston when he was from New York, and living at 'Horation Street'; by the time their records had him moving into Horatio Street, he had already moved out. They had him down as a 'former Professor' from Howard University, and as author of the novels 'Go Tell It to the Mountains' and 'Another World'. And, repeatedly, they had him down as a 'prominent member' of the Fair Play for Cuba Committee, when he scarcely had any interest in it at all. Thus the entire edifice manifesting the FBI's interest in Baldwin was based on a falsehood.

*

Baldwin never produced his threatened work on the FBI, but he had, as usual, a multitude of other plans in mind, including the slave novel – now retitled 'Tomorrow Brought Us Rain' – a screen treatment of *Another Country*, a musical version of *Othello*, a play called 'The 121st Day of Sodom', which Bergman intended to produce in Stockholm, and a text for a book of photographs by his old schoolfriend and fellow *Magpie* editor, Richard Avedon.

All of them, save the 10,000-word text for Avedon's photographs, published in 1964 as *Nothing Personal*, remained unwritten. What time Baldwin could steal for writing at this point he gave mostly to his play *Blues for Mr Charlie*, which, being based on the lynching of Emmett Till – in some ways a catalyst for the modern civil rights movement – was anyhow related to his public role.

Baldwin later put the word about that he wrote *Blues* in buses and aeroplanes while he went on the road for civil rights. Walter Wager, editor of the magazine *Playbill* (described by the FBI as 'the legitimate program of the official theater in that city' – i.e. New York), asked him on the eve of the play's Broadway production, 'Literally, *how* did you write it?' To which Baldwin replied:

On pads in planes, trains, gas stations – all sorts of places. With a pen or a pencil. Walter, this is a *hand-written* play.

It is not literally true, of course, that Baldwin wrote in gas stations – and what credit was due to him if he did? Here he is showing embarrassment at being caught in the ivory tower, with its air so different from that breathed by the black brothers and sisters on the picket lines and at the lunch counters. But in a figurative sense, the suggestion that Baldwin wrote *Blues* while on the road is not entirely false; for as the struggle raged around him, he found it difficult to concentrate on imaginative writing. 'I am *not* a public speaker. I *am* an artist,' he told the interviewers from *Mademoiselle* magazine. Yet he was aware that black and white comrades faced daily the threat of danger to their lives, and he wished his writing to reflect the times he was living through. *Blues for Mr Charlie* is, therefore, informed by the intense emotional energy of 'the cause', of what he could imagine of Emmett Till's defiance, and of Jerome Smith's electric terror when the time came to disembark at an Alabama bus station with a hundred thugs waiting and not a policeman in sight.

As far as literary critics were concerned, everything depended on how that emotion was shaped by the artist's hand. The most persistent criticism of Baldwin, retrospectively, has been that he lost his temper some time in the mid-1960s and never regained it, that he of all people, a writer and a preacher, failed to keep his head when all about were losing theirs. The charge overlooks the emotional heat in which Baldwin sat down to write, but it has some validity, especially when it cites a loss of control over the essentials of literary craft: a writer is of little use to anyone, in either the literary or political fields, if he is too angry to write well.

Baldwin's value to the movement was mainly symbolic. He was the intellectual with a fearsome articulacy, a worldwide readership, and – judging by his well-publicized meeting with Robert Kennedy – the ear of people in high places. He was neither a part of the rank-and-file of the civil rights movement, like Jerome Smith or Jim Peck, who also suffered severe beatings on the Mother's Day Freedom Ride, nor was he counted among its leadership, as he was later wont to claim. The leadership had to be careful of Baldwin, his fiery tongue, his sometimes peculiar company, and his sexual habits. The FBI recorded King's view of Baldwin in the summer of 1963. A conversation involving King was eavesdropped on by the Bureau on 1 or 2 June, in which a person whose identity is censored asked King if he would be willing to appear on a television programme with Baldwin. King, the FBI agent noted in his report, was 'not enthusiastic about the idea because he felt that Baldwin was uninformed regarding his movement'. King told his interlocutor that while Baldwin was considered 'a spokesman of the Negro People by the Press', he was 'not a civil rights leader'. The potential embarrassment which Baldwin's unconcealed homosexuality might cause was raised on a separate occasion; Baldwin was felt to be 'better qualified to lead a homosexual movement than a civil rights movement'.

Baldwin would have been hurt by these remarks, had he known. Although he had never been attacked at a segregated lunch counter, he bore emotional scars as real and deep as the scars on Jerome Smith's body. He had friends who had been clubbed to within an inch of their lives; he had heard from Smith how the police had stood idly by at bus stations while the Klan attacked the Freedom Riders; in June 1963 he received the news that his friend Medgar Evers, head of the NAACP in Mississippi, had been assassinated in front of his wife and children.

His despair was deepening, then, as Martin Luther King's crusade reached a peak in August 1963 with the March on Washington. A week before the main event, Baldwin had led a miniature 'march' of about five hundred people to the door of the US Embassy in Paris, where he handed in a petition. Then he flew back to Washington expecting to be among the speakers at the main event, only to learn, to his disappointment, of his exclusion. King did not want him, could not risk him. While King made his speech, Baldwin was ranked with the movement's celebrities, taking part in a television discussion with Sidney Poitier, Harry Belafonte, Charlton Heston and Marlon Brando.

On 28 August a quarter of a million people marched peacefully to the Lincoln Memorial in America's capital city to demonstrate their desire for black equality; there they heard King depart from his prepared speech and extemporize on the refrain of his 'dream' – 'a dream deeply rooted in the American dream' – that '*all* God's children, black men and white men, Jews and Gentiles, Protestants and Catholics, will be able to join hands and sing in the words of the old Negro spiritual "Free at last! Free at last! Thank God Almighty, we are free at last."'

Two and a half weeks after the March, they received the white South's response to their peaceful petition, when the Sixteenth Street Baptist Church in Birmingham, Alabama, was bombed and four young girls who had been attending Sunday school were killed. Other children who were in the church were grievously injured, and two black youths were also set upon by the mob and murdered the same day.

King held a meeting with President Kennedy (who had opposed the March), telling him: 'If you walk the street, you're unsafe. If you stay at home, you're unsafe – there's a danger of bombing. If you're in church, now it isn't safe. The Negro feels that everywhere he goes, or if he remains stationary, he's in some danger of physical violence.'

Baldwin was on a speaking-tour when he received the news of the Birmingham bombing. It first stunned him, and then accelerated his protest activity. The tragedy also marked a further weakening of his unquestioning support of King's policy of non-violent resistance. Appearing again on television, this time with the theologian Reinhold Niebuhr to discuss 'the missing face of Christ' – the face of Jesus had been knocked cleanly from a stained-glass window in the east wall of the Birmingham church – Baldwin questioned the white liberals' support for King's strategy: throughout American history, Baldwin claimed, 'the only time that non-violence has been admired is when Negroes practise it'. He made attempts to organize a nationwide Christmas shopping boycott, he signed letters on behalf of civil rights organizations such as the Congress of Racial Equality (CORE) and the Student Nonviolent Coordinating Committee (SNCC), and the so-called 'Monroe Defendants', three civil-rights workers being held on kidnapping charges; and he took part in the organization of rent strikes in Harlem.

Dear Friend,
   As you are reading this letter, young men and women are entering Mississippi to ... staff a wide range of programs whose goal is nothing less than to help bring the Mississippi Negro into the 20th century ... The gravest of dangers await these courageous workers ... I ask you to help give them a chance by sending a generous contribution for the Mississippi Summer Project and to send it NOW ...

Dear Friend,
   There's a lot of hidden suffering behind the civil rights headlines – students expelled from colleges for taking part in demonstrations, workers dispossessed and fired after trying to register to vote, youngsters held too long in jails for lack of legal defense ... An envelope is enclosed. Please be generous ...

Dear Friend,
   The rat, jumbo-sized and vicious, has become the symbol of the spreading rent strikes in the old-law tenements of Harlem, the east Bronx and the Bedford-Stuyvesant section of Brooklyn ... Won't you join me in sending a check today to the Community Council on Housing at the address above?

   Sincerely ...

In the second week of October, he had a confrontation at close range with the type of club-wielding Southern cop whom people involved with the movement on its home ground had to deal with every other day. James Foreman, executive secretary of SNCC, enlisted Baldwin's help to launch a voter-registration drive in Selma, Alabama, knowing that his presence would guarantee wide media coverage.

Blacks had the right to vote, but first they had to register to vote, and this was not made easy for them. The white opposition disrupted the registration process through a mixture of frustration and intimidation. In this they were fully aided by the police.

Baldwin understood the thinking behind this perfectly well. 'After all,' he told his fellow participants in the *Commentary* round-table discussion moderated by Podhoretz, 'part of the reason there is a battle going on in the Deep South is that as the Negro starts voting and becomes economically free, the power of the Southern oligarchy will obviously be broken.'

On Friday 6 October 1963 he flew with his brother David (and an FBI tail) to Birmingham, Alabama. Baldwin had expected to be met at the airport by a person whose name the FBI will not reveal, but when he arrived there was no one there to greet him. He contacted someone else (again name censored), and eventually made for the Gaston Hotel, where he tried to place a call to Robert Kennedy. All this was noted by the FBI.

On the morning of Monday 9 October, Baldwin proceeded to Selma, once more supervised by agents of the FBI, which was supposed by many people to be aiding the black struggle in the South. There, 325 applicants were lining up outside the courthouse, intending to claim their legal right to vote. The intimidation by the police began almost immediately. No one who left the line, for example to visit the toilet, was permitted to rejoin it. When Baldwin and his brother attempted to talk to the waiting people, the county sheriff, armed and helmeted, told them: 'Move along – you're blocking the sidewalk.' When they brought refreshments in the afternoon, they were forbidden to hand them over, the barked explanation being, 'I'll not have these people molested in any way.' When they attempted to accompany James Foreman into the courthouse to make an enquiry about the delay in admitting applicants, they were told by the armed guards at the entrance that they would have to go in by the side door; at the side door they were told they could only enter by the front door. At the end of a harrowing day, of the 325 people who had queued in sweltering heat to register to vote at the county courthouse, Baldwin estimated that about twenty had been admitted. (The *New York Times*, reporting on the same event, put the total at nearer fifty.)

Such activities, together with attendant pressures, made life more or less writer-proof. Baldwin's vanishing-trick – he made for Turkey, Puerto Rico and Paris that year – became his only respite. In Istanbul, as part of the traditional family life of Engin Cezzar, he could evade the daily harassments of the famous writer in New York: being recognized in the street, being asked for interviews, being asked for autographs, being asked to speak, being invited here, there and everywhere. He could become unofficial again, indulging the habits which gave him the most pleasure: music, whisky, conversations which lasted until dawn.

At the same time, he amplified the importance in his life of his own family. His sister Gloria became his money-manager; for the youngest of the family, Paula Maria, he helped organize a fashion show, while David frequently accompanied him on his travels, becoming, in effect, his lieutenant. And he bought a large house on Manhattan's West End Avenue, with a dream that members of his family, including his mother, would occupy its separate apartments.

This longing for family life coincides with the moment of his greatest fame, when he was called on almost daily to perform in the public circus. He was successful far beyond the boldest dreams of the boy who had fled Harlem for Greenwich Village, or the hopes of the struggling artist in Paris. But what of his private life? Well, he could say now, here I have my family all around me. Lovers and friends might come and go, but the family was for ever. He was wary, he told one interviewer, rehearsing a refrain that had by now become familiar, of trying 'to avoid the private life because you can hide in the public one'.

The self-awareness is characteristic, but there's a salty irony in the fact that he is making the admission – that his private life is being invaded – in a public situation. Here we are witnessing Baldwin in the process of parting company with his own privacy. He has exposed his personal life, his most personal emotions, his intensest feelings and most private thoughts, in the public arena, where, inevitably, it loses some of its personalness. Baldwin loses, at the same time, a certain sureness of taste – for what belongs to him, and what belongs to the world – and loses, therefore, something of his intimate relationship with himself. This can be seen in another way: as far as the security services of the United States were concerned, he had forfeited the right to privacy altogether. Baldwin, with some awareness of their intent, combatted them not by becoming more secretive, but by becoming yet more public.

Between 1948–59, roughly speaking, there were no public events in Baldwin's life, and therefore to reach a sense of the man we are compelled to trace the private biography, contained most concretely in his correspondence. After that, however, things change, and between 1963 and 1968, Baldwin's life consists largely of outer events, forming a story which can be told only by making constant reference to the public record.

Thus we find that, whereas in the 1950s Baldwin had been a prolific and candid correspondent to his trusted friends, in the next decade his confessor was the interviewer.

Chapter Sixteen

It was a year of platforms and microphones, spent before students and journalists hungry for the latest prophecy from the author of *The Fire Next Time*. Between spring 1963 and spring 1964, he published only five articles; all were the texts of speeches. He was expected to talk tough, to disturb the peace, to threaten the wrath to come. He excoriated Americans as 'the most unattractive people on earth', denounced America as 'a loveless nation'. Don't talk to *me* about integration, Baldwin said – who wants to be integrated into a burning house?

When a black man sings a gospel song, Baldwin told his listeners, he is not just singing; he's telling you what happened to him today:

Those songs and those sermons had less to do with the Old Testament than they had to do with our daily life. When the man sang the song:

If I had my way,
I'd tear this building down

he wasn't talking about Samson and Delilah – he was saying something very specific, and something very, very clear:

If *I* had *my way*! . . . [*Urgent whisper*:] I'd tear this building down . . .
People in this country still do not know what black people are talking about.

And his mainly white audiences loved it, an irony which disgusted Langston Hughes, who numbered Baldwin among the 'black ravens cawing over carrion'.

But this raven could change, miraculously, into a dove as his repentant flock looked to him for a guiding star, a promise of improvement. He presented them with a choice, which made them *want* to be better people; the choice he gave them was: hold each other, or watch the light go out. With love, Baldwin promised, we can change ourselves, change each other, change the country and alter the history of the world. 'I do not for an instant doubt, and I will go to my grave believing, that we can build Jerusalem, if we will.'

When he did, at last, get some writing done, there were hints of a different tone from that of earlier days, even from the tone of *The Fire Next Time*. Nineteen sixty-three was the year his voice broke; and it affected every element of his literary style – his rhythm, his syntax, his vocabulary, the way in which he made discriminations and reached judgements. It was the year Baldwin shifted away from the lyrical cadence that had been his signature tune. In years to come, it would make people wonder: what happened to Baldwin's great style? And it was done on purpose.

In a Christmas feature in the *New York Times Book Review*, wherein several authors were asked to comment on their literary techniques, Baldwin eschewed comparison with other writers and chose to liken himself to a jazz musician and a blues singer:

I would like to think that some of the people who liked [*Another Country*] responded to it in the way they respond when Miles [Davis] and Ray [Charles] are blowing.

What listeners were drawn to in both these musicians was some kind of 'universal blues', and he considered himself to be in the same mould, tossing off the laurel which had been placed on his head: 'I am not an intellectual . . . and do not want to be.'

Parallels with the world of blues and jazz began to be drawn frequently. In Britain for the launch of *Another Country* in February 1963, he repeated to a BBC interviewer that he did not think of himself in a great line of writers: 'I see myself as a blues singer,' he said. Back in the US in June, with the hardcover version of *The Fire Next Time* into its tenth printing only five months after publication, he complained to the journalist Nat Hentoff of his endless 'one-nighters' – 'I'm like a jazz musician.'

In *The Fire Next Time* he had written: 'For the horrors of the American Negro's life there has been almost no language.' Note, *almost*: the exception was the idiom of gospel, blues and jazz. In the same year he wrote an essay on the subject, 'The Uses of the Blues'. The title was not meant to refer to music, Baldwin explained, but to 'the experience of life'. He quoted the songs of Bessie Smith and Billie Holiday to support his assertion that the blues constituted a precise record of Negroes' daily existence, and referred to 'a certain beat' as if it were an ordering aesthetic principle. He stated that his models were jazz musicians, and that he tried 'to write the way they sound.'

It is a critical hour in Baldwin's career, when we find him proclaiming his disaffection from the classical literary tradition, to which he had consciously aspired previously, and aligning himself with black culture or, in the emerging vocabulary, black consciousness. From thinking about his art in association with jazz musicians, it was only a short step to writing in imitation of one: his rhythm became freer, a syncopated note is heard, an improvisatory feel affects his prose, as the order of sentences hitherto obedient to the structures of James and Hemingway begins to make way for that 'certain beat'.

This is all the more extraordinary for occurring at the very time when Baldwin was in high season as practically the most famous writer in the land. 'There is probably no literary career in America today that matches James Baldwin's in the degree of interest it commands,' Lionel Trilling had written in his review of *Another Country*. In the same month that he appeared on the cover of *Time* magazine, *Life* devoted a nine-page spread of words and pictures to him. He was described as 'the monarch of the current literary jungle', and interviewed over and over again, managing to make it sound fresh on each occasion. 'Rarely,' wrote Marvin Elkoff in a long *Esquire* profile the following year, 'has any American writer had so much public renown.' Baldwin was 'the hottest property in publishing'.

And yet this famous writer did not wish to be grouped with writers and intellectuals, but with blues singers and jazz musicians.

At the same moment – and not at all coincidentally – the mood of the civil rights marchers was changing. King's name was now heard no more often than that of Malcolm X. Malcolm criticized King for leading his marchers to Washington to plead for their rights, and many black people, tired of 'dreaming', backed him in doing so. He criticized Baldwin for condescending to sit down with Robert Kennedy; and Baldwin listened.

Baldwin was aware that his immense 'public renown', while pushing him to the forefront of his people's cause, had had the effect of removing him from those very people. When Baldwin spoke, he spoke on the whole to well-educated whites. His prose, in the words of F. W. Dupee, suggested 'the ideal prose of an ideal literary community, some aristocratic France of one's dreams' – hardly the kind of plaudit likely to seduce young blacks on the streets, in whom Baldwin invested so much hope. His reputation depended greatly on the intellectual salons, and scarcely at all on the ghettos. Lionel Trilling and the readers of the *New Yorker*, Philip Rahv and the National Institute of Arts and Letters, had no credibility there.

'In Birmingham and Harlem,' wrote the journalist who interviewed him for *Time*, 'most Negroes still do not know his name.' Those who did – the students, the artists, the 'hip' – might read *him* but the people whom *he* read – Henry James, Dickens, Dostoevsky – meant little or nothing to most of them. Their models were Miles, Ray, Bessie and Billie . . . and from now on, he claimed, so were his.

At the same time, there is a change in his humour; his temperament and his manners show signs of strain. In a long interview with *Mademoiselle* in May 1963 (the rate of publication of interviews now outstrips that of essays) Baldwin criticized the efforts of white liberals to join the civil rights cause. He claimed not an *equal* sense of identity to whites but a superior one, and raised the spectre of Auschwitz in seeking a parallel for the tribulations of American blacks.

The *Esquire* profilist recorded an incident in Smalls Paradise in which a young college student attempted to engage Baldwin in a conversation about T. S. Eliot, only to receive the rebuff: 'I'm pulling rank here, so let *me* tell *you*. T. S. Eliot doesn't write from personal experience. He writes from culture. He is *not* a poet.' Quite a change from the days when he wrote to his friend Stephen D. James recommending 'The Love Song of J. Alfred Prufrock' and the poetry of Milton.

While Eliot was emphatically not a poet, the anonymous slave who drew on his culture to write the lines 'The very time I thought I was lost, / My dungeon shook and my chains fell off', was among 'the greatest poets since Homer'. Culture in Eliot's sense was less important to the mature vision of life, and to art, than 'a certain beat'.

The vocabulary which serves the 'beat' begins to crop up in his prose: 'This play', he began the introduction to the published version of *Blues for Mr Charlie* 'has been on my mind – has been bugging me – for several years.' In 'The Uses of the Blues' he composed his words into a spoken idiom. 'All right, it's a mess, and you can't do anything about it. You can't stay there, you can't drop dead, you can't give up, but all right, okay, as Bessie said: "Picked up my bag, baby, and I tried it again"'.

That the new national awareness of the wretchedness and continued enslavement of his people should bring recognition of an entirely different sort to James Baldwin was an irony not likely to escape him. Nor would he have been blind to the fact that his fame had shut him into a kind of cage: as the world's most famous black writer, he was now expected to pronounce endlessly on the plight of black people. What is the nature of the problem? What is the solution? What can white people do to help? What do black people really want?

He could no longer write a novel such as *Giovanni's Room*, with an exclusively white cast, nor protest, as he did in the 1950s, that he did not want 'to become merely a Negro writer'. Nor would he be so inclined to resist special pleading for black people, as he had done in 1953, when he wrote that he would not wish 'to suggest that the Negro has it worse than anybody else'. His attitude now was, precisely, that the Negro had it worse than *everybody* else. The interview, currently his favoured form of expression, helped to change his tone of voice as well, since what most of his interviewers wished to talk about was what Baldwin himself had cursed as that 'monolithic abstraction', the Negro problem.

'I shouldn't be doing all this speech-making,' he told *Life*'s interviewer, who was following him around on a whistle-stop tour of the South. 'I never planned on it. It's much too easy for me. I should be saying what I have to say at the typewriter.'

Once he found his way to the typewriter, however, he exhibited the symptoms of the writer who is losing faith in his material. He repeated himself (with diminishing clarity); he wrote excessively about his personal past; and he wrote about writing. On one occasion he investigated the very reasons why he no longer felt confidence in his subject matter, or, indeed, trusted his language. In an essay called 'Why I Stopped Hating Shakespeare', Baldwin attempted to clarify his relationship with the English language. Although it disappeared from sight after it had been published in the *Observer* newspaper in 1964, it is an important essay, for at the very moment when certain critics were praising him as the best contemporary exponent of English prose, Baldwin himself was denouncing his language as tyrannous. The classic forms of English would not serve him in expressing what he, a 'blues singer', had to say. In 'Why I Stopped Hating Shakespeare' he set out the terms of his embattlement:

My quarrel with the English language has been that the language reflected none of my experience. But now I began to see the matter in quite another way ... Perhaps the language was not my own because I had never attempted to use it, had only learned to imitate it. If this were so, then it might be made to bear the burden of my experience if I could find the stamina to challenge it, and me, to such a test.

In support of 'this possibility', Baldwin cites 'mighty witnesses', his black ancestors. They had been forced to use a language which was not their own, a language which should have controlled their experience, but which they used in the service of it – a language out of which they 'evolved the sorrow songs, the blues and jazz'.

This passage holds a key to the direction in which Baldwin wished to take his writing after *The Fire Next Time* – to force the English language to contain his black experience. The effort required the formulation of a modern aesthetic which had its roots in the literary-musical heritage of slaves: the gospel and spirituals which W. E. B. DuBois in 1903 called 'not simply the sole American music, but ... the most beautiful expression of human experience this side the seas ... The singular spiritual heritage of the nation.'

If Baldwin could succeed in combining that culture with the resources of a tradition in English in which he was already a master, binding the two in the rhetoric of the preacher he had never ceased to be, then he too might become a great 'poet' in a line descended from Homer; the greatest named black writer ever; and, in an aesthetic sense, the blackest of them all.

PART IV
Tear This Building Down

No more auction block for me,
No more, no more . . .
Many thousands gone.

Traditional

Chapter Seventeen

'It was at about this point,' says Jim Silberman, 'that Jimmy started turning up with certain people. You know, there would be a young man who was a photographer, and it would turn out that Jimmy had bought all his cameras. That kind of thing.' Or he would just as likely turn up with Ava Gardner, or Nina Simone, or a college boy who had asked him for an autograph, or an Algerian girl with whom he could talk French, or a journalist who, having begun the day on an assignment, would end it at an all-night party. Baldwin was forever gregarious and, as his celebrity-rating rose, so did the scale of his conviviality. If he had an appointment at four, he might turn up three hours late and coax the people who had patiently waited for him into accompanying him to the house where he was expected at six. Then the combined parties, who had not previously known each other but by now were old friends, would be enjoined to escort him to a restaurant to keep his dinner date at nine (which he would announce, at the earliest, at ten). By midnight the group would have been augmented by an acquaintance met by chance in the street, the owner of the restaurant, someone to whom Baldwin had said, 'I'll be at So-and-so's later,' and perhaps two strangers from another table who on their way out had asked 'Are you James Baldwin?' and been rewarded with smiles, handshakes, glasses of wine and an invitation to join the party. The vast acquaintance was multi-national, multi-tongued, multi-ethnic . . . Baldwin's philosophy was tending towards blackness, but his temperament and his nature were rainbow-coloured.

At the same time, there was a growing staff of secretaries, drivers, money-managers and people who might be described as 'hand-holders'. Lucien Happersberger had now arrived in the United States as a long-term resident, and, as the most reliable and trusted of Baldwin's clan, was given the job, together with Baldwin's sister Gloria, of managing the money. Those with Baldwin-related positions in the middle of 1964, according to a caricature in the *New York Times*, included his lawyer, New York City Councilman Theodore Kupferman; his agent, Robert Lantz; his benefactor, Tom Michaelis; his photographer, Frank Dandridge; his song-writer, Bobby Sharp; his publisher, Richard Baron; his disk jockey, Frankie (Downbeat) Brown; his minister-friend, the Rev. Sidney Lanier; and a supporting cast, changing every few months, of well-wishers, advisers and hangers-on.

In the meantime, the seed which Elia Kazan had planted in Baldwin's mind for a play many years earlier had sprouted into *Blues for Mr Charlie*. His achievements in the novel, the essay and the short story were recognized, but he still harboured an ambition to succeed in the theatre. He was drawn to its mythology; he had a strong faith in the power generated between actor and audience, in the catharsis which effected change – change being, after all, James Baldwin's cause.

Here we hit another paradox. Baldwin's opinion of the American commercial theatre was low. A 'tepid bath' he called it during a brief stint as drama critic at the short-lived black magazine *The Urbanite* in 1961. Yet ambition, or vanity, drove him to seek a Broadway production for *Blues for Mr Charlie* instead of looking to one of the uptown theatres where the more avant-garde Leroi Jones and his like were working. Broadway meant fame, and fame – here Baldwin could dissolve the paradox – meant influence. If questioned about his decision to put on his 'blacktown' play in the heart of 'whitetown', he could say it was all for the good of the cause. Robert Cordier, who worked with him on *Blues*, recalls walking one evening to 52nd Street, where the play was showing, with Baldwin and Jerome Smith. 'Can you see those lights from here?' Baldwin asked anxiously, as they came near the ANTA Theatre. Smith replied: 'You can see those lights all the way to the Mississippi!'

But still he kept free of chauvinism. When questioned by the *New York Herald Tribune* on the subject of black theatre, Baldwin opined that he did not believe that 'there is a Negro theatre in the United States', or even 'that such a development would be worthwhile'. That type of black nationalist development he was not eager to sanction. His concerns were centrally based. It was crucial, he said, that 'the country' should listen to 'the black man's own version of himself and of white people.'

This mixed tough talk with integrationism, and, incidentally, justified his taking his play to Broadway. It was not a view that would have appealed to Leroi Jones, whose Black Arts Theatre in Harlem (opened six months after the première of *Blues*) barred whites altogether.

As America's most prominent black writer, Baldwin now found himself in the peculiar predicament of being resented by both the traditionalist old guard, in the form of Hughes, and the young radicals, such as Jones. Baldwin and Jones had met at Howard University in 1955, and had once been on comradely terms; shortly after Baldwin's return to New York from Paris, Jones had sought his assistance in setting up his Beat Generation-based magazine, *Zazen*. (Baldwin had replied that he was 'leery'.) By the mid-1960s, however, Jones's radical nationalism had taken him in the opposite direction from the older writer – that is, from Greenwich Village up to Harlem, rather than the other way round – and before long he would be joining the Black Muslims and changing his name to Amiri Baraka.

In 1963, Jones published an attack on Baldwin and the South African writer Peter Abrahams under the title 'Brief Reflections on Two Hot Shots'. A self-styled 'revolutionary' writer, Jones had little patience with Baldwin's artistic sensibility: part of every sentence he writes, Jones said, 'must be given over to telling a willing audience how sensitive and intelligent he is'. Through Jones's embattled eyes, America's great black writer was seen to be eating out of the hand of Mr Charlie (that is to say, whitey) himself. 'If Abrahams and Baldwin were turned white, for example, there would be no more noise from them ... they could be sensitive in peace. Their colour is the only obstruction I can see to this state they seek, and I see no reason they should be denied it for so paltry a thing as heavy pigmentation. Somebody turn them!'

Not only was Baldwin working in the heart of white man's theatreland, with a white company, white director, white producer, white backers and so on, he had even taken the idea for his play from a white man. Elia Kazan's suggestion, made while they were working together on *JB* and *Sweet Bird of Youth*, had been that Baldwin write a play based on the murder of Emmett Till, which Kazan would then stage at the Actors Studio. During the interval which had elapsed since he made his suggestion, Kazan had moved on to the Lincoln Center to launch a repertory company there, but as far as he was concerned he still had first claim on Baldwin's long-awaited play. However, while he was in Greece directing a film (and expecting to meet Baldwin, who failed to turn up), the actor Rip Torn, a powerful force behind the Studio, persuaded Baldwin to give his play to the newly established production arm of the Studio, the Actors Studio Theatre.

Kazan regarded this as treachery, and told Baldwin so. Baldwin, in response, offered a twofold justification: first, that there were no blacks on the board of the Lincoln Center, and second, that he was finding Kazan's 'father-figure' role a gross and impossible obstruction.

Kazan felt deeply wounded and greatly annoyed, but cannot have been surprised, for Baldwin was as notoriously unreliable in his personal relationships as he was famous as a charmer, a moralist, a preacher. He also had a paranoid fear of being patronized, especially by whites (which played a part in his dedication to courting them). He had used the convenient excuse before, when accused of repaying kindness with ingratitude, that the son had to slay the father. As for the motive that there were no blacks at the Lincoln Center, Kazan's rejoinder, that that was exactly the situation he was out to change, seems reasonable. In producing *Blues for Mr Charlie*, a play about blacks by a black playwright, with a majority black cast, he would have made a bold start.

According to Robert Cordier, an experienced Paris theatre director whom Baldwin had summoned to New York once the play went into production, Baldwin was driven by artistic snobbery as much as anything else. 'He wanted the Actors Studio badge, and all that,' he says. 'And he wanted to prove to Kazan that he had done it *his* way.'

In any case, Lee Strasberg, head of the Studio, gave him the guarantee he wanted: full-scale Broadway production. Baldwin made his usual flight from the city in order to finish the script, taking refuge this time in Strasberg's house on Fire Island, and in the autumn of 1963 had *Blues for Mr Charlie* ready for its first reading at the former church on West 44th Street which serves as the Actors Studio home.

It is hard on Baldwin that he faced criticism and opposition from sections of the black intelligentsia for giving his play to Broadway, for *Blues for Mr Charlie* sees a change in his love-thy-neighbour approach to civil rights issues, and marks the end of his season as white liberal America's black darling.

The play is set in the imaginary settlement of Plaguetown, Mississippi. Richard Henry, a black youth, is murdered by Lyle Brittan, beer-slugging redneck, for flirting with Brittan's wife. Lyle is arrested and put on trial, mainly due to the efforts of another white man, newspaper editor Parnell James. After a long courtroom scene in Act Three, however, Lyle is acquitted.

The time sequence of the play is complicated: the shot which kills

Richard is fired even before the first lights go up, followed by Lyle's words, 'And may every nigger like this nigger end like this nigger', but the confrontation between Lyle and Richard which results in the shot is not acted out until after the jury's verdict is delivered at the very end of the play:

LYLE: You facing my gun. (*Produces it*) Now, in just a minute, we can both go home.
RICHARD: You sick mother! Why can't you leave me alone? White man! I don't want nothing from you. You ain't got nothing to give me. You can't eat because none of your sad-assed chicks can cook. You can't talk because won't nobody talk to you. You can't dance because you've got nobody to dance with – don't you know I've watched you all my life? *All my life!* And I know your women, don't you think I don't – better than you!
(*Lyle shoots once.*)

Blues for Mr Charlie does not lack good writing and passionate speeches, but it is short on action and theatrical inventiveness. One of its most imaginative strokes is in making the set serve as both a black church and, in the final act, a courthouse. The aisle of the church functions as the segregating line which kept whites and blacks apart in a Southern courthouse, and also as the division between 'whitetown' and 'blacktown'. The action among blacks takes place on one side of the stage, that among whites happens on the other.

There was, however, plenty of dramatic action surrounding the production of *Blues for Mr Charlie*, most of it before the opening night. The first director slated to do the play was Frank Corsaro, an experienced Actors Studio hand, and – possibly a strategic ploy on the part of Lee Strasberg – a graduate of DeWitt Clinton High School, like Baldwin himself.

Corsaro nursed Baldwin through a primary set of revisions, but when the author witnessed a second rehearsed reading of his play and realized that the text had been cut by half in his absence, he declared a 'crisis of confidence' in his director, and shortly afterwards Corsaro was removed from the theatre.

What he was trying to do, Corsaro says, was to prevent the play from seeming like 'an epic against whitey'. But Baldwin saw things differently: cuts were tantamount to censorship. The problem with Corsaro, he argued, was that he would not be able to make the black actors listen to him.

The storm did not subside with the sacking of Corsaro, for by this time

Baldwin was in dispute with almost the entire Actors Studio. Uncut, the play would take over five hours to perform, which horrified everyone, in particular the theatre's general manager, Arthur Waxman. He told Baldwin that it was absurd to expect people to remain in their seats from seven o'clock until after midnight. Baldwin protested that if the Studio could stage a long play by Eugene O'Neill – *Strange Interlude* – then there was no reason why they could not do *Blues* at five hours. Waxman replied that there *was* a reason: Baldwin was not O'Neill. Baldwin told Waxman that he was 'only doing this to me because I'm a nigger'. Waxman told Baldwin not to use that kind of language with him.

And so on. There was a dispute about the difficulties which the audience might have in understanding the development of the play, since the action moved rapidly backwards and forwards in time. Baldwin said that if people were incapable of following plays, they shouldn't come to the theatre. There was a problem with what genteel people of the sort expected to patronize Broadway might refer to as 'bad language'. Cheryl Crawford, Strasberg's right hand and co-artistic director, reasoned that if the running-time did not stop people coming in, then repetition of 'motherfucker', 'nigger' and 'no-good black bastard' would certainly drive them out. Baldwin replied that in a play intended to explore the intensity of racial hatred, these words were unavoidable. To cut them out would be simply to pander to the illusion he wished to abolish. 'This is not *The Green Pastures* by Arthur Miller. If you want to produce *The Green Pastures* you go ahead and call up Arthur Miller and get a hold of his play. But in the meantime we're producing this one – and you're going to do what *I* say because I wrote it.'

A more delicate problem lay in the fact that Baldwin insisted on giving his brother David a role – that of Richard, no less, blacktown's leading man. David Baldwin had had little acting experience, but he had read for Corsaro and Corsaro had assigned him a part, though not the part of Richard. Now that Corsaro was gone, the new director, Burgess Meredith, was faced with the same ticklish problem: the author was insisting that his brother take one of the leading roles in the play, while the Actors Studio was by now saying that he should be dismissed. David Baldwin himself graciously offered to bow out, but Meredith and Waxman considered that unnecessary, and a compromise was reached in having him play the part of Lorenzo, much reduced from its original length.

Not only did Baldwin have his brother in the play, he had Cordier and

Jerome Smith on the payroll. Cordier was theatrically experienced, and at one stage might have directed the play (he was credited eventually as musical director); Smith, the Freedom Rider who had insulted Robert Kennedy, was employed as a 'special consultant' on the particulars of Southern segregation and civil rights strategies (his expertise was used in the play's opening scene, for example, which shows a group of black students being schooled in non-violent self-discipline). Stretching tolerance further, Baldwin arrived at the theatre every day – already in breach of the convention which holds that writers should stay clear of rehearsals – with his by now familiar retinue of relatives, friends and hangers-on in attendance.

As if this were not enough for the Studio brass, there remained in their eyes a basic problem with the play itself. Almost everyone, including some members of his own gang, advised Baldwin to tone down the polemical temper of the piece. As it stood, the racial demarcation – black: good; white: evil – was just too rigid. It was clear to more theatrically tested members of the team that the moral burden of a play must be kept for much of the time in the balance, so that the audience remains in doubt about the way in which the story should be resolved. In *Blues for Mr Charlie*, the opening scenes in blacktown and in whitetown, if not the opening words, make the author's standpoint obvious. Crawford, Cordier and others knew that when this is the case, the action cannot be the vehicle for inner change in the central characters, and audience interest inevitably wanes. As Cordier told Baldwin, you cannot expect people to be enthralled by a string of speeches, certainly not five hours' worth.

Baldwin clung to a more intimidating idea of what the theatre could accomplish: 'Most contemporary theatre is designed to corroborate your fantasies and make you walk out whistling', he told *Life*'s interviewer. 'I don't want to make you whistle at *my* stuff, baby. I want you to be sitting on the edge of your chair waiting for the nurses to carry you out.'

It is a rhetorical remark, made partly to impress a journalist, but it nevertheless exposes the flaw which now bedevilled his work, whether novel, short story, essay or drama. This belligerent idea of the cathartic power of art – that it achieves its effects by stunning the audience with doses of 'the truth' – is not greatly removed from the one he had criticized at the outset of his career in 'Everybody's Protest Novel'. The formula over which he had so valiantly done battle with Harriet Beecher Stowe fifteen years earlier – 'black equates with evil and white with grace' – was now reproduced, in reverse, in his own work.

The climate which gave birth to *Blues* was, of course, more tense, not to say bloody, than the one which nurtured the early Paris essays. Chants of 'We shall overcome' outside Southern schools and churches had failed to quiet the sounds of flailing clubs, of bombs and guns, and Baldwin felt he could not sit silently by while his play's most politically sensitive lines were snipped out and thrown in the bin. Attempts to persuade him that artistic and political responsibilities should be treated separately – a distinction he had not so long ago been at pains to point out to others – ran into an emotional block. Four dead Birmingham schoolgirls deserved to be spoken for. Anyone who reasoned with Baldwin that the loudest way to speak was not necessarily the best way, was likely to be rebutted with a louder protest still.

The scenes behind the scenes of *Blues* have ensured it a place in Broadway's anecdotal lore. There is a story about Baldwin climbing up a thirty-foot-high electrician's 'A' ladder in the auditorium and berating the lordly Lee Strasberg in front of his own company for sabotaging his play; another about him literally collapsing after seeing how the play had been cut; another about him threatening to kill Rip Torn if Torn entered the theatre after Baldwin had forbidden him to do so (Torn later played the leading white role). Baldwin reiterated his contempt for the Actors Studio's revered method-school of acting to anyone who would listen – 'it has *nothing* to do with acting' – and did not care if his words were repeated back at the theatre. Finally, when a journalist asked him if he would ever give another of his plays to the Studio, he replied, 'Not unless I'm attacked with leprosy of the brain.'

By this time the Studio was feeling much the same way. Cheryl Crawford named *Blues for Mr Charlie* as one of the plays which marked the beginning of the Studio's demise as a force in American theatre. For all the commotion, once premièred on 23 April 1964, Baldwin's play was not the hit he had hoped for. The audience on the opening night cheered loudly; the author took a bow; Diana Sands was universally admired as the leading lady in the role of Juanita. But while the *New York Times* – the most powerful constituent in the critical assembly – came out in favour, the rest of the reviews were mixed.

The public voted with its feet. They didn't like being hectored, and they didn't like the change they saw; St James, the preacher, who had delivered his 'we-can-change-the-world' sermon only eighteen months before, was sounding like James X, the black militant. 'If there is ever a Black Muslim nation,' wrote Philip Roth in the *New York Review of Books* in May 1964, 'and if there is a television in that nation, then something like Acts Two and Three of *Blues for Mr Charlie* will probably be the kind of thing the housewives will watch on afternoon TV.'

Now the real trouble started. Baldwin had insisted on special low prices of admission, with the intention of attracting audiences from the poorer uptown areas. But while the ANTA probably housed more black people during the run of *Blues* than any other theatre in Broadway's history, it was not enough. Exactly a month after the opening night, Cheryl Crawford ordered a one-week closing notice to be posted outside the theatre.

Baldwin was outraged. And it is suggestive of the sort of influence he carried that he was able to keep his play going for another three months, contrary to the artistic director's wishes. He viewed the attempt to close *Blues* as a triumph for racism – with a backhanded compliment delivered to himself. Hadn't he wanted to upset people with his play? Well, he had succeeded, and now they were trying to shut it down.

A meeting was held with the theatre management, at which Baldwin emerged, if not victorious, then at least confident that he had convinced the Studio's top brass that he was going to tear the closing notice down. A campaign was set in train: posters and leaflets were printed; two sound-trucks were mobilized; an advertisement was placed in the *New York Times* and other papers with the appeal to conscience that if *Blues* could be saved, then 'more than it could be saved'. A host of celebrities, black and white, supported the motion, pledged donations, and appealed to the right-thinking public for more.

It was literature as political act. As Baldwin had intended, his play was creating a furore. He had always expressed dislike for the effete principle of art for art's sake, and now his writing was fully reconciled with its own purpose and causing change: people were joining forces and giving their all to ensure that a political play, *Blues for Mr Charlie*, continued to run on Broadway.

Substantial funds were raised in the first two weeks of the drive (it was now the end of May), but not enough to keep the play going on a proper extended run. The actors were aware that every night might be the final night. After the curtain came down on what was supposed to be one of the last performances, Nan Lanier, a member of Baldwin's camp, gathered the actors together on the stage with a group of potentially helpful people.

Some small donations were pledged. When Nan Lanier appealed for more – 'All we need is another $10,000' – two female hands were raised. The ladies were sisters, Mrs Ann Pierson and Mrs Mary Strawbridge, and to everyone's astonishment and delight they offered to donate $5,000 each.

The show went on. The story was featured in *Time*, only now giving the sisters' maiden name: there was a photograph of Baldwin, grinning widely, on each arm a Rockefeller.

Blues for Mr Charlie finally closed on 29 August, when the ANTA Theatre had to be vacated to make way for another production. Baldwin was on his way to Istanbul via Paris and Marseille, and could fight no more. But the fuss over the play did not cease there. The Actors Studio had accepted an invitation to appear at the World Theatre Festival in London, in April 1965, and, as its representative productions, it elected to take Chekhov's *Three Sisters* and *Blues for Mr Charlie*. Baldwin's standing was high in London, and Strasberg calculated that a hospitable reception from the English critics would aid the Actors Studio cause.

Baldwin, meanwhile, had bowed to pressure from Burgess Meredith to allow certain changes in the script – chiefly in the matter of the confusing time-sequence – and replacements were found for Diana Sands, by now starring in a successful commercial production, and Rip Torn, whose 'corrosive attitude' had at last defeated the director's patience. It is unlikely that Baldwin regretted their departure, for each, in a separate way, had given him headaches. He had quarrelled with Torn over numerous issues, even threatening to kill him. As for his leading lady, she had gone off and got married – to none other than Baldwin's leading *man*, Lucien Happersberger, who had in the meantime been divorced from his first wife. Baldwin was greatly upset – according to Cordier, he smashed up his newly decorated apartment on West End Avenue – but the marriage lasted only a year before Lucien returned again to Europe.

If the New York production of *Blues for Mr Charlie* toiled upwards from a state close to failure until it became something of a defiant success, London was a straightforward disaster. There was difficulty with the lighting at the Aldwych Theatre, and the action took place in a crepuscular half-light. The critics in general shared the view of the anonymous *Times* reviewer that the author was 'exchanging creative writing for demagogic oratory'. As far as the eagerly expected Actors Studio troupe was concerned, far from deepening the play, they were 'coarsening it even more'.

A disturbing side-show was created, to make things worse, when members of the fascist British National Party stood up in the circle at the start of Act Two and shouted 'This is a lot of filth', and 'Go back to Africa.'

At a press conference the next morning, Strasberg committed the unpardonable sin of disavowing his author and actors. There was 'confusion' in Baldwin's play, he told the assembled journalists; the anger motivating the piece had not been properly worked into 'human emotions'. It was 'partly his fault, partly ours'. This clumsy attempt to salvage the Actors Studio's lofty reputation succeeded only in infuriating Cheryl Crawford, Burgess Meredith and, of course, Baldwin himself. His one consolation was that the critical and public reception of *The Three Sisters* was even worse.

Blues for Mr Charlie left its mark. In spite of its faults as dramatic art, it possesses, in common with *Another Country* and almost all of Baldwin's work, 'a certain emotional power'. It remains one of the few major works in the American theatrical repertoire by a black writer for a majority black cast, and it has been frequently revived, in Britain, the United States, and elsewhere.

Its original Broadway production left one other legacy: it gave the next crop of journalists and interviewers a ready-made headline: 'Blues for Mr Baldwin.'

Chapter Eighteen

The life of the 'hottest property in publishing' takes on an absurd aspect now. 'I can't go out in New York', he told an interviewer during a sojourn in Italy. 'I can't go out where I like to drink, to see people I like, to hang out. I'm a celebrity.'

Baldwin was more fascinated than anything else by his fame. He mentions it often, as if he could not quite believe it had happened to him – a Negro leader, a spokesman for his race, a public figure, 'a celebrity'. It fulfilled a fantasy he had had as a child in Harlem – 'a big Buick car, and I was driving it, wearing a grey suit coming from some place downtown. I'd drive up my block and everyone would notice me. My family . . . would be proud of their rich and famous son. We'd all leave Harlem in this car and go into the country.'

It was becoming hard *not* to notice him. Leslie Schenk, an old friend from his Paris days who was back in America, had the impression that Baldwin's face appeared on television every time he switched it on. Baldwin himself remarked, 'I'm probably the most photographed writer in the world.'

There is a touch of vanity in this, but there is more surprise, and even more self-defence, for this rich and famous son, this celebrity, still found it hard to get a taxi to stop in a New York street, especially when going in an uptown direction. 'I used to offer to hail him a cab when he was leaving the Dial offices,' Jim Silberman recalls, 'but he wouldn't have that. Instead, he would stand on the downtown side of the street and then, once he was in, have the driver turn around.' At other times, it was necessary to stand by a traffic light, then climb into the cab when the driver stopped at a red light. 'Once I was in,' Baldwin said, 'it was his problem.'

On one occasion, he and two of his brothers boarded a taxi by this method, only to hear the driver say, when they were seated, 'I'm sorry. I'm not going to Harlem.' By now Baldwin could reply – with what quantities of irony and bitterness one can only imagine – 'That's good. Neither are we.'

His defence against the onslaught of these humiliations alternated between fury and laughter. But the latter could only be the former in disguise when the incidents were as trivial and unpredictable as that recalled by Robert Cordier. It was at the time of *Blues for Mr Charlie*, and he and Baldwin chose to have lunch at Chez Nous, an 'exclusive' (what bitterness, again!) restaurant in midtown Manhattan. 'We arrived, checked our coats at the cloakroom, and went towards the dining-room. But it was smokey and overcrowded and noisy, so I said let's find somewhere quieter. Jimmy agreed. But when the cloakroom attendant saw us coming back, he smiled this cruel, stupid smile, and practically flung our coats at us – "Come to the wrong place, huh?"'

Once they were out in the street, Cordier continues, 'Jimmy kept it in for about ten minutes, but I could see that he was boiling over inside. Finally, we pass this jeweller's shop and he spots a Chinese jade ring in the window, priced about $4,000. "I want that ring," he says. I said, "Jimmy, don't be ridiculous." "Bobby," he says, "I *must* have that ring! I want to buy it for Betty Lou [Cordier's wife]." So we went into the shop and he bought the ring. It was all about "I'm James Baldwin, no one can talk to me like that, I can have whatever I want", etcetera. Ripping him up inside.'

There are other such stories, for example about the house he bought on West End Avenue in 1964. The agents first of all claimed not to want 'professional people' living there; then, when that didn't work, said they could not sell to a bachelor. Finally, Baldwin managed to move in at the end of the year, thanks to a ploy involving the white face of Lucien. The experience sickened him – Richard Wright had had similar problems just before he left the country for good, almost twenty years before – and he was aware that only his 'celebrity' status had enabled him to emerge the victor. 'If this is true for me and Lena Horne and Harry Belafonte, what about the local cat on the corner?'

Everything about Baldwin, including the mannerisms and hysterical tics highlighted in the long profile which *Esquire* carried in August 1964, has to be weighed against the counter-balance of this kind of daily tribulation. The author, Marvin Elkoff, witnessed an ugly confrontation in Smalls Paradise in Harlem between Baldwin and a young black man, in which Baldwin was harshly insulted. Jerome Smith went to square up to the man, but Baldwin stopped him. There was distress, even tears – a snub from his own race hurt him most. Then he disappeared for half an hour with his brother David:

> When Baldwin returned the tears were gone, but in their place was a jangling, lurching-doll quality, grimaces, overly intense looks, sudden inward disappearances and pointless smiles. He kissed too many faces, cupped too many heads in his hands, fell forward and backward into too many arms ... He moved or was pulled to different tables and different people, but he was not really *with* it, not *with* anyone.

An erratic performance, a transparent attempt at grace under pressure, a private way of dealing with too much attention and too many demands; in the context of the depredations against dignity which he had to put up with, the restraint of his literary temper, especially as it is manifested in his early essays, seems almost saintly. The surprise is not that he should occasionally let slip his rein, but that he could keep hold of it so often and for so long.

The title story of Baldwin's new book, *Going to Meet the Man* (1965), a collection of eight short stories, features a white policeman, Jesse, who as a small boy was taken by his parents to see a lynching. Jesse is a new type of character in Baldwin's prose fiction: he has been brought into existence solely to act as an emblem of American racism. He represents the 'ill-assessed motives and undigested history ... moral evasions and tremendous innocence' of his white countrymen, which Baldwin referred to in an interview the same year. Treating Jesse as a complex of those motives and evasions, Baldwin attempts to expose them.

Since he has never faced up to the nature of the crime he witnessed as a child, Jesse is unable to understand his part in it, or to forgive himself, and therefore, according to the theology set forth in the introduction to *Blues for Mr Charlie*, is condemned to repeat it. Like Lyle Brittan, the leading white character in the play, the policeman 'closes his eyes, compulsively repeats his crimes, and enters a spiritual darkness'. Multiplied one-hundred-millionfold, Jesse was Baldwin's vision of white America.

Using the policeman's reflections as a vehicle while he lies in bed beside his wife awaiting the dawn, Baldwin then introduces the theme of the white fantasy of black sexual superiority. This fiction has a definite purpose: it is to show how these two horrors – the one, the lynching, real; the other, the black man's uncontrollable lust, invented – are shaped in Jesse's imagination into a nightmarish cycle of envy, self-disgust, cruelty and guilt.

Jesse touches his half-sleeping wife in the dark. Then:

He thought of the morning and grabbed her, laughing and crying, crying and laughing, and he whispered, as he stroked her, as he took her, 'Come on, sugar, I'm going to do you like a nigger, just like a nigger, come on, sugar, and love me just like you'd love a nigger.'

Like *Blues*, with its portrait of Lyle, 'Going to Meet the Man' is offered as an attempt to 'understand this wretched man'. But again like *Blues*, the moral ground has been staked out before the story has begun, and thus the author is writing from a position of moral bias. Understanding – particularly of a kind of wretchedness which one finds repugnant – requires a neutrality which Baldwin was finding harder than ever to maintain. 'Going to Meet the Man' was not intended as an anti-white tract, nor was *Blues for Mr Charlie*, but Baldwin could no longer prevent it coming out that way. He allows his own emotions to get too close to the action, the moral key to the story is too quickly disclosed, and hence dramatic tension is lost. The policeman is shown as pitiable, indeed, but his creator can spare no pity on him. He allows him the appearance of generosity – as, for example, when Jesse is made to offer a black boy some gum – but is unwilling to concede that somewhere, somehow, this corrupted man might incorporate genuine goodness. Baldwin has deprived his character of a soul.

Going to Meet the Man contained better work than the title story, but it was not well received by the critics. In bad moments, Baldwin read the decline in critical fortunes which was now besetting him as some kind of political conspiracy. The portrayal of Jesse, the white policeman, and Lyle Brittan, as uncompromising racists, together with the espousal in his current essays of opinions unpalatable to white liberals, was, he thought, a signal to those liberals to turn against him.

What this theory fails to take account of is the possibility of an actual decline in the quality of his work. The energy demanded by the civil rights campaign, in addition to the emotional pressure it put him under, made it difficult for him to concentrate on writing for lengthy periods. And there was also a reduction in the extent to which he would allow his work to be tampered with editorially once it had left his desk. In his early years,

Baldwin had been helped by some first-rate editors – Rahv, Warshow, Levitas – who were now as good as fired, since Baldwin no longer wrote for their low-paying magazines, nor was he a first-time novelist. Now that he was a star, he could write as he wanted, giving free rein to the rhetorical mannerisms to which he had always been prone. This was about as far as he had come in formulating a new 'jazz and blues' aesthetic.

'In my most anti-English days', he opened the article 'Why I Stopped Hating Shakespeare', 'I condemned him as a chauvinist ("This England", indeed!)'. The confrontational self-stylization, 'my most anti-English days', is not a phrase which would have got past the author of 'Nobody Knows My Name' or 'Equal in Paris'. Had it done so, he could have depended on Philip Rahv or Robert Warshow to scratch it out. The same goes for the rhetorical point that the parenthetical '"This England", indeed!' is aiming to score. But who, on the glossy magazines that he wrote for now, was going to stand up to the author of *The Fire Next Time*, if he wished to throw his weight around in brackets and sardonic exclamation marks?

The shift in critical standing that Baldwin was starting to suffer was no different, basically, to that endured by thousands of artists before him. Critics scent a weakness, and go for it. And the weakness here, diagnosed not only by hostile reviewers but by friends as different as Philip Roth and Robert Cordier (even at times by Baldwin himself), was that the politician had sabotaged the writer. Like any artist of stature, Baldwin had set himself a standard which he was expected by critics and readers to maintain, if not exceed. Failure to do so would inevitably be regarded as a fall.

Although he defended himself, blamed the critics, blamed the liberal public, he continued to harbour doubts about the efficacy of his political role. In the course of an interview on BBC television in February 1965, he admitted to Colin MacInnes that he approached his typewriter nowadays with a feeling of trepidation, sensing 'a kind of audience at your shoulders ... saying to you – "What will this do to the cause?"'.' In his heart of hearts, he knew what his proper role was, and that the more he sounded like a politician rather than an artist, the more he usurped his essential self:

MACINNES: Richard Wright ... was in a sense your precursor. And in two of your
    essays, I think you did suggest that at a certain point he became an emblematic
    figure. Right? Is there not a certain danger for you in the present context ... ?
BALDWIN: Oh yes.

*

He was now out of favour with sections of the mainstream, mainly white, intelligentsia, but it is important to keep sight of the fact that he had never been greatly *in* favour with its black equivalent. Richard Wright, Langston Hughes and Leroi Jones had all attacked him, in one way or another, and in his discreet way Ralph Ellison had done so too.

They were not the only ones. Back in 1962, in the winter issue of the black magazine *Freedomways*, the journalist Sylvester Leaks had launched an intemperate attack on Baldwin. Having detached himself from 'black folks', Leaks wrote, 'Mr Baldwin may not be capable of understanding Negroes in depth'. One did not feel his 'love of his people in his writings'. Had a white writer created Rufus and Ida of *Another Country*, 'a boycott of the novel would have been immediately instituted by most Negro organizations and intellectuals – labelling the writer as racist, chauvinistic and anti-Negro.' The reviewer of the novel in the black magazine *Jet* also complained that Baldwin knew 'nothing about Negroes'.

The next number of *Freedomways*, Spring 1963, contained another attack, this time by the novelist Julian Mayfield. Most black writers did not care to know Baldwin, Mayfield claimed; in their minds he was 'an "arty" upstart and the coloured darling of the avante garde [*sic*] magazines who would soon be exposed for the dilettante phony he was'. Mayfield quoted blacks who, he said, considered Baldwin to be the worst thing that ever happened to the race. One of them – 'a learned college professor' – likened him to 'a rebel cow': 'The market wouldn't take her milk and the children wouldn't drink it, but she had a vast following; indeed, she was a best smeller . . . '

In addition to these insults, Baldwin had to put up with the nickname 'Martin Luther Queen', and it happened more than once in a public place – as in Smalls Paradise – that a black person would approach Baldwin and, instead of asking for his autograph, offer a venomous tribute of his own. In the case of a white adversary, Baldwin would probably have responded with a volley of super-articulate fury; confronted by black opposition, he was just as likely to break down in tears.

To have come so far that he had stepped out of reach of his black brothers and sisters – that was not what he understood by 'making it'. What kind of success was it if, while he was describing himself to listeners of the BBC as 'a blues singer', his one-time neighbours in Harlem were jibing at 'the fair-haired boy in high places'?

Now, whenever a way of escape opened, he went down it. And when he found time to take a deep breath, he privately renewed his purpose: not to sacrifice all his energy to the movement, but to contain some in his art. The book of stories had been published, and there was a new novel, a long one, in the typewriter. But with the mood outside the study so tempestuous, when he wanted to work he found it necessary to leave the country. Paris, London, Helsinki, Rome and Istanbul were among the places where he turned up between the summers of 1964 and 1965.

At the end of 1964, one project came to fulfilment which brought a great deal of unselfish pleasure: his old friend Beauford Delaney held a one-man exhibition at the Galerie Lambert in Paris. Eighteen months earlier, Baldwin had established a Sponsoring Committee to raise the $5,000 which would make the exhibition possible. In a letter sent to potential sponsors, he described Delaney as 'my spiritual father', and pledged the first $500 himself, stating that this was not intended to pay off his debt to the painter – 'only my life and work can do that'.

For the catalogue, Baldwin wrote a brief essay, which was translated into French and given the title 'Par lui j'ai découvert la lumière':

I learned about light from Beauford Delaney, the light contained in every thing, in every surface, in every face. Many years ago, in poverty and uncertainty, Beauford and I would walk together through the streets of New York City. He was then, and is now, working all the time, or perhaps it would be more accurate to say that he is *seeing* all the time; and the reality of his seeing caused me to begin to see.

This assumed fellowship with a dedicated artist – Delaney was not one to involve himself in politics – revived Baldwin's acquaintance with the artist in himself, and his belief in art's power: 'Beauford's work leads the inner and the outer eye, directly and inexorably, to a new confrontation with reality.' Beauford Delaney was a great painter and a great man: 'I do know that great art can only be created out of love, and that no greater lover has ever held a brush.'

His hopes of sustaining this essentially spiritual vision of the combined force of art and love were almost immediately dashed. On 21 February 1965, while Baldwin was in London, Malcolm X was shot and killed as he addressed a meeting of his newly formed Muslim Mosque at the Audubon Ballroom on 166th Street. Malcolm had once told Baldwin, 'I'm the warrior of this revolution and you're the poet.' Temperamental and philosophical opposites in so many ways, they had nevertheless been on comradely terms, and Baldwin had lately been echoing the tenor of Malcolm's demands. The splendid dreams of King, after all, were still only dreams.

Dining at the Hilton Hotel with his sister Gloria and some friends, Baldwin was sought out by journalists. The papers next day reported him as saying, 'You did it. You killed him. All of you!'

They didn't, of course. As news came filtering through, it emerged that Malcolm X had been killed by two renegade members of the Nation of Islam, from which he had broken a year before, plus one other man, all of them black. But for Baldwin the death of another Negro leader was like the death of a part of himself. To one who was now apt to look at the world, his world, with tunnel vision, all it required was a slight adjustment in the focus of his rhetoric to encompass the information that Malcolm X had, in fact, been killed by a rival faction of his own religious-political sect. Disembarking from a plane in New York City the next day, Baldwin told reporters, 'The hand that pulled the trigger did not buy the bullet. That bullet was forged in the crucible of the Western world.'

Chapter Nineteen

He had jetted to London in February from Istanbul; once back in New York, he tarried only a short while before returning once again to his Eastern hideaway. Istanbul is a little enigma in Baldwin's life. He never introduced it into his writing. Mention of the town to those unfamiliar with his movements provokes surprise: 'James Baldwin? ... Istanbul?' It doesn't fit.

Yet the unravelling is not hard to begin. In London in February 1965, for example, he had met Bertrand Russell to discuss membership of the philosopher's War Crimes Tribunal, which condemned American action in Vietnam; he had addressed students at the Cambridge Union and debated 'the Negro question' with the conservative American journalist William Buckley Jr; he was interviewed repeatedly, in the studio, in the street outside Lord Russell's home, and at the airport; when Malcolm X was shot he had been immediately harried for quotes, accusations, dark promises of vengeance.

In Istanbul, on the other hand, while he was respected and occasionally interviewed by friendly reporters who were flattered to have among them a famous American writer, he was left alone.

Although he never bought property in the hermaphrodite Euro-Asian city, Baldwin occupied several addresses there. Throughout the 1960s, from the autumn of 1961 until the very last days of the decade, his Istanbulite friends could half-expect him to be in town at any time, or to be on the next plane.

Engin Cezzar, the Turkish actor with whom Baldwin had teamed up for the projected dramatization of *Giovanni's Room* in New York in 1958, and had since remained friends, expected him on the next plane for two whole years. The first mention of heading for Turkey in Baldwin's correspondence with Cezzar occurs in August 1959; five months later, in January 1960, he promised to arrive within a few days; two months further on he admitted, 'I assume you know that I'm not in Turkey.' By the time he got there, it was October 1961.

Even then, he kept Cezzar and his new bride, the actress Gulriz Sururi, in a state of prolonged anticipation, sending telegrams which threatened imminent arrival for at least a week before finally knocking on the door in the middle of a party. The Cezzars were celebrating their wedding. Engin Cezzar remembers Baldwin, at the centre of the throng, after several drinks, asleep with his head on the lap of a Turkish actress met only a few hours before.

On this first visit – theoretically, a stage in his circumambulatory pilgrimage to Africa – he stayed for about four months, finishing *Another Country* at last and posting it off to his agent, Robert Mills. He liked this teeming, overexcited, half-Eastern, half-European antheap of a city. Istanbul appealed to several different senses. It was a place unique in Islam: ambitious to adopt Western appearances, it was oriental in its values, its manners, its atmosphere. It was not Christian; its streets crawled with the visibly downtrodden, the dispossessed, among whose souls Baldwin instinctively felt his own soul belonged.

In Istanbul, people were greatly hospitable; strangers were naturally sociable; young men had no shame in touching one another; homosexuality was quite common, and, in its underground form, accepted without fuss. People were socially gentle, occasionally naïve, mostly undemanding; it seemed to a visitor that there could be no Turkish word for loneliness. Baldwin himself, naturally gregarious, must have felt that he had landed in an ideal place – another country, indeed.

A seed was planted in 1961, and he returned again twelve months later, this time with Lucien Happersberger. Fame and its responsibilities kept him away the following year, but between the end of 1964 and the middle of 1967, Baldwin was semi-resident in Turkey.

At first, after the wedding-party, he had found a bed at the Cezzars', and then, when Engin went off on military duty, at his brother's house. 'I had meant to move to a hotel,' Baldwin wrote to Bob Mills in November, 'but they all considered this to be an insult . . . I've gained a little weight here and this is taken, apparently, as an enormous justification for Turkey's existence.' Life, he adds, has been 'very restful'.

The Cezzars' party had given Baldwin an entry into Istanbul society, and he met there a man who was to become one of his closest Turkish friends, the novelist Yashar Kemal, author of *Memed, My Hawk* (1955) and many other novels since. It was not long before he eased his dependence on his gracious, but otherwise very busy, host and hostess. 'He slept all day,' says Cezzar, 'went to the local bars in the evening, came back at midnight, and then worked till dawn.'

At this rate, they hardly ever saw him, and soon he had his own social circle, drawn from the bars and nightclubs in the backstreets. When he returned to Turkey in 1964, Engin moved him into an apartment just yards from his own house. It was in Ebe Hanim Sokaği, reached by going downhill from Taksim Square, then down a steeper, narrow street, and finally half-a-dozen steps. It was a small place, shaded and cool, surrounded by some of Istanbul's ancient, unpainted timber houses. Here, totally independent but among friends, Baldwin began another novel.

It was exile of a different stamp from his first flight to Europe in 1948. For one thing, it was done in fancier style. This time it was not the poverty and anguish of being an outcast that he fled from, but the poverty and anguish of American success. The exhilaration of fame produced a weary hangover; flattery left a bitter morning taste. But fame also afforded extravagant luxuries, such as commuter exile. 'I want to be alone,' Baldwin could say (being a star permitted one a touch of camp), and board a plane the next day.

The feeling of being an outcast in his own land was not transformed either by success or by flight. No American carried his historical baggage with him like the Afro-American, a stranger at home as much as abroad. Yet Baldwin, as he himself put it, could 'breathe' in Istanbul. Engin Cezzar and Yashar Kemal agree that he was not made to feel like a 'Negro' in Turkey.

'As far as I was concerned, Baldwin was not black,' says Kemal, 'for there are no "blacks" in Turkey in that sense. We didn't experience the slave trade; we don't have the category; they are only people with darker skins. Jimmy's nickname here among his friends was "Arab".'

Baldwin was fascinated by an incident in Kemal's earlier life in Adana, Southern Anatolia. It concerned a schoolfriend of Kemal, a black boy, who was the son of the village priest. The boy grew up and found work in the local prison, and when Kemal was first imprisoned, in 1950, his old schoolfriend became his jailer. 'Jimmy loved that story,' says Kemal. 'It contained everything that appealed to his symbolic imagination: the prison, the priest, the conflict of loyalties, and the boy's blackness. He was always saying he wanted to write about it. But for me the fact that my old friend was black did not come into it.'

Kemal, who has been imprisoned several times on account of his political allegiances, is not a man to be lighthearted about Turkish liberties, but he understood why Baldwin experienced relief from racial pain in Istanbul. He used to tell Kemal: 'Yashar, I feel free in Turkey,' to which Kemal replied: 'Jimmy, that's because you're an American.'

There was also less difficulty here over his other conspicuous difference: homosexuality. 'He said, "Yashar, does it bother you that I am a homosexual?" And I replied, "Well, since you're such a great fellow, it would seem quite a healthy thing to be." Anyway, it's part of Mediterranean culture, and people have always been less afraid of homosexuality here. I think that made him feel comfortable in Istanbul, too.'

In the middle of 1966, Baldwin moved out of the little apartment near Engin Cezzar and the riotous Taksim Square, into a residence more fitting to his celebrity. It was high up on a hill on the campus side of the English-language Robert College, and it had the best view in the city, over the Bosphorus to the Asian shore. The Pasha's Library, as Baldwin's new home was called, was a 200-year-old house with large rooms and a great walled garden. There Baldwin could accommodate not only his 'sad tribe', which was how he described to Cezzar the constant and constantly changing entourage which encircled him, but also friends such as Marlon Brando, who spent some days being ferried round the city in Cezzar's little car while a decoy limousine made dummy runs up ahead.

It was in the Pasha's Library that Zeynep Oral, a young journalist with *Yeni Gazete*, first met and interviewed Baldwin, in October 1966. He was in Istanbul not for a short visit, but to complete a novel, and he explained to Zeynep Oral that he found it impossible to live and work in New York, and that he took succour from the warmth and vitality of the Turkish people. When asked if he wanted to settle in Turkey, however, he replied: 'Staying here forever would be running away, which I cannot do.'

Zeynep Oral thought Baldwin a wonderful man. She returned to her office and filed her copy, which was to appear in the next day's edition of the paper. That evening, she went to a restaurant on the Bosphorus called the Burç, where, at another table, she saw her friends Engin Cezzar and Gulriz Sururi. Baldwin was with them. A well-known singer was performing in the latest fashionable idiom, the bland hybrid of Turkish folk and Western pop music. When Zeynep sat down with her friends, she shook hands again with Baldwin, and, for something to say, remarked: 'Isn't it beautiful music?'

Baldwin exploded. 'Beautiful! How can you call it beautiful? This is *my* music – stolen! This is my rhythm – raped!' He ranted on, clearly drunk, in her eyes, about his ancestors, about chains and slavery. He told her that he could never trust her, that he had lost all respect for her, both as a journalist and as a human being. He went further: 'I forbid you,' he screamed at Zeynep, 'even to write *one word* about me!'

Zeynep Oral remembers the incident vividly. 'Engin and the others, they had to pull us apart. Everyone in the restaurant was staring. He was shouting and waving his arms around. I thought he was mad. And he kept on repeating, "I forbid you to write a single word about me".'

Since the pages of *Yeni Gazete* were already rolling through the presses, that was beyond Zeynep's control. She gave Baldwin her opinion of his manners, and left the restaurant in a kind of shock, not least at having seen the intelligent, charming man of her afternoon assignment transformed into a frenzied black militant by night (and by drink).

'I was sitting in my house the next day, very worried about the article having appeared, because he really seemed to mean what he said and I had no idea what someone like that might do, when the doorbell rang. I answered it, and it was a messenger with a bouquet of roses and a note which read, "Sorry about last night. The piece was beautiful".'

Zeynep Oral was only half-mollified by this handsome gesture – 'Which was the real man: the one who screamed at me, or the one who sent the flowers?' – and she had no further contact with Baldwin until three years later. After that, she wrote many articles about him. 'He said I was never to write a single word about him, but I ended up being the person who wrote the most about him in the whole of Turkey.'

Baldwin travelled to Turkey to avoid America. In Istanbul he could mingle with the crowd and not be threatened by it. He gave his time, as always, to journalists, but he was not besieged by requests and demands and pleas and impossible questions. Yet he carried his personal geography with him, surrounding himself with people who could understand him even when he ranted. He had come to Istanbul for peace and quiet, but he had seldom to be alone. During his first visit, in 1961, he had met a young white American teacher from Robert College, David Leeming, who introduced him to the teaching staff and later became his secretary, both in Istanbul and in New York. His brother David came to stay, as did Beauford Delaney, the man who, he told Engin Cezzar, 'helped me grow up'. Lucien had been back and forth, and he also became friendly with a black singer, Bertice Reading, to whom he read sections of the

work-in-progress, *Tell Me How Long the Train's Been Gone.*
In ten years of commuting to Turkey, he learned scarcely any Turkish beyond the words for please and thank you. And this afforded another sort of freedom, from the treachery of language. Here, in this great, unpretentious, hospitable city, whose inhabitants were largely screened from the false witnesses of the American Dream, Baldwin was safe even from the assault of communication.

When he did communicate with non-English-speaking locals, it was via a lexicon of grunts, hand-signals and Injun talk, the esperanto of travellers everywhere. Or else by another type of body language, which is sexual. Or by means of an intense fellow-feeling which supersedes language and takes literature as its referents, such as fired his friendship with Yashar Kemal. Beyond Kemal, there were few contacts with the Turkish literati. But so much did Baldwin enjoy the atmosphere of the city and the quality of Turkish life that at times he did think of buying property there. What prevented him was the difficulty of functioning from Istanbul as a best-selling writer. Turkish telecommunications in the mid-1960s were unsophisticated, and Baldwin was always having problems getting through to an agent or a lawyer or a publisher, or else had trouble getting to his money. He had found a place where he felt able to function as a man, but to the international author it introduced constraints.

There were other reasons for not staying there. In Turkey, Baldwin took time off from his own stardom, but that stardom was hungrily sought, assiduously cultivated. Other American writers – Paul Bowles is one – have retreated seriously from the soap opera of success and fame in America, but Baldwin, though he execrated its specious glitter, craved success and used it as a means of wreaking vengeance on the merciless republic.

In one chamber of his heart, however, he genuinely wanted the simple life. Engin Cezzar has a late photograph of Baldwin in Turkey which expresses his attachment to the country better than any other. It was taken at a farm near the southern seaport of Bodrum, where the Cezzars had rented a house during the summer of 1980. Baldwin spent three months there, writing a screenplay which he and Cezzar hoped to work up into a film. The photograph was taken at night, without a flashbulb. It shows a small square of yellow window in a large area of darkness, and behind the window-frame the vague, watery shape of a man at a desk, head down, working. The farmhouse had no electricity and therefore the desk is lit by two large candles, one on either side of the paper on which Baldwin is writing. He appears to be concentrating intensely, and to be content. The bright lights of Broadway and Times Square have been gently blown into the candlelight of a primitive farm somewhere unmarked on the Anatolian coast.

It is perhaps an effect of Baldwin's freedom to breathe in Istanbul that neither of his two closest Turkish friends feels strongly that the political activity which occupied and dominated him throughout the 1960s was having a deleterious effect on his literary work. This bears out his own claim that in Turkey he could concentrate on the job of being a writer.

Not that he took up residence abroad as an excuse to abdicate his political role. When Yashar Kemal was rounded up and put in prison for a month during the *coup d'état* of 1971, along with other leading intellectuals, Baldwin campaigned from afar for his release. 'Jimmy organized petitions,' says Kemal, 'got publicity in the papers, did everything he could do.' At the time, Baldwin was acting as a judge in a literary competition in France, and he nominated Kemal for the prize, no doubt having in mind the headline 'Imprisoned Turkish writer gets literary award'. The nomination, says Kemal, failed by one vote to gain acceptance. 'Jimmy cabled the prison to tell me.'

Baldwin was well aware of the perils of being an expatriate. The danger is, he told the Turkish monthly magazine *Cep Dergisi* in 1967,

that as time goes on, the expatriate may find that he has no real or relevant concerns, and no grasp of reality. He is living, really, on the hazards and energies of other people; he has ceased to pay his way.

Flying to France in 1948, he had been prepared never to return home – only to find, the moment he touched down on French soil, that he was unalterably American. From 1957 until 1964, he had given his time and energy – his 'hazard' – to the civil rights movement, but nowadays when they wanted him, often, he just wasn't there. Although he might insist, while sipping tea with Turkish journalists, that he could not run away, that was just the way they saw his prolonged breathers back at movement headquarters.

'Do you believe you are in danger of being criticized for deserting the cause of civil rights?' the *Cep Dergisi* interviewer asked. It was a familiar question, with a twist: it enquired not about the internal damage caused by voluntary exile abroad, but about being rejected at home. Baldwin's reply was cool. 'I have never stopped fighting for civil rights, but I must do my work or I'll be of no use to anyone. I have been criticized for so many things, and for so long, that I am quite unable to look on the possibility of being criticized as a danger.'

This was a prescient remark, for when he flew back to the USA from the Pasha's Library in August, another row with the black intelligentsia was looming. It centred not on himself, but on a white novelist and a close friend of his, William Styron. While it reconfirmed Baldwin in his independence, in the eyes of his black critics it offered proof that the worst names he had been called had substance: that he was an Uncle Tom, that he was a deserter, that he was out of touch with the new moves in the struggle.

Styron had dared – the black critics' interpretation of this word was very different from Baldwin's – to write a novel with a black protagonist. In itself, that would probably have been enough to cause trouble in the heat of 1967, but Styron had chosen to make his fiction out of the character of a historical personage, the leader of a slave revolt and a black folk-hero, Nat Turner.

In August 1831, in Southampton County, Virginia, Nat Turner led the most famous slave insurrection in American history. Sixty or seventy rebels were involved in the dawn uprising, in which over fifty whites were killed, all members of slave-owning families, in their beds. Nat Turner went on the run, but was caught and hanged, leaving behind a 6,000-word 'Confession', in which he described how he knew from an early age that he had been chosen for a 'great purpose'; he claimed visions of 'The Spirit', believed that his massacre was divinely inspired, and identified himself at last with the crucified Saviour.

Baldwin, an expert on false gods, was never tempted to worship Nat Turner, but he saw no contradiction – as others have done and still do – between his idolization and his bloody hands. If whites were shocked at his elevation to heroic status, that was just another proof of their lack of understanding of the depth of black resentment and the will to express grievance.

Styron, somewhat appropriatively, called his novel *The Confessions of Nat Turner*, after the original pamphlet which was released following Nat Turner's execution. On the eve of publication, Styron gave an interview to the Paris magazine, *La Quinzaine*, in which he said, 'I asked James Baldwin to read it and he liked it. But I imagine the black . . . radicals will hate it.'

He could hardly have been more correct, and it was not only the radicals. Blacks of many different political and literary styles read Styron's action as an attempt by the whites to plunder yet again the black man's history and property. It created a cacophony of protest which was eventually orchestrated into a unique book: *William Styron's "Nat Turner": Ten Black Writers Respond.*

Some of the objections were just, others less so. One of the most cogent was by Michael Thelwell, who objected to Styron's language, claiming that the real Nat would have spoken the language of the spirituals – 'Styron's Nat speaks . . . no language at all.' The most common charges were perhaps the most predictable: racism (Loyle Hairston, Charles V. Hamilton, Ernest Kaiser and others); the presumption that all blacks were striving to be 'equal' with whites (Alvin F. Poussaint); the attempt to reduce a black 'giant' to a 'child of pathos' (John O. Killens).

Baldwin, as usual, had his own view, and he was caught in the crossfire. He had anticipated the storm when *Newsweek* interviewed him on publication of the book, saying that Styron was likely to 'catch it from both black and white. It'll be called effrontery but it isn't that.' Baldwin proclaimed Styron's *Confessions* 'a very courageous book that attempts to fuse two points of view, the master's and the slave's'. And he ended with a tribute that was to anger many of the 'ten black writers' but which reflected his steadfast idealism: 'He has begun the common history – *ours*.'

Baldwin's reasons for liking the novel were, to an extent, extra-literary, for he read the 'confession' less as Nat Turner's than as William Styron's. It so happened that he had been staying with Styron at his Connecticut house during part of the writing of the book, and Styron had read portions aloud to him. The grandson of a slave watched as the grandson of a slave-owner wrestled with the American torment, and attempted to shape the experience into art. In such areas, Baldwin transcended mere racial allegiance; the gist of his response to the ten who united against Styron was: if you don't like *his* Nat Turner, write your own.

Chapter Twenty

From America's racial agony there seemed to be no release. In the summer of 1966, James Meredith, the young man who had become the first black student to be admitted to the University of Mississippi, announced that he would take a 'walk against fear' through the state. Meredith set out from Memphis on 5 June, planning to end up in Jackson, the state capital of Mississippi, sixteen days and 220 miles later. On the second day, he was shot down.

Meredith was not killed. Besides being injurious, however, the shooting was at least as symbolic as the walk which provoked it, and one black commentator marked it down as the blow which broke the non-violent spirit. 'Civil rights', and the values which the term implied, Milton A. Galamison reflected in the journal *Freedomways*, fell with the wounded Meredith. When the news of the shooting was broadcast, 'Civil rights leaders from across the nation rushed to continue the march Meredith had begun. There ensued some division, some struggling for leadership, some pushing and shoving. A manifesto was issued which was endorsed by most of the leaders. But there echoed across the land a term the people had never heard before. It was Stokely Carmichael's Black Power.'

Carmichael was rapidly filling the space left by Malcolm X. For the time being, Carmichael was working within the framework of the old Southern organizations; at the time of the Meredith shooting, he was chairman of the Student Nonviolent Co-ordinating Committee (SNCC). But at the same moment in California, an entirely new creature was coming into being, under the triumverate leadership of Huey P. Newton, Bobby Seale and Eldridge Cleaver: the Black Panther Party for Self-Defense. In time, the Panthers and SNCC would merge, and Carmichael became the Black Panthers' 'Prime Minister'.

Comprised of young men with a liking for guns, berets, leather jackets and the outer forms of military discipline, the Panthers must have seemed at first a doubtful quantity to Baldwin – just as he appeared to them a leftover from the reign of King, whom they openly despised. Whatever impatience he might exhibit with the slow pace of change, Baldwin was yet responsive to traditional forms of debate. He had lately allowed his name to be included among the members of Bertrand Russell's War Crimes Tribunal, for example, which reported on American misdeeds in Vietnam. It laid him open to charges of anti-Americanism – he had never been afraid of that – but it was nevertheless in line with conventional methods of subversion.

Young men bearing guns and taking their political direction from Mao's *Little Red Book* came into a different category. The Panthers totemized their weapons – the most prominent Panther image was of Huey Newton on a fan-shaped wicker chair, African spear in one hand, rifle in the other – and attempted to banish all recognized authority from the ghetto, so as to control the streets themselves. They were America's homegrown Viet Cong, preparing to engage in a guerrilla war against the official forces of their native country. After all, they protested, the country had for long enough been waging civil war on *them*. If you asked a Panther sympathizer what he understood by his 'people', he would deliver a certain reply. He was *black*. Baldwin's old-style terminology – he still referred to 'Negroes' – and his investigations into the complexity of American identity, had no place here.

Baldwin first met the Panther leadership at the house of a friend in San Francisco in October 1967, shortly before Huey Newton was arrested and charged with the murder of a policeman. Also present at the dinner were Bobby Seale, the Chairman of the Black Panthers, and Eldridge Cleaver, Minister for Information, who was about to become a best-selling author.

Cleaver had already made public the new-image, black action-man's view of the older-generation, sexually ambiguous writer. In 'Notes on a Native Son', an essay collected later in his book *Soul on Ice*, Cleaver accused Baldwin of 'antipathy towards the black race', and interpreted his homosexuality as a 'racial death-wish'. In flamboyantly offensive terms, Cleaver skewered Baldwin on his own confessions for the greater glorification of – of all people – Norman Mailer, whose essay 'The White Negro' Cleaver praised as 'prophetic and penetrating'. The subtle analysis of Baldwin's early essays – the title of which Cleaver had adapted to mock their author – was lost amid the certainties of Marxist-Leninism and the *Little Red Book*.

Even after his ex-officio fellowship was recognized, Baldwin still came in for criticism from the Panthers for his scepticism and hesitancy. Reporting on a meeting at a church in Oakland, California on 18 May 1968, for example, the *Black Panther Black Community News Service* compared Baldwin's ambivalence unfavourably with the 'gutsy' contributions of the other two speakers, Bobby Seale and Revd John Eckles. 'Baldwin eased out early in the evening', wrote the reporter; his 'vague position' was in 'sharp contrast to the others who were very much together on what to do and how to do it'.

Yet Baldwin embraced the Panthers. By the time they met, he knew what Cleaver had written about him, but he chose not to retaliate. He wanted to discover what the young were doing and thinking, and he was seduced by the personal charm of all three Panther leaders. He was 'very impressed by Eldridge', he wrote, and felt him to be 'valuable and rare'.* He struck up a lasting friendship with Bobby Seale and later wrote a preface to Seale's second book. He liked Huey Newton at that first meeting too, but his feelings about Newton were only brought into focus some weeks later, when Newton was arrested and put in prison.

Baldwin showed himself almost automatically loyal to black leadership. Even the 'faker', Elijah Muhammed, had answered his need for a father-figure and his call to moral authority. And his admiration was inevitably transfigured into adoration when he witnessed the black leader's martyr-dom. He himself, the boy-preacher turned man of the people, 'odd and disreputable' as he put it in *No Name in the Street*, reflected in mirror-image the conversion of Saul to Paul, exemplifying the soul's victory in the heathen midst. And the persecuted black leader was cast in his biblical imagination as the crucified Christ.

The metaphor applied whether or not the figure in question had previously appealed to him. He had said little that was positive about Malcolm X, for example, until after Malcolm was killed. In an interview recorded just a few days before the assassination, he said, 'I would never have sent any child of mine to school to Malcolm, and I would – for myself – rather die than become that kind of theologian.' Nothing of this sort is on record after Malcolm's death.

---

* Baldwin wrote this in *No Name in the Street*; although it was published in 1972, the book carries the dateline 1967–71; it follows a fragmented, diary form, and it seems safe to quote Baldwin's remarks on certain events as if they were written at the time. Baldwin was later very scathing about Cleaver in private, but never put his change of heart into writing.

Although the two were barely acquainted, Baldwin went to visit Newton in prison in California. He found him 'lucid', 'good-natured', 'well-bred', 'old-fashioned in the most remarkable sense, in that he treats everyone with respect'; he was 'beautiful', 'always listening and always watching', speaking with 'perfect candour'. These and similar qualities he found specially impressive because, at that very moment, Newton was 'standing in the shadow of the gas chamber'. (Huey Newton was eventually convicted of voluntary manslaughter, but his conviction was reversed because of a judge's error and he was released after three years in jail.)

Baldwin went further, adapting his own political stance to fit in with the young hero's: 'Huey believes, and I do, too, in the necessity of establishing a form of socialism in this country.' Such a system would be 'formed by', and responsive to, 'the real needs of the American people'.

Here Baldwin is at his most ingenuous. His grasp of *realpolitik* – 'all that sociology and economics jazz' – was never so feeble as it was now. 'Huey believes, and I do, too', does not, for example, answer the question of whether he subscribes to the Panthers' rule of compulsory political re-education to bring the 'real needs of the American people' to the fore of the American consciousness. Nor does Baldwin elaborate on the type of socialism he envisages, nor venture a definition of what Americans' 'real needs' are.

Huey was plain about the political system *he* wanted: one founded on the principles of Marxist-Leninism. He believed firmly (and had acted to prove it) that power emanated from the barrel of a gun, and he disseminated the Maoist doctrine throughout the ghetto by distributing free copies of the *Little Red Book*. Baldwin the Marxist-Leninist? He is queasy about guns, and on shaky ground when it comes to different shades of Communism: the best he can offer, in fifteen pages, is to follow the Chairman of the Black Panthers, Bobby Seale, and call for a '"Yankee Doodle type" socialism'.

Baldwin's importance in the social debate concerning blacks had shrunk considerably since the early 1960s, and his blind support for the new, young militants illustrates the reason why. His strength was in intuiting and articulating the people's buried feelings, and in past times these intuitions had guided his intelligence and directed his means of expression, steering him safely clear of practical politics. This was generally recognized. When, at the *Commentary* round-table discussion in 1964, Norman Podhoretz had asked, 'Mr Baldwin, is it conceivable to you that

Negroes will within the next five or ten or twenty years take their rightful place as one of the competing groups in the American pluralistic pattern?', Harold Cruse, author of the magisterial study *The Crisis of the Negro Intellectual* (1967), commented: 'Nothing that Baldwin has ever written indicates that he could deal, even superficially, with the implications of that question.'

In 1961 he had had wit enough to point out to the young Black Muslim who drove him from Elijah Muhammed's mansion to keep his appointment with the 'white devils' that the estimated 20 million dollars annually at the disposal of blacks – which the Muslims took as the foundation for a putative black economy – was dependent on the total economy of the United States. But now he could skate over the Black Panthers' canonization of Mao, over the compulsory political education programme, over the question of how they intended to pull down the world's most powerful state, and how they would sustain its replacement – by a vague appeal to the 'real needs' of the American people.

Other black intellectuals had for years watched in unadmiring wonder at the way the white world hugged Baldwin to its breast even as he chastised it. Now, partly in a spirit of capitulation to his black critics, he wrote in a way which the white audience found less agreeable. But, according to his own reading of things, his decline in popularity occurred only because the white liberal public had had all the truth it could bear.

An instance of the kind of confusion this led to occurred at the close of 1967, when Stokely Carmichael, returning from North Vietnam and Cuba, had his passport lifted by the American government, placing him, in effect, under house-arrest. Baldwin drafted an open letter, 'In Defense of Stokely Carmichael', which he offered to both *The Times* in London and the *New York Times*. Both declined to published it, and Baldwin interpreted the decision as a political one: he was being censored.

In fact, the real reasons were more likely to have been journalistic. A cogent defence of a newsworthy figure such as Carmichael by James Baldwin would have stood every chance of being published in London, and probably in New York too. Shortly afterwards, for example, the *New York Times* printed a statement by Baldwin in which he set down a 'truth' which could 'no longer be ignored – white America appears to be seriously considering the possibilities of mass extermination'. They were prepared to publish *that*. The Carmichael letter, however, is sloppy and repetitious, calling once again on old anecdotes such as his presence at the voting registration drive in Selma and the meeting with Robert Kennedy.

Baldwin had been away for too long: he had given up his old position but failed to find a new one. Yet the paranoia which forced him to believe in a conspiracy of silence surrounding his Carmichael letter has to be understood in context. The litany which had begun in modern times with Emmett Till was growing longer, it must have seemed, by the day: Medgar Evers of the National Association for the Advancement of Colored People, who was shot outside his house, Malcolm X, four Birmingham schoolgirls, not to mention the nameless thousands of lynchings and disappearances before and since.

Then there was Martin Luther King. Baldwin eventually read his Carmichael 'Defense' aloud from the stage of the Carnegie Hall at a Centennial Celebration for the late W. E. B. DuBois on 23 February 1968. It was the last time he saw King alive. He bought a suit to wear especially for the event, so he wrote to Engin Cezzar, and he put on the same suit six weeks later for King's funeral.

The killing reached him in Hollywood, where he was working on a screenplay of *The Autobiography of Malcolm X* for Columbia Pictures. The Los Angeles office of the FBI had welcomed him to California with its usual array of pretext phone calls, interviews with neighbours and mail checks. Hoover was assured on 14 March 1968 that 'all known details on BALDWIN's temporary residence and itinerary plans' would be 'discreetly verified', and his activities followed.

Baldwin was staying at a rented house in Palm Springs. There, on 4 April, while sitting on the edge of the swimming pool with the actor Billy Dee Williams, whom he wanted for the leading role in the film, he received a phone call from a friend:

He said, 'Jimmy – ? Martin's been shot,' and I don't think I said anything, or felt anything. I'm not sure I knew who *Martin* was . . . David said, 'He's not dead yet' – *then* I knew who Martin was . . .

The small martyrdoms of Huey Newton and Stokely Carmichael had caused a sort of tribal genuflexion, but King's assassination was almost more than he could stand. It was a moment of recognition that there is, finally, no justice in the world, that the atonement of his white American brothers and sisters for the sin of slavery would never be made. Faith was felt to be superstition, and something died inside him: '. . . something has altered in me, something has gone away.'

In place of the redemptive vision was conjured up a nightmare of genocide. Slavery, to Baldwin, was a crime to be measured on the same scale as the Nazi holocaust, 'the crime which was spoken of in the Bible, the sin against the Holy Ghost which cannot be forgiven'. When he placed Huey Newton in the shadow of the gas chamber, he did not do so under the protection of a careless metaphor. Should any vagueness surrounding the allusion have remained, Baldwin spelt out exactly what he meant for readers of the *New York Times* in the summer of 1968. Asked for a summary of his current project, Baldwin ignored the brief and attacked 'white America' for considering 'the possibilities of mass extermination'. In the view of the American government, black people were expendable: 'For saying this I may be dismissed as paranoiac. So were those unhappy people (shortly to be reduced to corpses) who saw the real significance of the Reichstag Fire.'

It was not just a case of post-assassination hysteria. The horror of the holocaust had entered his imagination, and would be expressed frequently in his writing from now on. In a television interview the year after King's death, Baldwin shocked his host, David Frost, by suggesting that white and black were beginning to see that their present path was leading them to 'the same gas oven'.

FROST: Gas oven?
BALDWIN: Gas oven.
FROST: That's overstating the point, isn't it?
BALDWIN: So were the Jews in Germany told that.
FROST: But there's no parallel, surely.
BALDWIN: There is a parallel if you live in Harlem.
FROST: But you've never had a policy here like the one in Germany.
BALDWIN: I will tell you this, my friend, for every Sammy Davis, for every Jimmy Baldwin, for every black cat you have ever heard of in the history of this country, there are a hundred of us dead.

'*What will happen to all that beauty?*' he had asked in a refrain which runs through the final pages of *The Fire Next Time*. As he looked at the infant children in Harlem streets, then turned his head and saw their elder brothers and sisters on the needle, or in the brothel, or in jail, he was bound to feel that many of those children would not survive. Blacks were not wreaking this destruction on themselves – the beauty of the children proved that – it had been, and was being, done to them.

Medgar Evers, Malcolm X, Martin Luther King ... Baldwin began to fear – and who could say that he was not within his rights? – that he would be next. Someone might have easily considered it a useful strike against Black Power, or just against blacks, to take a shot at the highly visible, outspoken writer.

Yet his trepidation, while justified, was also disproportionate. Baldwin's importance to the movement was considerable, but not as great as he seems at times to have believed it was. What did he mean, for example, by telling Engin Cezzar just a week after King's death that he was now 'the black elder statesman', and that he was 'the only mobile black American left'? And although the FBI was certainly keeping a close eye on his movements, it was overstating the case to assume, as he did, that they had his every change of direction covered and his conversations taped. 'Medgar, Malcolm and Martin' – he frequently repeated the tragic refrain – were, each in his own way, in a different category of civil rights leadership from Baldwin, as was their contemporary avatar, Stokeley Carmichael, to whom Baldwin considered himself the 'older brother'.

'He seriously believed that he was in as much danger, physically, as Martin Luther King and Malcolm X,' says Kenton Keith, a friend from Istanbul days, and cultural attaché to the US Embassy there. 'He wasn't.'

Yet Baldwin persisted in his belief, once more involuntarily compressing the matter of his daily life into legend, as the details of actual experience began to fade. During the eleven years of their acquaintanceship, he had met King at irregular intervals, had been ever ready to speak at marches, and had exchanged sporadic correspondence with him. Yet in a *Life* profile of 1971, he is found casting their relationship in terms of public and political equals: referring first to 'Medgar, Malcolm, Martin and me', he continued, 'We [Baldwin and King] had been young together, we had tramped all over the South together, we had even dared hope together.' In an interview the year before, he pointed to the catalogue of assassinations – 'I loved Medgar. I loved Martin and Malcolm' – and continued: 'We all worked together and kept the faith together ...

I'm the last witness – everybody else is dead.' Within a few years, he would be telling readers of the *New York Times* how he thought of Martin Luther King as his 'younger brother'.

Even allowing for the figurative language of deep spiritual kinship, this suggestion, and Baldwin's claim to have 'tramped all over the South' with King, are considerable overstatements. As we have seen, King himself was wary of too great an involvement by Baldwin in the civil rights crusade. Other observers of the political and cultural scene, while not undervaluing Baldwin's contribution to the movement, also feel that he tended to exaggerate his closeness to its leaders, King in particular. 'He could not have spoken the same language as someone like King,' says Norman Podhoretz. King was cautious of Baldwin's homosexuality; he had been forced to cold-shoulder an old trooper, Bayard Rustin, on account of that very tendency. Moreover, in his last months, King could scarcely have approved of Baldwin's latest flirtation: the Black Power movement threatened his base of support, the Panthers' weaponry was anathema to his dream of non-violent conciliation, and he regarded Carmichael as a troublemaker.

Baldwin's exaggeration can be regarded as a symptom of the devastation which King's death wrought inside him. If he inflated his importance within the top echelon of the black leadership, it was to help prop up a spirit that died a little each time a limb of that leadership was broken off. All but the last glimmer of Baldwin's vision of 'relatively conscious whites and . . . relatively conscious blacks' joining hands to 'change the history of the world' was extinguished with the man, both younger brother and father-figure, who was truly his idol.

Whether or not Billy Dee Williams would have made a good lead in the film version of *The Autobiography of Malcolm X* will probably never be known, because shortly after attending King's funeral, Baldwin returned to Hollywood and got into a fight with Columbia over the studio's interference with his script. He told them they would do his picture, 'or *no* picture', and walked out.*

His objections were well founded but they revealed a lack of appetite for work. The new novel, almost entirely written in Istanbul, was finished

---

*The screenplay, *One Day When I was Lost*, was published in Britain in 1972, in the United States a year later.

and about to be published, but he had no enthusiasm for the event. When the galley proofs were sent to him by his publishers for correction, he failed to return them. 'I think he stopped caring,' says Richard Baron, then head of Dial Press. Baron and E. L. Doctorow were the editors in charge of *Tell Me How Long the Train's Been Gone*, and Baron recalls going to Baldwin's house to discuss changes to the typescript. 'Jimmy said, "Do what you like." That was shocking.'

He had all but given up the essay form, where his talent had flourished, and his current project – *No Name in the Street*, a memoir of the 1960s – although finally published in 1972, was never properly finished.

'That's not writing, that's typing,' Truman Capote allegedly told Jack Kerouac; Baldwin was fond of the remark, and even quoted it, without a thought for hubris, during the composition of *Tell Me How Long the Train's Been Gone*. The novel was completed before King's death, but that event and the book's critical reception, coming just two months after the shooting, have a morbid congruity. 'Martin has reached the end of his rope', Baldwin had once said, and the critics were saying the same thing about him. The novel's publication signalled the second assassination of the year.

He had written *Tell Me How Long* while weighted by a great many burdens, and had frequently left the US in order to find the peace to work. The book is long – over 400 pages – but the main effect of its size is to display its faults in abundance. There is no plot. The novel's emotional centre is, as usual, a relationship – between a black actor called Leo Proudhammer (Leo, king of cats; Leo was also Baldwin's astrological sign) and his elder brother, Caleb. Other significant characters in the book, benign and malign, include Barbara, a white actress with whom Leo has an affair; Saul San-Marquand, a theatre director who is based on Lee Strasberg; and Christopher, a young black militant, whose 'we need guns' sounds the story's final chord.

It is assertion without authority, however, for almost everything that can go wrong with a novel has gone wrong here. Baldwin's basic skill as a writer of fiction had often been questioned; his successes had been attained by keeping a firm rein on the novel's shape and characters. His most disciplined novel is *Go Tell It on the Mountain*, but it is also, of his first three, the least vital. In *Another Country*, the reverse applies: the book is overflowing with life, but betrays a poor control of form. When Baldwin opened one channel of his talent, it seemed automatically to shut off the other. But in *Tell Me How Long*, there appears to be scarcely any application of control at all.

The narrative is presented largely in the form of flashbacks, a device which had irked critics of the earlier novels and of *Blues for Mr Charlie*. The story has no firm structure, and therefore no sense of inevitability. Most disappointing of all, the language is uninventive, and the book as a whole is lacking in artistic daring. Baldwin's exciting declarations of intent about the role of a blues singer result merely in a kind of flat hip-speak:

One night, quite late, there were only about five people there, I was sitting on my stool, singing, and Caleb walked in. And when he walked in, I'll be damned if I wasn't singing 'Sometimes I Feel Like a Motherless Child'. I did, too. He was in the joint practically before I knew it. I saw this big, black man stooping through the doorway, and I thought, *Shit, I wonder where he comes from, fuck it. I am not serving anybody else tonight*, and then, so to speak, my vision cleared, and I found myself staring at Caleb.

Well, he looked wonderful – big and black and shining; safe and proud. I hadn't seen him for the longest while. I forced myself to finish my song, while he stared at me, smiling. Hilda looked at me, and I finished my song and I said to Hilda, 'That's my brother, Caleb.'

Another danger which had always threatened to wreck the fabric of his fiction was the opinionated voice of the essayist, and it intrudes freely into this novel. Leo's voice is James Baldwin's voice, but the character can merely mimic his creator, and the result is parody. Nowadays, Baldwin was likely to reach moral judgements based on the 'white equates with evil; black with grace' principle, and *Tell Me How Long* harbours much tedious commendation of black nobility and condemnation of white shame. In the scene, from which the above quotation is also taken, where Leo recollects his days as a singing waiter in a Greenwich Village restaurant, he supplies a long, unflattering description of a typical night's (mainly white) customers – 'just the usual fools' – sparing a few kind words only for a 'brilliant, ageing Negro lawyer', a 'nice blonde girl' from Minneapolis who has a black musician husband, and a black girl, Sally, whom Leo likes very much, though she lets herself down by associating with 'two white, male NYU students . . . I thought they were full of shit.'

White people in general in the novel are 'snooty', 'bored', 'distrustful', 'dangerous', 'brutally cruel', 'hateful', 'successful and vocal Fascists', 'weeping and sweating'; they are also likely to be deceptive, rude and supercilious, lacking in passion, drunk, vulgar, and, at the same time as despising their black 'servitors', deeply in awe and envious of them. Blacks, on the other hand, are 'very impressive' (the owner of the restaurant), 'cool and sleek' (Sally), 'wonderful – big and black and shining; safe and proud', which, along with just about every conceivable epithet of praise, describes Leo's brother.

Baldwin thought of Leo as Rufus (of *Another Country*), without Rufus's need to kill himself – Rufus triumphant and victorious. Leo was '*Rufus qui n'est pas un suicide*', as Baldwin told the French interviewer, Christian de Bartillat. But Leo fails to engage our interest precisely because he lacks Rufus's tragic dimension. Whatever has gone wrong in Leo's life is wrong only because society has made it so, and has nothing to do with his personality. He is diminished from a character to a symptom.

Reductiveness of this sort is not only tiresome to read about, especially in a novel without compensations of structural design, but involves a suspension of character judgement in favour of colour-coded prejudice. The hallmarks of Baldwin's moral outlook – equivocation, ambivalence, doubt – have all but vanished.

The critical reception of *Tell Me How Long the Train's Been Gone* was disastrous. Baldwin had dispensed with 'art-making power' (the *New Republic*); he had 'almost ceased to be an artist' and was committed to 'self-indulgence' (the *Nation*). In an extended response in *Harper's*, Irving Howe referred to a 'speechmaker's prose' – but it was not that of the speechmaker who had electrified audiences a few years before; this prose was 'without clarity or firm relation between object and word'. Perhaps the most disappointing thing of all, which none of these critics mentioned, was that the new aesthetic purpose which had earlier fired him – based on the 'certain beat' of the black artist's musical heritage – had not resulted in innovations of style or form. Baldwin's improvisations seemed more like bad discipline.

Chapter Twenty-one

Salacious stories inevitably cluster about the persona of an exotic noncon-
formist like Baldwin, not all of them flattering. Some are unpleasant, even
to the most indulgent eye. Most concern his sexuality, and if you probed
deep enough, many of them would undoubtedly say more about the
storyteller than the protagonist.

Baldwin was open about his homosexuality, almost from the moment he
had realized it as a fact, but he was irked, and even puzzled, by the
emphasis placed on it. 'I've loved a few men and I've loved a few women,'
he would say, and the word 'homosexual' did not explain what it was he
felt himself to be. In a 1984 interview with the *Village Voice* on the subject,
he said, 'There is nothing in me that is not in everybody else.' His
interviewer insisted on marking him down as 'gay', however:

VOICE: Is it problematic for you, the idea of having sex only with other people who
    are identified as gay?
BALDWIN: Well, you see, my life has not been like that at all. The people who
    were my lovers were never, well, the word gay wouldn't have meant anything
    to them.
VOICE: That means they moved in the straight world.
BALDWIN: They moved in the world.

While Baldwin himself would have attributed the urge to pass on dirty
stories about others as the conscious mind's defence against its own
unconscious and forbidden longing, the gossip none the less persists.
Jimmy only liked fair young boys, reports one of Baldwin's friends; Jimmy
only liked truck-driver types, says another, the bigger the better. Jimmy
only liked white, Jimmy only liked black . . .

Here are two quotations:

I think it was at that party that I heard Baldwin boast (?) of just having fucked a 10-year-old 'white boy' with 'a tight asshole'.

I have handled a great many children, washed them, spanked them, put them on the toilet, tied ribbons in their hair; and, though I am trying to, I find that I am unable to imagine a child as a sexual object.

The first comes from a letter sent to me by someone who claimed to have overheard Baldwin speak at a New York party; the second is from Baldwin's original essay on the Atlanta child killings, 'The Evidence of Things Not Seen'.* Like most lovers, no doubt, his sexual tastes were varied, changed with the years, and strayed at times towards the taboo. It is hardly rare for ageing men to seek the consolations of freshness and innocence in bed, and the majority of Baldwin's lovers were younger than he; but he was a confessional writer, and paedophilia does not feature anywhere, at any time, among his preoccupations, in the millions of words he wrote, in books and letters, that I have read. Moreover, his own remarks about not being able to see a child as a 'sexual object' have a straightforward candour and authority.

A different charge, relating to a different sort of offence, is, in its own way, more disturbing, if only because it issues from what is at first sight a more reliable witness. The place is Puerto Vallerta, Mexico, the year 1969, and the source the diary of the actor Richard Burton:

(April 5) As we arrived back at the house we were hailed by a Negro. It turned out to be James Baldwin and a French boy who spoke no English. He was down here, escaping from Hollywood he said. We discussed Black Power, Black Panthers, Black is best, Black is beautiful and Black and White. He said quite openly and not at all sneakily: 'Richard, can you let me have 20 dollars?' ('Let me have', mark you, not 'lend'.)

I was rather surprised, as I would have thought he was fairly affluent and said 'Twenty dollars?'

'I mean 200 dollars,' he said. I said certainly and Jim is going to give it to him today. We are seeing him again tomorrow.

(April 9) We think James Baldwin is a thief! Val had 220 dollars or so stolen from her purse when J. Baldwin came to lunch on Monday, and after several reductios

* *Playboy*, December 1981; to be distinguished from the book with the same title which he wrote later.

ad absurdum have decided that the guilty feller is Baldwin. It may be his French friend but then that's the same thing.

(April 10) Well, we decided that J. Baldwin had stolen Val's money for the following, mostly psychological, reasons: the servants have not stolen anything in 7 years, despite my habit of leaving money all over the place in trouser pockets, etc, and E. leaving baubles all over her dressing table and other locations. The children have never stolen anything in their lives ... [The other guests were old and trusted friends.] Neither E. nor I did.

I have already recorded in this diary that Baldwin had asked me for 20, no 200 dollars. Two days later he asked Jim for a further 50. Then a further 100. Some couple of years ago he had borrowed 10 dollars from Jim (while travelling 1st class on *La France*) and has never payed him back. He was sitting at the table with us over lunch when he saw me give the money to Jim to give to Val (I had been holding it for her) who put it into her handbag. She had later taken it to her room in the lower house and James had made a tour of the houses alone. We shall never be able to prove it and the money doesn't matter, but why does he do it? Does he steal also from black men or does he think that the white man owes him a living? I must find out from others if James has a reputation as a kleptomaniac.

The obvious defence against this hideous accusation is to say that Burton made a mistake, or that the thief was Baldwin's French friend – not quite 'the same thing'. Baldwin, as we have seen, was a habitual borrower and a bad debtor, even, as the above shows, when successful and well off. The failure to repay is always annoying, but in his own way Baldwin honoured all debts in kind, by virtue of a magnificent, boundless generosity, which asked no return and was itself frequently taken advantage of. For every anecdote featuring Baldwin's failure to pay back, there are one hundred of his talent for giving. Burton's story is unique in casting him as a crude thief.

Was the mind which had let slip the relation between 'object and word', as Irving Howe said of his last novel, also losing hold of the connection between honour and deed? Baldwin had, after all, taken large sums of money from the Ford Foundation, among other bodies, then written courteous and grateful letters to the chairmen, only to scorn their benevolence when their backs were turned and the money was spent. 'Does he think the white man owes him a living?' Burton asks his diary, and from a certain point of view, at certain times, it could be answered, yes, he did think so.

He had, moreover, experienced dire poverty during his childhood – empty-belly, bare-feet poverty – and probably never overcame his fear of not having enough. The compulsive borrowing of his early Paris days had been rendered unnecessary by financial success, but it seems the compulsion remained, independent of its original conditions. There is also the consideration that Baldwin might have been motivated by a topsy-turvy desire to impress the Burtons by so casually borrowing $200 from them. But of the dozen or more of Baldwin's close associates who were asked for their opinion of the incident – including Engin Cezzar and Lucien Happersberger, who knew him for almost thirty years and forty years respectively – every one recoiled at the suggestion that Baldwin could be guilty of simple thieving.

Cezzar provides what is surely the answer to the charge: Baldwin's companion at the time was a young Frenchman, who flew around the world with him. In Istanbul, he gave Cezzar little reason either to respect his manners or to trust his honesty. On at least one occasion, Cezzar suspected this boyfriend of being a thief, and some years later Cezzar discovered that he had ended up in prison on a charge of armed robbery. The last Cezzar heard of him, he was keeping company with an internationally known playboy on a luxury yacht in the Bosphorus.

The Burton misadventure falls within the worst period of Baldwin's adult life, the time immediately following the assassination of Martin Luther King. His optimism and morale had fallen, and his critical reputation went tumbling after. 'The rapid decline in James Baldwin's stature as the major Negro writer in America is one curiosity of the 60s', the critic Robert E. Lee told an MLA meeting in Denver in 1969. The new political mood required a new set of voices, and Baldwin was no longer recognized as being in the front row.

He realized this himself. By 1970 he was talking of 'beginning again'. He needed a 'certain privacy', he told *Ebony* magazine, 'a place where I can find out again . . . what I must do'. He was speaking once more from Istanbul, a city where for almost a decade now he had sheltered from storm clouds. And it was here, in conjunction with Engin Cezzar and Gulriz Sururi, that he took his new departure – as a theatre director.

In December 1969, the FBI, which had monitored the Security Index subject's movements throughout the 1960s ('advised . . . James Baldwin arrived in Istanbul, Turkey, from Athens, Greece, via Air France on July 13, 1969'), clipped and filed an interview which had appeared in the daily *Milliyet*. The reasons for it catching the informant's interest may have had to do with the anti-American implications of Baldwin's sentiments

expressed in the piece, but the thrust of the article was the announcement of a new partnership formed with Cezzar and Yashar Kemal. It was
projected as the launch-pad for translations of books, theatre and film
productions, in and about Turkey. Its first and only fruit (in which
Kemal played no part) was the presentation of the play *Fortune and Men's
Eyes*, by the Canadian playwright John Herbert.

The play, which is about homosexuality in a Canadian reformatory for
young men, had already been staged successfully in London (by Charles
Marowitz) and in New York (by Sal Mineo). For his Istanbul production,
Baldwin gave the leading role of Smitty – the boy who enters the prison
jungle as a naïf and leaves it more vicious than the rest – to Cezzar
himself. Gulriz Sururi was the producer for the all-male play, and the
American jazz musician Don Cherry, whom Baldwin met by chance on a
street corner at an early stage in the preparations, composed and
recorded the music. The play ran for 103 performances during the
winter and spring of 1969–70.

Baldwin's obsession with the theatre went back to the very beginning
of his career. From his schooldays on, he had had aspirations to be
playwright, actor, critic. In October 1966, he watched Cezzar give a
performance as the clerk in a stage adaptation of *The Overcoat* by Gogol,
and afterwards gave his friend his impromptu thoughts on the performance:

I have a feeling that if you bring down the makeup slightly, over the eyes and
forehead, you will have added a value. I mean, the clerk's bewilderment is not
only in his body but also in his face. The clerk's eyes are really frightening,
possibly you give his eyes too much work to do which you can balance by the
candour of the forehead; or the clerk is a child, and you can use his forehead to
tell us, and for this all you need to do is use a little less makeup on it. It's an
extremely impressive performance, to say no more than that, but the extreme
tension of your performance is somehow centred there, and this connects with
the really unbearable innocence and passion of the clerk. If we were not so
innocent, and, also, therefore, so easily corrupted, could we ever be defeated by
the problem *The Overcoat* presents?

Baldwin had always liked the sense of community gained from working
in the theatre, but the role of director was a new one. *Fortune and Men's
Eyes* presented special difficulties, moreover, for it was being staged at

234 TALKING AT THE GATES

Cezzar's 'Milky Way Theatre' (Ümit Tiyatrosu) in a Turkish translation,* and Baldwin knew scarcely more Turkish now than on the day he
had first arrived in the country in 1961.

Another difficulty that cropped up was of a sort he was more accustomed to: the Istanbul authorities considered the play to be outrageous
and a threat to public order, and the police tried to ban it. When Gulriz
Sururi first heard that Cezzar and Baldwin were considering producing
the play, she told her husband: 'You'll never get away with it, not here.'
The original version contains some scenes that would not have been
allowed on the English stage ten years earlier, such as the coercion of
one youth to become the sex-slave of another, and the ultimate breaking
of this bond by similar ploys; but the journalist Zeynep Oral, whom
Cezzar had persuaded to forget the restaurant-and-roses incident and
act as Baldwin's personal assistant, says that in Turkish the play's
obscenities were, for her, literally unspeakable – 'Even now'.

The producers remained uncowed, however, and somehow bluffed
their way out of trouble. Cezzar was summoned to the prosecutor's office
to explain his intentions in staging such a play: he explained that it was
going ahead as planned. On the opening night, thirty policemen turned
up at the door, saying they wished to 'observe' the proceedings. Cezzar
charged them admission and gave them standing room, since the theatre
was otherwise sold out.

Cezzar considers, and Zeynep Oral agrees, that Baldwin could have
made an exceptional theatre director. 'He was wonderful,' says Cezzar, a
director himself. 'He directed from the inside. He had fantastic insight
into these characters. We spent a month just sitting round a table and
talking with him before rehearsals even began, which is very unusual in a
Turkish theatre, so that by the time we got going, everyone knew each
other's character as well as they knew their own. Jimmy spoke about his
reading of the play with a passion that fired the actors. By the time we
went on, we were living our parts.'

ROCKY: So come on, baby, let's me an' you take a shower before bedtime.
SMITTY: A shower?
ROCKY: Sure! I like one every night before lights out!

* The Turkish translation, by Oktay Balamir, was called *Düsenin Dostu (Friend of the
Fallen)*.

SMITTY: Go ahead! I had one this afternoon when they brought me in and gave
me a uniform.
ROCKY: It ain't gonna kill ya t'take another. I like company.
SMITTY: Tomorrow, Rocky.
ROCKY: Right now!
SMITTY: No . . . thanks!

In the character notes which he wrote down on sheets of paper and distributed to each member of the cast, Baldwin directed the actor playing Rocky to

remember the pain that only you know, and never talk about, and try to forget that you were ever a boxer: since you actually *were* a boxer, that will be there, and, if you don't use it, then you *can* use it. This is exactly the same thing as my asking you, whenever you feel the impulse to shout, to lower your voice. You use your fists and your voice when you are frightened: if you use the fear which prompts the volume and the gestures, instead of using the voice and gestures to hide the fear, you will achieve a portrait of Rocky . . .

To Engin (Smitty) he pointed out that 'the play stands or falls on Smitty's journey' –

To have seen love fail – twice – and to have seen how the world destroys love – or how one's father is willing to destroy his son – is to have a lot to 'pay back'. People who reach this point become saints or tyrants or poets.

Like any director, Baldwin scribbled all over his script, and his notes reveal a depth of analysis into another writer's characters which was now seldom present in his own. Baldwin compared John Herbert's play to Chekhov's *Cherry Orchard*, remarking in his programme note that Herbert's play was about homosexuality in 'precisely the same sense' that Chekhov's was about cherries:

As Chekhov's play ends, we hear, from far away, the sound of an axe beginning the destruction of the trees – the destruction of a human possibility doomed by human folly. The boys in *Fortune in Men's Eyes* are, like those trees, cut down, and, in this case, before our eyes.

The production was rapturously, even gratefully, received by the

Turkish press, and, in particular, the theatre world. Writing in the American stage journal *Variety*, the Turkish playwright and journalist Refik Erduran commented:

If Baldwin had not lent his name and skills to this production, it would have been ignored by Istanbul's mass audience and instantly denounced by the left as another example of Western decadence. Now it has provided the first occasion in a long while that seems to have brought together the city's theatrical factions on a middle ground. 'This play is subversive in the deepest sense,' mused a well-known Turkish radical columnist: 'What I don't understand is why the reactionary sitting next to me had tears in his eyes.'

After his success in the Milky Way Theatre, Baldwin, typically, began to plan other stage presentations. He wanted to direct *St Joan*, he wanted to do *Tamburlaine the Great*, he wanted to work with Cezzar on a Turkish version of *Blues for Mr Charlie*, he planned to stage a play inside a real prison. But shortly after *Fortune and Men's Eyes* was over, he fell ill. Kenton Keith took him to the German Hospital in Istanbul, where hepatitis was diagnosed. He was advised to give up cigarettes and alcohol, but Baldwin stubbornly insisted that the affliction was psychological, and refused to surrender his addictive crutches. He left for Paris again, where once more he collapsed – his young French lover had by this time deserted him, which contributed to his misery – and was admitted to the American Hospital for a lengthy stay.

It was another crossroads. What had laid him low, in fact, was distant shrapnel from the bullet that killed Martin Luther King. Two years and two changes of continent were not sufficient to heal him after the Memphis assassination. He felt now that he simply could not return to America. Nor, however, would he remain for ever in Istanbul; he felt at home there and had many friends, but his time had at last run out.

Although his name was still used for fund-raising and the like, Baldwin had found himself somewhat adrift since the change of mood, and the change in the guard, of the civil rights movement. Even a Turkish magazine, interviewing him in Istanbul, had felt bold enough to imply that he had deserted the cause. He maintained contact with the new, more militant leadership, but nowadays *he* took his cue from *them*; the days when Baldwin was the first to tell the white world what blacks were doing and thinking were over. The wasting of non-violence had coarsened his eloquence. Although he continued to protest against injustice wherever he encountered it, his silences were deeper, his absences longer. When he spoke, it sometimes sounded off-key. Increasingly lengthy sojourns in Europe and Istanbul were seen as practically a second exile – when they were noticed at all, that is, high season for a writer in America being perilously dependent on media exposure. When a reporter, catching Baldwin at the airport, asked: 'Are you home for good?' the newspaper-reader next morning could be forgiven for saying, 'I didn't know he'd been away.'

His magazine appearances were becoming rare – he all but disappeared during this period from the popular monthlies, *Harper's*, *Esquire*, *Mademoiselle* – and when they occurred it was more often than not to make a statement. In addition to the civil rights cause, he spoke out against Vietnam; he resigned in protest from the board of the black magazine *Liberator* over evidence of anti-Semitism in its pages; at the request of Stan Weir, an old friend from Greenwich Village in the 1940s, he became embroiled in a dispute involving white and black long-shoremen who had been deregistered and prevented from working; and for seven years he conducted a harrowing and expensive campaign to have a young friend, Tony Maynard, released from prison, where he was being held on an unsubstantiated murder charge.

He was aware that this effort kept him away from his work, but he persisted in his belief that it was no less his 'work' to protest against injustice. Here he is reconciled at last with 'committed' French writers such as Sartre and Camus; no other American or English novelist this century has been so consistently willing to lend his name to good causes as Baldwin. The charge made by Robert Kennedy, that he did it to gain publicity for himself, is shallow and, in fact, only shows up Kennedy's own idea of the uses to which a cause might be put. A speech delivered at the 1965 protest march from Selma to Montgomery caught the eye of the media – that was why he made it, to draw attention to the marchers – but an attempt to influence the outcome of a long-shoremen's dispute in San Francisco interested scarcely a soul beyond those directly involved. Baldwin wrote to influential people and publicized the case in a magazine article. In the struggle to clear the name of Tony Maynard, Baldwin devoted substantial amounts of time, money and emotional resources to visiting Maynard in various prisons, and in ensuring that he had competent legal representation.* In a letter to Stan Weir, the old friend from

---

* The story of the early part of the Maynard case is set out in *No Name in the Street*.

Village days who was among the legally embroiled dockers, he wrote of an exhaustion which had hit him 'like a hammer'. He had been spending

I don't know how long now, from early morning until late at night, in the corridors and court rooms of the Tombs, trying to help a friend fight for his life ... I kept thinking of ... the DA who asked me to persuade him to plead guilty, and then, since he's already been in prison nearly two years – without trial – after a year or so, they'd let him go. Honor, as it were, among thieves. But Tony had already turned down the bargain, which, in any case, I could never possibly advise him to accept. The offer seemed – it was – so confident and brazen, and the morality which produced it so pervasive, that every human effort began to seem to be unutterably futile and all of my own effort mere doomed pretensions.

In fact, his effort was as heroic as his self-questioning was sincere. 'Once you can say, why bother?' he wrote, 'you are free to become wicked.' But Baldwin knew that a writer, unless he really does want to give up and become a politician, has to concentrate, and concentrate hard, on writing. '*It's not your job*', he had stamped his foot and fumed at Mailer, on first hearing that Mailer intended to run as Mayor of New York in 1961. Now Mailer and others were saying the same to him: *It's not your job*.

For a decade now, rival political and artistic commitments had competed inside him. In such a contest, in such a man, there was only one proper victor – literature – but that was not the result. Nor was politics the winner, however. Instead the outcome of Baldwin's active daily conflict was something like 'match abandoned'.

Chapter Twenty-two

When he left hospital in Paris, his new agent Tria French, a black American woman domiciled in France, took him to convalesce in St-Paul de Vence, a fashionable *village perché* in the Provençal department of Alpes-Maritime, about ten miles by road from Nice.

St-Paul was well known for its illustrious residents long before Baldwin arrived: among *les hôtes de St-Paul*, at one time or another, can be numbered the writers Maeterlinck, Bernard Shaw and Jean Giono, and the painters Paul Signac, Max Jacob and André Derain, among others. The restaurant to the south of its broad central *place*, the Colombe d'Or, had on its walls, until they were removed for conservation purposes, paintings and drawings by the likes of Picasso, Matisse and Braque – executed, so the legend goes, in lieu of payment for meals and drinks. The French actors Yves Montand and Simone Signoret lived there, and they quickly befriended Baldwin, introducing him to the select society of the region and finding him a decent place to live.

With Simone Signoret's help, he left Le Hameau, the hotel where he was living half a mile outside the village on the route de La Colle, and took a room in an old stone farmhouse just across the road, with tall iron gates and a gatehouse. Several acres of slanted garden and fields overlooked a valley which dipped down to the Côte d'Azur. There was even an air of culture here: in 1950, Georges Braque had had a studio in the very room which Baldwin made into a study.

The elderly French woman who owned the house, Mlle Jeanne Faure, kept half of the old house for herself, and let out the other part, room by room. As Baldwin's friends and relatives came to visit, sometimes staying for weeks at a time, he rented one room after another as they fell vacant. One day he realized that he had taken virtually every available room in the house. Then he thought, 'Why not stay here?'

Mlle Faure was not known for her hospitality towards blacks. She was a *pied noir* who had lived in Algeria during the heyday of colonial occupation, and she remained a committed imperialist. When, eventually, she sold part of her large house and grounds to Baldwin, she did it only out of financial exigency, and even then with reservations. The house is L-shaped, and Baldwin at first occupied one leg of it. When he first moved in, Mlle Faure blocked the connecting door with a heavy, wooden *armoire*, telling her neighbours: 'You never know what to expect from these "nee-gers".'

According to Bertrand Mazodier, who then worked in the post office and is now a jeweller in the village, she was not the only one to have suspicions about Baldwin. 'When he first came to live in St-Paul, people didn't know what to make of it. There was a police watch on the house, keeping an eye on the goings-on through binoculars. They thought he was some kind of black militant. There was hate-mail arriving at the post office every day for him – sheets and sheets of it, all sorts of crazy things. It went on for ages.'

Ignoring the suspicions, and hence allaying them, Baldwin began to make friends in the village. 'There have been lots of famous people who have lived in St-Paul,' says Mazodier, 'but Jimmy was the only one who would stop and talk to you in the street, or come up and buy you a drink in the bar, or let you buy him a drink.'

The imperious Jeanne Faure's experience of her once-feared tenant was also to be transformed: from barricading her door with a heavy wardrobe, she was soon sufficiently charmed by his elegant manners to invite him to dine with her, and to accept his invitation in return. They became friends, and when Mlle Faure's brother died many years later, Baldwin took up a position at the head of the funeral procession by her side. Later still, in 1986, when he was invested with the Légion d'Honneur by President Mitterand, Baldwin showed his sense of occasion by inviting just a few close friends to the ceremony – including his housekeeper, Valerie, and Mlle Faure.

Baldwin on the Riviera? Eyebrows were raised at home, too, but for entirely different reasons. An exile in Paris, where there was an established American colony, even a black colony, was one thing; the fashionable resorts of the south of France quite another.

'Brother Baldwin,' the magazine *Black Scholar* grilled him in 1973, 'how do you see yourself as a black man here in the "sunny hills of Southern France" and your relationship to black people who are struggling all over the world against racism and exploitation?'

The question, and its pointed form of address, succeeded in making him wriggle. 'I could say, you know, that I have found a haven although I know very well that that's not true . . . I am *not* in exile and I am *not* in paradise. It rains down here too.'

The final remark was droll, but it was also meant to be taken figuratively. Certainly it rained, the same terrible rain – for example, when he saw Angela Davis portrayed in chains on the cover of *Newsweek*. The image prompted an open letter, 'Dear Sister . . . ', in which he raised the spectre of slavery in the opening sentence: 'One might have hoped that, by this hour, the sight of chains on black flesh . . . would be so intolerable a sight for the American people, and so unbearable a memory, that they would themselves spontaneously rise up and strike off the manacles.' The article, signed 'Brother James', was dutifully filed by the FBI, whose agent made special note of Baldwin's pledge to 'fight for your life as though it were our own – which it is.'

It rained, too, when, in late August 1971, the news-vendor brought the afternoon editions to the garden of the Colombe d'Or containing news of the shooting to death of George Jackson in San Quentin Prison, along with two other prisoners (three guards were also killed in the shoot-out). Like Angela Davis and the Black Panthers, Jackson was inspired by Communist ideals, but Baldwin saw him as a leader in the tradition of Malcolm X. He was already planning a film project based on Jackson's collection of prison letters, *Soledad Brother*, to be made by his own production company which was then in the process of formation (in the end, the project, like the company, came to nothing).

E. M. Passes, an Englishman on holiday in St-Paul, was the person who actually brought Baldwin the news of Jackson's death. 'I often used to see him in the Colombe d'Or, and this afternoon when I heard the newspaper-seller shouting "*France-Soir! France-Soir!*", I went outside and bought a paper. The headline said that George Jackson had been shot and killed. I went back inside, and Baldwin was sitting alone at a table. He said: "What's in the papers?" I just put the newspaper down silently in front of him, and when he read it he put his head in his hands and wept: "Oh, the bastards, the bastards."'

He had rarely to be alone in St-Paul, but the companionship, though genial and adoring, did not always bring intellectual stimulation. His guests at table might include a publisher, an agent, a chauffeur, an ex-junkie from Detroit, a promising actor from Marseille . . . 'Jimmy was very lonely in his later years,' says Michael Raeburn, a London-based film-maker who worked for some years with Baldwin on a project to make a film out of *Giovanni's Room*. 'I mean lonely in an intellectual sense. There were plenty of people around who could entertain him, or whom he found attractive in one way or another, but not many that he could talk to about books, or about a play, or about his current work.'

He developed an everyday conversational manner to match his platform style – a speechifying, declamatory monologue, in which he interpreted history and prophesied the future through a series of increasingly abstract figures of speech. From his usual company, he could expect little interruption. If contradicted, Baldwin would either raise the speed and heat of his delivery so that it burned up the objection of his interlocuter, leaving it a scorched threat of wrath before his or her own eyes, or else he would take his foot off the pedal and slow down completely, flattering his adversary with sweet, absorbed attention. 'I never thought of that,' he might say, wonderingly, or 'You're one step ahead of *me* there.'

Of the many friends and lovers who came to visit, a few stayed. He had not found a partner to match the seriousness of his early bond to Lucien, and the want of such a love in his life created a lonely gap. As usual, he required not only lovers but secretaries (sometimes one and the same), whose duties might include cooking supper as well as getting him to the station on time, or ensuring a proper supply of whisky in the cupboard. He had a way of charming the most casual acquaintance into performing such tasks, so that with a sense of urgency and importance the visitor could find himself calling the airport to confirm a seat, or phoning Paris to check the time of an appointment, or else tracking down someone he had once known in Istanbul to ask if she still had the script of that uncompleted novel he had left with her in 1965.

In St-Paul, this function was eventually fulfilled by Bernard Hassell, a black dancer whom Baldwin had first known in Paris in the 1950s. They were reunited there in the late 1960s and when Baldwin moved south, Bernard followed, eventually settling into the gatehouse which guarded the ancient residence on the route de La Colle.

All along the affluent road leading out of St-Paul, the houses are protected by burglar alarms, security systems, barking dogs, or just a warning: 'Chien méchant'. Baldwin had no alarms, frequently forgot to lock the door, and left his iron gates open.

*

This period of transition, in which he made a positive step out of the United States into Europe after dallying on the frontiers for so long, was a productive one. Between 1971 and 1976, he published seven books in all: a novel, two works of non-fiction, two book-length 'dialogues' (with the anthropologist Margaret Mead and the poet Nikki Giovanni), a film script and a children's story. Yet not a word is said, in the whole lot, about his present life in France. Not even the large autobiographical portions of the essays *No Name in the Street* and *The Devil Finds Work* provide a hint that he is now based outside the United States. 'Havens are high-priced', he had written in the Introduction to *Nobody Knows My Name* in 1961, and the price of his new haven seemed to be to deny that he had found one.

From now on, Baldwin bounced himself back and forth between Europe and America, neither in one place, really, nor the other. This was a different situation from the early years. Baldwin's stay in Paris in the 1940s and 1950s had given him the education his own country had withheld. Returning home, he had entitled the opening essay of his first book to be published while he was living in the US, 'The Discovery of What It Means to Be an American'. It served as both a farewell to France and a reunion with his native land, for better or worse.

And worse it certainly had been (Medgar, Malcolm, Martin . . .). It snuffed his flame. Fury there was, but less fire; an increase in polemic, a reduction in self-enquiry. 'Europe', in Baldwin's latest writings, was not so much a place as a concept, a metaphor for colonialism and oppression which, even in retreat, had left a cancerous blight on the world.

This was the theme of *No Name in the Street*, which received many critical, and some puzzled, reviews. In several places the book contains evidence that, when it came to non-fiction, the moralizing essayist had lost none of his capacity to attack a subject from a hidden vantage, to play behind the beat, to say something unexpected when the case seemed to be summed up:

In the private chambers of the soul, the guilty party is identified, and the accusing finger there is not legend, but consequence, not fantasy, but the truth. People pay for what they do, and still more, for what they have allowed themselves to become. And they pay for it simply: by the lives they lead.

Here and elsewhere, Baldwin's electrifying style is undimmed. Indeed, it has been given a new charge. But just as often the rhetoric is hollow, as in the apologia for the new black militancy, and in the long jeremiad on 'the decline of the West' which closes the book. As a whole, *No Name in the Street* wants the industry which would have imposed a scheme on its random narrative. It was billed as a fully argued statement on 'what happened in and to America' during the 1960s, but it has instead the tone of a notebook or diary, and would probably have benefited from having been presented as such. Baldwin had begun writing his account before the death of King, but the assassination starved his will to continue, and it was his brother David who came to St-Paul de Vence in 1971 and packed off the pages of what became *No Name in the Street* to New York, when Baldwin himself was ill and unable to complete it.

The essay's lack of design and chronology seemed to vindicate his critics, who could now say that Baldwin was so tired out and passé that he no longer took the trouble even to finish his books. Yet the reader of *No Name in the Street* is rewarded with many pages of mesmerizing prose. His new novel, *If Beale Street Could Talk*, offered little of that.

Baldwin took the bold step of making the narrative of *If Beale Street Could Talk* female: nineteen-year-old Tish, a perfume sales assistant in a downtown shop. She lives with her family in Harlem, and is pregnant; but her boyfriend, Fonny, has been arrested and jailed on a false charge of rape.

Some inspiration for the novel came from his experience of the doubtful case brought against his friend Tony Maynard, who had been in prison since 1967. Baldwin's loyal attendance had taken him first to Hamburg, where Maynard had run off to, then, once he was deported to New York, to the Tombs, where Maynard might otherwise have been absorbed without trace into the 'dark, dark mass'. But the opportunity to write something hard-edged about the way that 'the wretched . . . fare in the halls of justice' is squandered amid behavioural clichés and the corruptions of sentimentality. *Beale Street* is a protest novel: Baldwin's blacks in the novel are poor, but so beautiful, and – in the case of Tish and her wronged lover – so saintly, that they represent a strong case for keeping the ghetto intact.

Here is the teenage salesgirl from Harlem talking about love:

Only a man can see in the face of a woman the girl she was. It is a secret which can be revealed only to a particular man, and, then, only at his insistence. But men have no secrets, except from women, and never grow up in the way that women do.

It is very much harder, and it takes much longer, for a man to grow up, and he could never do it at all without women. This is a mystery which can terrify and immobilize a woman, and it is always the key to her deepest distress.

Of the relationship between herself and her father, Tish says:

I was his daughter, all right: I had found someone to love and I was loved and he was released and verified.

In trying to bless his young narrator with a depth of self-knowledge and a vocabulary which, on any realistic measure, should have been out of her reach – nothing could be more jarring than the word 'verified' from Tish in the above quotation – Baldwin only does her harm, for he deprives her of a character of her own. Tish's voice is drowned in the absurdity of sounding like the author of *No Name in the Street*. Was Baldwin so bent on reminding white people that they had no idea of how blacks thought and felt that he had lost sight of it himself?

Beale Street also raises the charge that Baldwin has misrepresented and undersold black speech. Whereas the intelligence of Harlem street-talk is locked in its ironic wit, its poetic double-edge, its full-speed-ahead, rhetorical 'rapping', Tish conveys her thoughts through an analytic literary medium. The other members of her family are no better served by being confined to coarse slang.

If Beale Street Could Talk was followed by a non-fiction work, an essay 120 pages long, which once again wove the thread of personal reminiscence into the woof of the ostensible subject, which is the role of blacks in the American cinema, from *The Birth of a Nation* to *Lady Sings the Blues*.

The Devil Finds Work proves that Baldwin's essay-writing was still more engaging than his fiction (a judgement that continued to cause him some pain). Less heated, though no less energetic than *No Name in the Street*, its literary character is similar: patchy and repetitious in places, it is studded with insights and offers passages of brilliant, poetic writing. There is the attempt to create a free-flowing improvisation in prose, to draw his lyric gift and rhythmic sense into a literary blues. After a discussion of the 'mindless and hysterical banality' of the film *The Exorcist*, at the end of which the 'demon-racked little girl murderess kisses the Holy Father, and ... remembers nothing', Baldwin hastens to a powerful conclusion: 'Americans should certainly know more about evil than that,' he writes; 'if they pretend otherwise they are lying' –

The grapes of wrath are stored in the cotton fields and migrant shacks of this nation, and in the schools and prisons, and in the eyes and hearts and perceptions of the wretched everywhere, and in the ruined earth of Vietnam, and in the orphans and the widows, and in the old men, seeing visions, and in the young men, dreaming dreams: these have already kissed the bloody cross and will not bow down before it again: and have forgotten nothing.

Once again the book is autobiographical in tenor, but the absence of any mention of Baldwin's current mode of life raises an unignorable conundrum: while his books often seem to give warning that he has capitulated to the racially exclusive ranks of black power, his close circle of friends, and his everyday acquaintance, was equally apportioned between black and white. Life and work, at certain moments, seemed to be parting company.

On a Baldwin page in the 1970s, 'white' was almost by definition guilty, if only by association, while 'black' was elevated to a perch of impossible virtue. Black men, when they walked, moved with a 'marvellously mocking, salty authority'; white men, by comparison, 'seemed to be barely shuffling along'. When a black person laughed, his face opened up and his laugh came 'rumbling up from his balls'; white people had 'shrivelled faces' which indicated 'how matters were with them below the belt'.

The confusion to which this simplification leads is illustrated in *The Devil Finds Work*. We are told that 'white men invented the crime of rape' and that the 'guilty, furtive European notion of sex' is something that 'obliterates any possibility of communion', though no evidence is offered in support of either of those remarkable assertions. What is 'European' meant to convey here? Surely Baldwin cannot mean – although he seems to – that the French, Italians, Poles, etc. never really make love? And is he implying that non-European peoples – specifically, black – have bigger, better, fuller sex-lives than whites? This is the very racial stereotype over which he had fought for years with his old adversary Norman Mailer, who had stubbornly, sometimes goadingly, argued the case.

The autobiographical dimension of the latest long essays, which in the past had been the strength of Baldwin's non-fiction, was also a shade of what it once had been. Baldwin had used his early life for fiction in *Go Tell*

It on the Mountain, and again in a different form in his two greatest essays, major examples of the genre, 'Notes of a Native Son' and 'Down at the Cross' (or *The Fire Next Time*). After writing the latter, he continued to examine his childhood and adolescence, but without extracting anything new in detail. Both *No Name in the Street* and *The Devil Finds Work* give prominence to the early part of his life, but they only reheat material which has been more freshly treated elsewhere.

This raises the question, once more, of Baldwin's relationship to his own experience. Fame, in one sense, froze his early self – pre-1963 – and made it a stranger to the new phenomenon, the saviour, the star. His own past had become a legend and a myth. 'To tell the truth I can't remember much about those years', he told Fern Eckman in 1964, when she was trying to gather information on his literary apprenticeship in Greenwich Village. It is an extraordinary thing to say, and yet it is borne out by his own repetitiveness when talking on the subject.

It led to meaningful distortions. For example, in 1970, Baldwin spoke to Ida Lewis of *Essence* magazine about his life in Paris twenty years earlier:

My friends were Algerians and Africans. They are the people who befriended me when I arrived here broke. In a sense, we saved each other, we lived together. So when the war began, my friends began to disappear one by one. What was happening was obvious. When the hotels were raided I was let alone, but my friends were taken away.

This is self-dramatizing and also disingenuous, on several counts. The people who 'befriended' Baldwin when he arrived in Paris did include some Algerians – he was introduced to them by Themistocles Hoetis – but they remained at the margin of his acquaintance. His real friends, the ones who fed him, lent him money, kept faith with him in harsh circumstances and helped him get published, were Swiss, English, Norwegian – and American, white, black and Jewish.

Nor did he commonly 'live together' with Algerians and Africans, but in the main in cheap hotels, on the bohemian Left Bank. Baldwin moved from black to white, from rich to poor, from heterosexual to homosexual, but when he returned to the US in the late 1950s, he told Harold Isaacs of *Phylon* that his meetings with black Africans were disastrous: 'we almost needed a dictionary to talk.'

Furthermore, if the story of his 'friends' disappearing 'one by one' is given credence, anyone looking into Baldwin's life and work is bound to say that he has taken an unconscionably long time to mention it. Persecution of Algerians in Paris certainly did occur, but the snapshot Baldwin presents of his friends being led away to an unimaginable fate while he was spared (because of his American passport) is misleading on a point of emphasis. In among hundreds of pages of correspondence to friends in the 1950s, and in several essays, there are no more than incidental mentions of the Algerian war.

It would seem fair to attribute these exaggerations to the traumatizing effect of the assassinations and other events of the past decade. It is in *The Devil Finds Work* that Baldwin transforms *HMS Pinafore*, the matinée he saw on the day he quit the church, into the more significant *Native Son*. Whatever the reasons, he was developing the habit of stretching his past life at the corners, to make it fit the dimensions of a present idea.

Chapter Twenty-three

The English language was still as much foe as friend. Baldwin had not yet resolved the conflict between the literary English in which he excelled and the idiom of gospel, blues and jazz, for which he felt not only a natural affinity but an ethical responsibility. As a result of this, among other things, his critical reputation had dwindled by the mid-1970s. The last big Baldwin novel had come out in 1962: *Another Country* had been destined for best-sellerdom even before its publishers saw the typescript, so grand was Baldwin's standing. Things had changed since then. His personal analysis of the 1960s, *No Name in the Street*, had failed to recuperate his position, but, according to publisher's gospel, a major novel would.

'We always wanted the big novel from him,' says Richard Baron, ex-head of Dial Press. 'The non-fiction might have been more important in the long run, in what it achieved – but a novel sets people talking.'

Baldwin was not unaware of the false gods of commerce – nor of his falling foul of them. On publishers' row, he would scoff, you're only as good as your last best-seller, uttering the words with a salt of scorn, convinced that it was a worthless measure of value and that the real index was drawn up by time. He had never chosen his own heroes simply by the latest fashions. 'If you depend on the market, you might as well become a travelling salesman,' he quipped; and he quoted the exchange between Picasso and Gertrude Stein when she saw his portrait of her. Stein complained: 'I don't look like that.' Said Picasso: 'You will.'

Yet it rankled that he no longer commanded the heights on the best-seller list given to other fellows of his old school, such as Mailer, Styron, Roth and Capote, whom Baldwin judged to have created, in *In Cold Blood*, a clever book 'but a dead end'. He had hoped to emulate their successes with the slave novel, which had fermented in his working notebooks since the 1950s. Though he had given it yet another title, it had made little progress. 'He used to say, "Would you publish a book with the title *House*

Nigger?"' Richard Baron recalls. 'I'd say, "Jimmy, if the quality's good enough, we'll publish it – with any title you want."'

The next novel to be handed in to Dial, by which time Baron had left the firm, was not called 'House Nigger', nor was it set on a Southern plantation on Emancipation Day, as the slave novel was to be. However, it did return to the themes which had occupied him during the early part of his career, Southern life and black religion, and it took its title from an old song sung by Ida in *Another Country*:

> Just above my head,
> I hear music in the air.
> And I really do believe
> There's a God somewhere.

In terms of length at least, *Just Above My Head* was Baldwin's biggest novel yet.

The defects inherent in all his novels, with the exception of *Go Tell It on the Mountain*, were again plain to see in the new one: too many bloodless characters, too neatly divided into goodies and baddies; too strong a dependence on colour as an indicator of virtue ('I cannot make my alignments on the basis of colour,' Baldwin had said in 1964; but in fiction, nowadays, he almost always did); too many rambling conversations and descriptions (the book is 600 pages long and has no plot); too many rhetorical passages which belong not to the narrator but to James Baldwin.

Yet in spite of these faults, there is a magnificence in the conception of *Just Above My Head*. Like *Go Tell It on the Mountain*, it has the possibility of redemption at the core. Whereas Baldwin's first novel bore witness to the effort of one youth to strike a bargain with God for his own identity, *Just Above My Head* moves the drama into the arena of American history, and introduces the variable treachery of the individual memory.

The burden of memory is to clarify the event, to make it . . . bearable. But memory is, also, what the imagination makes, or has made, of the event, and the more dreadful the event, the more likely it is that memory will distort, or efface it.

Baldwin might have been talking about himself: if one's memory is not to be trusted – and apparently his was not – then how does one prepare to face one's own experience, and how, in the end, is it to be recorded?

This is the question that Baldwin tackled in *Just Above My Head*, and the answer he gave is to listen to the 'sorrow songs' – gospel, blues and jazz – for the history of black people in America is contained in them, as nowhere else. 'History' as the schematic patterning of events he had all but rejected; his idea of history depended on the spiritual witness. That and only that, he believed, offered a genuine introduction to the inner life of the people.

The main character in the novel is Arthur Montana, a famous gospel singer. His story is told by Hall, his elder brother and manager, a middle-class family man. Hall had once had an affair with a former child-preacher called Julia. Her occupation, and Arthur's, provide Baldwin with the opportunity to serve up great helpings of evangelical rhetoric in the form of Julia's sermons, and chunks of gospel song. The stanzas are often accompanied by a line-by-line commentary by Hall on the significance of this music for black people.

Just Above My Head was Baldwin's most ambitious attempt to outwit the English language and the 'nightmare called history' which he believed it defended. The vocabulary of gospel and blues constituted a more specific record than most white people realized. 'Music don't begin like a song,' Hall says. 'Music can get to *be* a song, but it starts with a cry. It might be the cry of a man when they put the knife to his balls . . . people spend their whole lives trying to drown out that sound.' And he says: 'When a nigger quotes the gospel he is not quoting; he is telling you what happened to him today.'

While Hall struggles to do justice to the trials of Arthur, Julia and himself, he is ever prepared to admit to the unintended distortion in his account – 'Memory does not serve me.' And it is precisely this that creates the need for a second voice in the novel, the voice of gospel music, which renders an alternative, abstract narrative, and therefore an alternative history. The book opens and closes with Arthur's death, but this particular life-story is being told in order to serve another story. One of them, Baldwin is saying, is of a man, born to live and to die; the moral of the other story can never die.

A large enough number of personal references are buried in the opening pages of the novel to indicate its autobiographical character. The central relationship is between Arthur and his brother Hall, as the deepest bond in Baldwin's life by this time was with his brother David, who, like Hall to Arthur, occasionally acted in the capacity of 'manager'. The age gap between the real-life brothers was seven years, as it is in the novel (although the order of seniority is reversed). Like Arthur, David Baldwin had been in his youth a member of a gospel quartet. Hall's wife is called Ruth, the name of one of the Baldwin sisters; Arthur was James Baldwin's middle name, and Arthur's lover in *Just Above My Head* is called – of all things – Jimmy.

In one passage, Hall mentions Arthur's unfulfilled desire to buy a house in Istanbul: 'he had been there a few times, sometimes to work and sometimes to rest, and he liked it there'. In another, he attempts to cope with the unease of his son concerning Uncle Arthur's private life, an embarrassment which James Arthur Baldwin himself surely feared his own expanding brood of nephews and nieces would have to face:

> 'What was my uncle – Arthur – like?'
> 'Well – why do you ask? *You* knew him.'
> 'Come on. I was a baby. What did *I* know?'
> 'Well – what are you asking?'
> 'A lot of the kids at school – they talk about him . . . They say – he was a faggot.'. . .
> 'Well – you're going to hear a lot of things about your uncle.'
> 'Yeah. That's why I'm asking you.'
> 'Your uncle – a lot of people –'
> 'No. I'm asking *you.*'
> 'Okay. Your uncle was my brother, right? And I loved him. Okay? He was a very – lonely – man. He had a very strange – life. I think that – he was a very great singer.'

Arthur, the black singer, the essential Afro-American artist, died at the age of thirty-nine. Did Baldwin pluck this figure out of the air? It was in *his* thirty-ninth year, in 1963, that he began to speak of himself self-consciously in terms of a black singer: 'I see myself as a blues singer'; 'I'm like a jazz musician', etc. In effect, it was the age at which he exchanged art for politics, the patient scrutiny for the hasty judgement, *le mot juste* for *le mot fort*, the age at which the artist in him went into temporary retreat. Proclaiming disillusionment with the Western literary tradition, yet unable to forge a new, black aesthetic to express the reaches of his vision, he died a little death, just as in the novel Arthur, lover of Jimmy, dies a real death.

To his brother David, Baldwin once said, 'When it comes to words, I can do as much as anyone. But words are not enough – it has to go beyond words.' In *Just Above My Head*, Baldwin attempted to graft the black oral tradition, to which he felt he belonged, on to the Western literary tradition in which he had studied; the introduction of the parallel, 'alternative' narrative – the gospel – was his attempt to move the realist novel, the great edifice of words, beyond words. 'Time,' Hall says in *Just Above My Head*, 'attacked my brother's face . . . Time could not attack the song.'

A continuing disappointment surrounded the failure of *Giovanni's Room* to reach the screen. Baldwin had long harboured a desire to work in movies and *Giovanni's Room* was probably his favourite book. Several attempts were made to film the novel during his lifetime, and in 1978 he began working with Michael Raeburn, the Rhodesian film director who was resident in London. (Baldwin also wrote an introduction to Raeburn's book of short stories, *Black Fire*.) In 1979, they went together to the film festival at Deauville, Normandy. As they sat down one day to watch *Star Wars*, a woman next to them asked, 'Are you James Baldwin?' She went on to inquire if he had ever thought of making a film of *Giovanni's Room*. Baldwin said, 'Yes. And' – pointing to Raeburn – 'he's directing it. Why?' Because, the woman said – she knew Robert de Niro, and he was very keen to make a film in which he could play a 'positive' gay character.

Since Baldwin already had a spoken commitment from Marlon Brando to play the part of Guillaume, the loathsome café-owner, he took this suggestion seriously – two star names on the bill would make Raeburn's task in attracting finance much easier. Negotiations moved slowly, but, at Baldwin's fifty-sixth birthday party in 1980, it was announced to the assembled company that Baldwin and Raeburn were going to prepare a script and make the film of *Giovanni's Room* together.

Raeburn tried to seal the arrangement formally, but after two years of frustration he ceased working on it because Baldwin's agent would not sign a contract without show of a substantial sum of money – 'Money which I just could not get,' says Raeburn.

In the meantime, Baldwin and de Niro had met in Paris but had fallen out over some comments which Baldwin made about de Niro's role in *The Deer Hunter*. 'Jimmy *hated* that film,' says Raeburn. A meeting had also taken place between Baldwin, Raeburn and Brando in a St-Germain hotel, to discuss Brando's part as Guillaume. They made deal, shook hands, and Brando left in a tiny French car, preceded as usual by a decoy in a limousine. That was the last Michael Raeburn heard from him.

Today, the film version of *Giovanni's Room* remains no more than a screenplay, 411 pages long, in Baldwin's own typescript. If performed without cuts, it would take an estimated five hours to perform. Baldwin was eager to be involved in the filming himself, and insisted on having a veto on the final version of the script – conditions which made Raeburn's task of attracting financial backers even more difficult.

The screenplay is of interest for the introduction of one or two incidental black characters into what was famously Baldwin's all-white cast. The only speaking black part is given to the 'Princess', a ruined transvestite who features among the clientele in Guillaume's café. Another notable augmentation to the original is the speech given to Giovanni on the concept of 'gayness' –

'Chez Guillaume they are always talking about *gaie* Liberation. But they are afraid – to be free. That is why they always sound like a barnyard. *Gaie!* They are always asking me, I say them, it is nobody's business, sometimes I am *gaie* and sometimes I am sad, and I do not have to join no club to love – whoever I love. And I do not have to answer to nobody, except just the good God who made me.'

Giovanni's usage is anachronistic, of course; although 'gay' could mean homosexual as early as the 1950s (according to the *Oxford English Dictionary, Supplement*), the political implications – '*gaie* Liberation' – did not follow until more than a decade later. Once again, Baldwin is employing his character to speak for him. He expressed precisely the same sentiments as Giovanni, with only a little less impatience, to Richard Goldstein of the *Village Voice* in 1984. Concerning his early realization of his sexual nature, he said it was 'really a matter between me and God'.

During the 1970s, Baldwin returned frequently to the United States – in 1977 it was even announced in the *New York Times* that he was back for good, 'and glad to be back' – but he kept his base in France. While the frantic babble of the American metropolis repelled him, it did stimulate his pen. He never forgot, however, that in that throng he had almost lost his life – his '*real*' life – which was the reason for his taking refuge in Europe in the first place. And he was still consoled by Europe's ancient resonance. Paris had given him the best years of his youth, and probably the best years of his writing. Paris, he said, was 'a real city'; he liked the French because they left him alone; in Europe he had found the space to breathe. 'In New York you're always looking up if you want to see the sky. And you can never look very far.'

PART V

The Price of the Beat

'*Ah! si j'avais à écrire une histoire des noirs, je devrais interviewer les blancs.*'

James Baldwin, unpublished interview with Christian de Bartillat, 1974

Chapter Twenty-four

In February 1978, James Baldwin received an invitation to address students at Edinburgh University. It was an informal request – so much so, indeed, that it came without the endorsement of the university or of any student body, and with no mention of a fee or travelling expenses. In fact, it was scarcely more than a letter of response to Baldwin's writing, with a postscript asking him please to come to Scotland.

He was not short of invitations, but for some reason he accepted this one. Scotland was one of the few European countries he had yet to visit, and he was touched, or so he told me later, by the personal approach, and by the 'authority' of the letter.

My invitation to Baldwin to come to Edinburgh was not just 'personal': it was impossibly inept and naïve. I wrote without a thought in the world of how to pay his fee, whatever that might have been, of how to transport him from St-Paul de Vence to Edinburgh, of where to put him up for the night, or even of how to feed him while he was there.

When Bernard Hassell replied, saying that Mr Baldwin would like to 'speak to the students of the Univ of Edinburgh in April when he is on his way to California', I was elated – and then appalled. What was I going to do with him, assuming he got here under his own steam? Offer him a pallet on the floor and a pint in the pub? My resources would stretch to nothing grander – I *had* no resources. A literature tutor with whom I discussed the problem (it had suddenly become a 'problem') gently suggested that the great American writer might expect to receive some money once his obligation to speak to the students was fulfilled. I had even less experience of money than of arranging for famous people to visit ancient universities.

The whole thing collapsed, with just two days to go, when a telegram arrived saying that he was unable to make it after all, owing to a bad bout of flu, and that I should contact him to arrange an alternative date.

Disappointment was edged out by relief. I telephoned him at his home in St-Paul and he offered a date in August, when, alas, the students would be on holiday. We agreed to call it off. It was a 'dead letter', Baldwin said. He hoped he would visit Scotland one day. He said he liked my accent. We left it at that.

Or at least *he* did. Nine months later, I wrote to Baldwin again. By this time I had assumed the editorship of a small-circulation literary quarterly, the *New Edinburgh Review*, and I folded my letter into a review copy of a book: *The Making of Jazz* by James Lincoln Collier, a white American music historian. While there were many allusions to jazz in his essays, I prodded Baldwin, he had never devoted a piece to the subject on its own. Perhaps he might welcome the opportunity to do so?

There was no reply, so after some weeks I sent a reminder. 'It looked a fairly interesting book to me,' I wrote, 'and I thought the possibility of writing something might catch your fancy.' And I added matily, 'Hope this finds you well.' This elicited a note, scrawled at the foot of my own letter, which was returned to me: 'Would love to do a long piece: but cannot do it within the dead-line. Am not free before the end of May.'

It amounted to a written agreement. Again I was thrilled, but my joy had to compete with dread that, as before, it might fall through. A long piece? I thought of *The Fire Next Time*; I thought of 'The Black Boy Looks at the White Boy'; perhaps Baldwin's next great long piece would appear in the *New Edinburgh Review*, and I would be his editor.

Of course, we had no money. Our contributors received £20, perhaps £30 for a very long piece or an exceptionally good short story. They were supposed to be motivated by the energy of literature itself. I remembered reading in Norman Podhoretz's *Making It* that Baldwin had been paid about $12,000 by the *New Yorker* in 1962 for the article which became *The Fire Next Time* (the true figure was closer to half that amount). What on earth would he say to £20? In one issue of the *New Edinburgh Review* I had reprinted a short piece by William Burroughs – which I had actually got from him for free some years before for another little magazine – and then posted him a cheque for £10, to be drawn on my own bank account. Burroughs, disgusted, sent the cheque straight to his English agent, who returned it to me, stating acidly that I had insulted her client.

I telephoned Baldwin, said I was delighted that he had agreed to write something for the magazine, but mentioned my embarrassment.

'Don't worry about money,' he replied in an amicable, low-slung growl.

I had a feeling that 'not worrying about money' could mean one thing to me and another to James Baldwin, so I persisted. If he wrote 4,000 words, we could stretch to an unprecedented £80.

'Eighty pounds?' Baldwin paused. 'That's OK.'

The deal was done. We agreed a July deadline. On the appointed day, a telegram arrived.

I FEAR YOU HAVE AN ESSAY I CANNOT DO JUSTICE IN THE LENGTH PROPOSED
HAVE BEEN TRYING TO CALL YOU PLEASE CALL ME
JAMES BALDWIN IN ST PAUL DE VENCE

Cannot do justice in the length proposed? How long did Baldwin want to go? As far as I was concerned, he could have an entire issue of the magazine – he could have the next year's worth if he wanted it.

I called. This book had given him a great deal to think about, he said; it was a heavy burden to carry; I had forced him into a confrontation with something 'very important about my life'; he had been re-reading *Uncle Tom's Cabin* in the light of Collier's account, and there was a connection he needed to explore . . .

He told me to ring him at the end of the week, which I did, then again at the beginning of the week, then in the middle, then at the end, then at the beginning of the next week . . . Almost every time I rang a different person answered the phone. They got to know me. Friendly, confident, black voices. 'Oh, Mr Campbell! How are *you*? Jimmy's not up yet. Can you call again in an hour?' Or else Baldwin would come to the phone: courteous, asking after my health, or about Scotland, or the weather . . . 'I'm working on the piece right now . . . but it's very hot down here.'

Finally, he wrote it. I don't believe he ever would have, had I not told him – ingenuously expecting contributors to hand in their copy when they said they would – that we had had the cover printed and that his name and photograph were on it.

'I'm on the *cover*?' Baldwin gasped. 'I'd better get to *work*.'

When the essay arrived, it was not quite as long as I had hoped, and perhaps had been led to expect, though it was close to our original target of 4,000 words. No mention was made in it of *Uncle Tom's Cabin*. It was called – the title was created first, as was often his practice – 'Of the Sorrow Songs: The Cross of Redemption', after the final chapter of W. E. B. DuBois's seminal work, *The Souls of Black Folk*.

Following an introductory attack on the limitations of Collier's book, it settled into a meditation on the music which 'begins on the auction block'. It was not a great essay, in the style of 'Notes of a Native Son', but it was a good one, and it could not have been written by anyone else. It was driven by the need to affirm the connection between art and life: art was important because the life it sprang from was more important –

the slave mother . . . weep[s], until this hour, for her slaughtered son . . . whoever cannot face this can never pay the price for the *beat* which is the key to music and the key to life.

Music is our witness and our ally. The *beat* is the confession which recognizes, changes and conquers time.

*

I did not actually meet Baldwin for almost another two years, and once again the encounter followed a somewhat comic pattern.

After 'Of the Sorrow Songs' was completed, he rounded off our dealings with an open invitation to visit him in St-Paul – 'if you ever happen to be down this way'. He also gave me some phone numbers where I could contact him in New York, those of his brother and his mother, saying that they always knew where he was, and that we should keep in touch.

The hand of friendship extended in this way greatly flattered me, and I resolved to make sure that I would 'happen to be down this way' before long.

The opportunity occurred early the next summer, which I spent in Paris. I rang Baldwin from a telephone box. 'How are you, baby?' he asked. I was fine – and him? Baldwin chuckled. 'A li'l tight, a li'l tight . . . but that's OK.' I explained that, if it was convenient, I would like to take up my invitation to visit him, in the middle of the following week. Baldwin didn't hesitate; he said he would be delighted. We fixed a day for my arrival, and I asked: 'Shall I phone you before leaving Paris?'

'Only if you have time,' he said. 'Call me when you get to Nice.'

I said I would. 'Goodbye, then.'

'*Ciao*, baby!'

In fact, I did not call before leaving, not wanting to tempt a postponement. As a present, I bought a record of the great pianist Mary Lou Williams, and took the early-morning train from Paris to Nice. Nine hours later, I crossed the road from the station to a café, where I dialled

Baldwin's number. For the first time in our telephone life, he picked up the receiver himself.

'Mr Baldwin –'

'Hey, baby, how are you? Where are you?'

'I'm in Nice.'

Baldwin exploded. 'You're in *Nice*, man! Oh baby . . .' his voice decelerated to a crawl, 'you should've let me know.'

Before I had a chance to protest that he himself had said it was unnecessary to call in advance, he asked: 'Do you have any French money?' Yes, of course I did. I had been in Paris for weeks. 'OK, look. Take a cab to St-Paul de Vence. Do you know any French? Ask the driver to let you down at a restaurant called the Colombe d'Or. He'll know it. I'll be there.'

I reached the Colombe d'Or but he wasn't in the bar. When I asked the barman about 'Monsieur Baldwin', he shrugged and looked vague. I lugged my bag across the road to the large café which took up one side of the *place*, and waited in the open air, watching the men playing boules. Within quarter of an hour, Baldwin appeared at the junction about fifty yards away: small and slight, in sunglasses and a short-sleeved shirt, with a mincing walk; looking all around, he seemed like a stranger himself. My mental image of him was out of date. With grey in his hair, he was no longer the young man I had read and read about.

I approached.

He took off the sunglasses.

'Are you him?'

We went into the Colombe d'Or, where the barman now looked very pleased to see both of us. I was not an autograph hunter; I was Monsieur Baldwin's – Jeemy's – friend.

He seemed nervous and shy. After two or three drinks, he asked: 'Where are you staying?'

I must have betrayed my alarm, because he answered for me: 'You're welcome to stay down at the house, if you like.'

Bernard Hassell joined us. He stared at me wonderingly and said my name very slowly as we shook hands, as if what he saw was the solution to a puzzle.

He went ahead, taking my bag with him, and Baldwin and I walked downhill together from St-Paul on to the road which led to the village of La Colle, and, before that, to Baldwin's venerable stone house. It was 14

July and very hot. Baldwin gave me a drink and we stood in the garden talking as the celebratory fireworks began to be launched from the village on the hill. He looked me in the eye. 'You're home,' he said.

It was not until long afterwards, thinking once again about my awkward entrance and the abundant hospitality in the week that followed, that I realized he had forgotten all about our conversation of a few days before. 'A li'l tight,' he had said over the line to Paris. I don't think he ever remembered. When he asked, 'Do you have any French money?' (I was to discover that he was quite used to people coming only to borrow money), he thought I was newly landed from Edinburgh.

Each time I suggested I might leave, Baldwin or Bernard would tell me to stay another night. 'There's a party tomorrow evening in Grasse,' Bernard said one day. 'Why not hang around for that?'

We travelled in a taxi, which was waiting for us when we came out several hours later. As we went through the door to the house, Bernard leading, a well-known English thriller-writer was standing by the entrance. Our arrival had been keenly anticipated. He grasped Bernard's hand.

'James Baldwin. I'm *so* pleased to meet you. We travelled on the same plane together from Paris to Nice the other day. I saw you in first class and I thought to myself, that *must* be James Baldwin.'

Bernard withdrew his hand. 'I'm Bernard Hassell. *That's* James Baldwin.' Later, he sneered: 'Sees a black man travelling first class and thinks he must be James Baldwin. Shit.'

At the party, Baldwin performed the role of celebrity superbly. Theatricality was central to his nature. No less characteristic of him than his integrity was his self-dramatization, a certain campness in his poise, an unflagging willingness to perform, and a weakness for flashbulbs and recognition in public places. He was as likely to allude to Marlon Brando and Sammy Davis, in discussing his contemporaries, as he was to mention Saul Bellow or Ralph Ellison. I remember him half-sitting on the round table in the middle of the floor, one foot up on a chair, at the centre of a ring of people. He was telling a funny story about the difficulty he had in getting *Giovanni's Room* published. I noticed how he undercut his pride with a self-deprecating humour, but without compromising it. He told them how the writing of *The Fire Next Time* came about almost by accident.

'I was supposed to write about Africa for the *New Yorker*, but it didn't work out. I couldn't. So I had to do *something* for them, to prove I hadn't been in Africa for three months jerking off – on *their* money!'

He had a precise and practised delivery, a fond wit, and a tremendously engaging way of throwing back his head and laughing when you said something funny or when you shared one of his jokes. He was at home with the adoration and the awe, but he appeared genuinely trusting and generous with people, irrespective of colour, class or gender. He knew he was a celebrity and an exotic species, yet far from indulging himself in the attention he commanded, he seemed to give something in return to each of his admirers individually.

In the taxi on the way home – Bernard had gone on ahead – I asked him why he did it, why he played the role, somewhere between prince and court jester, to people who clearly *were* autograph hunters. All they knew about *Giovanni's Room* and *The Fire Next Time* was that somebody famous had written them, and that they were rubbing shoulders with Somebody.

Baldwin had no time for my superciliousness. 'I've *smashed* enough glasses!' he said in the back of the cab, widening his enormous eyes and fanning the fingers of one suddenly upraised hand. 'I've *made* enough speeches! That doesn't help. People have to learn to *touch* – each – other.'

He liked the fact that we had, as he put it, 'worked together', and enjoyed introducing me to people as 'one of my editors'. He asked me to read the typescript of an essay he had just finished, and some poems; the essay was for *Playboy* and was the original for his book about the Atlanta child-killings, *The Evidence of Things Not Seen*. It was stamped with many of Baldwin's fine hallmarks, but I could see that the compact, epistolatory, intimately lyrical manner of the 1950s and early 1960s had deserted him for good, as a singer's voice will coarsen or a painter's style congeal. I liked the poems less, but of one long poem, 'Staggerlee wonders', I said that it fascinated me to find his voice released from the necessity of discourse and left free to play in the abstractions of verse.

Baldwin looked at me as if I had said something original when in fact I had been struggling to find anything to say at all. 'Released from discourse', he kept repeating, over and over again. 'Released from discourse.'

By chance, I found out that he was being paid a huge sum for the *Playboy* article, which was not much longer than the one he had written for the *New Edinburgh Review*. Yet, without being asked, he offered to write for the *New Edinburgh Review* again. Such magazines were important, he said. Reputations were established in their pages. He had started out in journals like that himself.

Later, I saw that writing for a little magazine like the *New Edinburgh Review* brought him an alternative wealth: it put him back in touch with his early days in Paris. Not in the nostalgic way that flicking through the pages of one of his first books might have done, but by enabling him to be as he had been then, one of a circle of young writers, artists and editors, when such magazines were the only ones to open their pages to him. He had known the honour inherent in intrinsically necessary creative work, and it had given him the courage to go for broke, become a writer or nothing at all. In the *New Edinburgh Review*, he welcomed the opportunity to hark back to those values, that climate, that writer; to write on behalf of the energy of literature itself.

His achievement really had been to plant seeds in stone, to carve a form out of rock, the rock of ages. 'The rock claimed me,' he said. It was a religious calling, primarily, a mission for the sake of the have-nots, which had got tangled up in an American mix of aggrandisement, gold and fame. The whiff of puritanism coming off the pages of a small, amateurish journal from Scotland rallied the struggling artist in him – the artist he was trying to revive.

He did not rise before noon. The newspapers came, one in English, one in French, and in fine weather he sat outside at the canopied table where dinner had ended well after twelve the night before, and drank a Johnnie Walker Black Label on the rocks.

When he showed me his study in the lower part of the house – what he called 'the torture chamber' – I noticed many books on the shelves on black subjects and by black writers. On the table was a novel by Ishmael Reed, a member of the west-coast avant garde and the new *enfant terrible* of Afro-American letters. Baldwin had publicly expressed admiration for Reed's work, but Reed had scorned and insulted him, saying that Baldwin was 'a hustler who comes on like Job'. Like the taunts from other quarters about his homosexuality, it wounded Baldwin deeply.

It hurt him to discover that writers of Reed's age regarded him as part of an older generation, as being 'past it', when he was not yet sixty. Hardly had he got used to being a grand old man than they were trying to extinguish him, just as he had shut off his own mentor, Richard Wright.

Baldwin would not accept retirement. 'I am *just* beginning as a writer,' he proclaimed one evening in the Colombe d'Or. A phone call had come through to the bar from *Playboy*, redirected from the house by Bernard, saying that they liked his piece. Baldwin looked as if he had won a prize. He raised his glass. 'I am *just – beginning –* as a *writer!*'

He wanted to find his way back to the artist he had been before the outbreak of the civil rights war called him to national service. He had wandered off-track. But now the map had changed. Ishmael Reed had changed it. Alice Walker had changed it, and Toni Morrison. Ralph Ellison, who had published *Invisible Man* in 1952 and very little since, was still changing it. Was Ellison, more or less a one-book man, going to outpace the prolific Baldwin at the post? Baldwin's intention, stated first in 1964, to 'challenge the language' to contain his experience, had not come to much. His intellectual powers were uniquely strong and subtle, but he required an aesthetic stimulus, a new rapport with characters and ideas. Without that, high standing as an artist, which at the outset his career had promised, would elude him.

In my view, at that time, the terms 'black writing' and 'black writer' did not fit him anyway. I had no difficulty in avoiding concepts like those. Baldwin the novelist was an old-fashioned American realist. No more was I, a non-American, inclined to think of him as a black writer than of Mailer as a Jewish writer, or Robert Lowell as a Boston writer. His subject, like theirs, was our common predicament. In fact, I could see that Baldwin and I shared a culture – Calvinism – and fragments of a common history. Born 'James Jones', he bore the name of a Celt, as I did. One of his preoccupations was the miscegenation of the races in America and he himself had white relations. Perhaps Celtic blood flowed through his veins.

If he was forced to take the view from the margin, that again was something I was familiar with – Burns, Scott, Stevenson, MacDiarmid and all Scottish writers down to my own generation were also on the outside looking in, and had seen themselves as such. 'Jimmy noticed that you billed him as an *American* writer in the *New Edinburgh Review*,' Bernard told me one day, 'and not as a black writer. He liked that.'

So what about launching this new beginning from a port where not all the natives were black? What about women's liberation as a subject? Vietnam? The US Indians? What about an essay on the differences between Tolstoy and Dostoevsky, as he'd been explaining them to me last night? What about Henry James, what about Hemingway?

My motives were partly selfish: I wanted to see, hear, feel, Baldwin's virtuosic prose range over subjects that were important to me. I had just written something about Hemingway, for example; it wasn't bad, but it wasn't outstanding. I longed to focus Baldwin's pen on it, as if it were a shining light, to create something 'unexpected', as William Shawn said of *The Fire Next Time*.

'Hemingway?' Baldwin looked puzzled. 'I don't think so. Faulkner, maybe. Something, you know, that I could connect with.'

Later, however, he told me he had re-read *The Sun Also Rises*, and had liked it better than he had expected to. So perhaps he could have connected, after all, and written something fresh and distinct about Hemingway, about the Paris expatriates of the 1920s and the novels they wrote.

But I had begun to see, by then, that the black writer he had become was standing in his way.

'The price a Negro writer pays for becoming articulate is to find himself, at length, with nothing to be articulate about.' This at first sight gnomic statement, made in 1952, is revealed in mocking clarity by the end of Baldwin's life. He experienced great difficulty in having his final book published. *The Evidence of Things Not Seen* was turned down by several houses – including Dial Press, which had been publishing him since 1956 – before being bought by Henry Holt and issued several years after it was completed.

Perplexed pride made him light on 'political reasons' as the cause of the delay in publication: his report was too controversial, he said. A true account of the black experience entailed 'great violence to the assumptions on which the vocabulary is based'; but, he told an interviewer, 'they won't let you do that' – meaning by 'they', presumably, the publishers, or the establishment or possibly even the American government.

Did Baldwin think he was being censored or banned? He seemed to – or at least he seemed to want to think so. In 1984 he told me about his 'political' difficulties with *The Evidence of Things Not Seen*, and gave me a copy of the typescript to read. To me, the reasons for the publishers declining it were plain to see; there was no need for a conspiracy. In expanding the *Playboy* essay about the Atlanta child murders from 6,000 words to 60,000, he had found nothing more to say. The book was padded out with anecdotes about his childhood, and polemics directed against the

'Republic'. If he had done violence to the language, it was only to render it incoherent.

Nor did he undertake proper research. Baldwin believed that the convicted killer, Wayne Williams, was not guilty, but he was not the sort of journalist to conduct lengthy interviews, ask awkward questions, sniff out leads, and collate the facts. He worked by instinct. But more than instinct is required in a murder case.

I had come down to St-Paul this time to interview him for *The Times* on the occasion of his sixtieth birthday. When I phoned from London and told him that I would be arriving the following week, he said, 'Come before that. Come *this* week.' His charm and magnetism were no less grand than before, but tiredness showed through, and occasionally despair. During one of our talks, he lifted my copy of *Notes of a Native Son* from the table, turned to the essay which had launched his career, 'The Harlem Ghetto', and read aloud: '"Rents are 10 to 58 per cent higher than anywhere else in the city; food, expensive everywhere, is more expensive here and of an inferior quality."' He looked up and said, 'Nothing has changed.' Then he began to read again: '"I can conceive of no Negro native to this country who has not, by the age of puberty, been irreparably scarred by the conditions of his life."' Again: 'Nothing has changed ... "All over Harlem, Negro boys and girls are growing into stunted maturity, trying desperately to find a place to stand."'

Baldwin closed the book, returned it to the table, and widened his eyes in that dramatic way of his: '*Nothing – has – changed!*'

That evening we went out to dine at a restaurant in Vence at the invitation of a young black man and his wife. The man was a photographer, and he wanted Baldwin to write the text for a book of his pictures of famous black Americans. I could tell pretty quickly that Baldwin was never going to fulfil the commission, and couldn't see why he was spending time on this man, who struck me as oafish and vain. It was quite clear that they hardly knew each other, since Baldwin could not remember the photographer's name when he attempted to introduce us. But the photographer was not the type to waste time before reaching first-name terms.

'So, James, when do you think you'll be able to get started on our project?' he asked as we drove to Vence.

'I'm busy right now,' Baldwin grumbled from the back of the car. 'But maybe in the fall.'

I remained mainly in the background, but as dinner progressed I began to feel that our host was exploiting me as a whipping-boy, as whitey. Since I would not have been so rude to him, I objected, silently, to his attitude to me. Most of his remarks I disregarded and my revolt, when it came, was triggered by something quite harmless. Baldwin was out of the room at the time, and a conversation started about the wave of black women writers, who, I remarked nonchalantly, appeared to have taken the vanguard from the men.

The photographer would have none of it. He snapped back that their 'success' was nothing but a strategy on the part of the white establishment to separate black women from black men – 'just as they did when the slaves stepped off the slaveships' – so as to suppress both.

As he embarked on a concise history of the slave trade, I ventured the opinion that this theory, though neat, was worthless. It was just as easy to interpret it the other way: the success of black writers, male or female, undermined the white supremacy on which the Republic was founded. If there was a plot to suppress Alice Walker, putting her on the cover of *Time* magazine was a funny way to go about it. I didn't give much for *Time*'s dedication to literature, but I didn't go for simpleton conspiracy theories either.

How can *you* understand, the photographer sneered, you are white. I protested that if understanding was what we were after, his insistence on demeaning me was certain to prevent it.

At this point, Baldwin returned to the room. 'I don't see what it's all about,' he kept saying above the shouting, and I don't think he ever did, but he took the side of black against white anyway, and proceeded to lecture me in his own fashion. I objected to being categorized as 'white' and I objected to being lectured – 'Even by you,' I said.

'Consider yourself lucky!' Baldwin barked back. 'Most of you do not even *get* that. Black people' – and he waved a finger like a metronome in front of my eyes – '*long a-go!* . . . stopped talking to white people.'

We moved from the restaurant to a café, and to another café, still arguing. The photographer's wife sloped off, then the photographer himself, and Baldwin and I retired to his terrace, where, at about five a.m., we held up our gloves, called it a draw, and each staggered off to bed. By the next afternoon, everything was as normal, and the subject was never mentioned again (nor was the photographer).

When we next met, a year later, in Scotland at last, there was laughter and the by now familiar marathon drinking sessions, during which

Baldwin would appear as curious and youthful as he had ever been, searching for something new to say on every topic that passed before him: to 'find out', he once said – 'what a wonderful phrase!'

Yet I had seen with my own eyes how that trusting touch and that fabulous laugh were controlled by rage, a rage as old and deep, finally, as that of the first slave mother, weeping still for her slaughtered son.

Chapter Twenty-five

Baldwin was not the sort of a writer who worked exclusively on a single piece – novel, essay or play – until it was water-tight, or to the point where he felt that more work would be to its detriment. He always had two or more things going at a time. During the 1980s, three major projects occupied him: a novel, *No Papers for Mohammed*, a play, *The Welcome Table*, and a 'triple biography' of the black martyrs Medgar Evers, Malcolm X and Martin Luther King, to which he gave the working title *Remember This House.*

When I first met him, I did not doubt that these books, once completed, would make significant additions to his *œuvre*. I discussed with him his change of style, and the effort I had sensed since *No Name in the Street* to forge a new idiom. Baldwin said that it was no longer possible for him to write the way he had written thirty years ago, but made an adjustment to my estimation of his aesthetics: to 'a new idiom' he preferred 'a new morality' – 'which in my terms,' he said, 'comes to the same thing'.

As the years passed, however, and he was still working on his book about 'Medgar, Malcolm and Martin', doubts grew about whether he retained the stamina to complete such a massive project as *Remember This House* was bound to be. What type of research was he going to do? I could scarcely imagine Baldwin compiling index systems, or sitting in a library studying the archives of King's Southern Christian Leadership Conference, or making a cool investigation of the political intrigue which had split the Nation of Islam. Blues singers didn't work that way, and Baldwin, increasingly attached to vatic statements such as 'There is no refuge from confession, but in suicide, and suicide *is* confession', was not about to start now. The book would follow the impressionistic, epistolary pattern that he had made his own and that had been his strength.

Also on his desk was *No Papers for Mohammed*, a novel he had been thinking about since before the publication of *If Beale Street Could Talk* in

1974. Its roots were sunk in Turkey, but also in a personal conundrum. Baldwin's stay in Istanbul coincided with the first waves of Turkish immigrant workers flooding into Germany and Switzerland. Regarding himself as an outcast of a different continent, he identified and sympathized with their situation. Yet when he came to live in St-Paul some years later and took charge of a spacious garden, he found himself the employer of a team of Arab workers who saw him as the master of the plantation, who changed their way of talking when he approached, who kept a friendly distance between themselves and him which was too wide to be bridged. 'In a certain degree,' Baldwin told Christian de Bartillat during their lengthy interview in French in 1974, 'I have seen in Mohammed, in his eyes, his voice, his actions, myself; and at that moment, I become the oppressor.'

The idea is pregnant with possibility, but, like the triple biography, the novel was never finished. However, he did complete *The Welcome Table*. It has never been published or performed, but exists in a typescript of ninety-eight pages, and although Baldwin wrote 'First draft' in the top right-hand corner of the title page, the play is complete. It is a comparatively short work, suited to studio production; all of the action, except for one brief scene at the beginning, takes place in a large house in the south of France. As described in the stage-directions, the house greatly resembles Baldwin's own house in St-Paul, and *The Welcome Table*, like *Just Above My Head*, contains many autobiographical references – though here they are given a unique psychosexual twist.

The play's main characters are Edith, a creole woman from New Orleans, described as 'an actress singer/star'; Laverne, her cousin and girl Friday; Peter Davis, a black American journalist; Daniel, an 'ex-black panther', and Mlle LaFarge, an aristocratic Frenchwoman from Algeria, exiled in France since the colonial war. All these characters, with the exception of the last, are black. In addition, the cast includes Regina, 'Edith's oldest friend, recently widowed', Rob and Mark, all of whom are white. Rob and Mark are lovers, as are Rob and Edith.

The play returns to the territory of *Another Country*, in the way that Baldwin mixes black and white, male and female, homo- and heterosexual; the text is sprinkled with remarks which would have fitted comfortably into that novel, such as Rob's 'love isn't something you can take back to the store for a refund'. When the same character says 'a person's lovers are a kind of key to that person – and it ain't always peaches and cream, darling, when that key turns and you see what's behind the door', and 'love is where you find it', he is again harking back to the themes of the novel.

One difference between *The Welcome Table* and *Another Country*, however, is that while the latter takes New York low-life as its setting, the scene of *The Welcome Table* is the Côte d'Azur and the cast is made up of 'stars' and people whose function it is to reflect the stars' brightness.

Edith is jaded by her success: it is the thing that prevents her being who she is. Early on in the action, we are told that she looks into a mirror and 'doesn't like what she sees'. Yet she has, according to someone else, 'a quite remarkable face'. She bought her house near Cannes from the ninety-year-old Mlle LaFarge, just as Baldwin bought his from the real-life *pied noir* Mlle Faure; and she is, underneath it all, 'a blues singer'.

In short, gender apart, Edith bears a strong resemblance to her creator. But even that seemingly definite distinction yields a personal element, for androgyny is the motor of the play. *Androgynous*, not *gay*, was Baldwin's chosen 'gender', and was a vital factor in the morality of his New Jerusalem. 'The last time you had a drink,' he wrote in one of his last published pieces, 'whether you were alone or with another, you were having a drink with an androgynous human being; and this is true for the last time you broke bread or . . . made love.'

There are other autobiographical clues in this work; Laverne, though she is related to Edith by blood, carries out the duties of a secretary/factotum, and has a tongue as sharp as Baldwin's own secretary in St-Paul, Bernard Hassell. The role of the rock-steady journalist, Peter, was written, so Baldwin himself said, with his brother David in mind (Peter is the only character who carries a surname: Davis), and one of the play's subplots is dramatized in a reassuring father-to-son type of conversation between Peter and the former radical, Daniel, which is the name of David Baldwin's own son.

Two central events are taking place on stage simultaneously: a birthday dinner in honour of the elderly Mlle LaFarge, and an interview given by Edith to Peter Davis, during which the journalist disassembles the star's protective armour and penetrates her defences. Baldwin himself, of course, gave so much of his time to interviewers that there evolved something like a 'form' answer to a question, and Edith has had similar experiences. A further dominant motif of *The Welcome Table*, mirroring another of Baldwin's personal preoccupations, is the corrupting effect of fame, its function as a refuge of the self *from* the self. At the hands of Peter Davis, Edith is forced into self-interrogation from which her stardom has previously protected her – and thus is thrust towards the 'confession' which, Baldwin believed, warded off all evil.

The very strategy that Baldwin has employed to pursue his autobiographical exploration in this case – making his alter-ego female, with a bisexual lover – represents his belief in the androgynous nature of each and every person. In 'Here Be Dragons', his late disquisition on the subject, he wrote: 'Love between a man and a woman, or between any two human beings, would not be possible did we not have available to us the spiritual resources of both sexes.'

Far from being licentious and orgiastic – charges flung at him in the 1960s, especially after *Another Country* – Baldwin's sexual ethics are puritanical, in that he stresses the place of love and self-knowledge in every sexual event. 'You cannot learn how to touch a woman,' he once said, 'until you know how to touch a man.' It was not *he* who was 'bent', but 'macho men – truck drivers, cops, football players'. Even here, however, his sexual politics were inclusive rather than exclusive (the reason for his disassociation from the gay movement, which he called 'a club'):

I know from my own experience that the macho men ... are far more complex than they want to realize. That's why I call them infantile. They have needs which, for them, are literally inexpressible ... I think it's very important for the male homosexual to recognize that he is a sexual target for other men, and that is why he is despised, and why he is called a faggot. He is called a faggot because other males need him.

Although he himself saw that the play required more attention – especially in the central scene, the unmasking of Edith by Peter – and although the 'hip' idiom in which many of the characters speak is at times irritatingly camp, *The Welcome Table* is nevertheless a fascinating work. Its dramatic method of letting several conversations run at once, subtextually contributing to one another, is skilfully executed and gives a sprightly, playful surface to deep concerns. The scene in which Peter interviews Edith is counterpointed by Laverne, Regina and Mlle LaFarge at table, Daniel and Terry (Peter's photographer) at the bar, and Rob and Mark having a lover's quarrel. Each of these brief scenes is successively spotlighted for a few lines at a time, while the other groups remain on stage, before the audience but temporarily cloaked in darkness. As the last work to be completed, *The Welcome Table* marks a more satisfying end to Baldwin's career than the ragged *Evidence of Things Not Seen.*

The play was the first thing he had written since coming back to live in France in 1972 which made mention of his adoptive country. In the 1950s, almost everything Baldwin wrote was touched by his experience of France; now, though he might reside in Europe all year round, he based himself mentally in the United States. If, as he liked to claim, he lived in both places, it was also the case that he lived properly in neither.

He was always on the lookout for an excuse to return home, and when he went back to America part-time in 1983, it was not to New York – his 'ghastly' birthplace – but to Amherst, Massachusetts, a peaceful town of white timber houses and wide lawns, famous for its associations with Emily Dickinson. Baldwin moved into the house of a white female colleague in the neighbouring town of Pelham, and took up the position of Five College Professor at the University of Massachusetts. It entailed lecturing on literature and the history of civil rights, and conducting seminars on creative writing.

It was yet another curious departure for the barefoot boy from Harlem, the starving Left Bank artist, friend to Bertrand Russell and Huey Newton alike. Speaking engagements apart, he had scarcely seen the inside of a classroom since the end of his schooldays in 1941. And, as Professor Baldwin, he drew a mixed reaction.

Hugely popular on the personal level, and a prestigious addition to the faculty, he nevertheless disappointed many students, who were unprepared for his impromptu approach to the lectern. Some 'lectures' consisted of a brief reminiscence from the great man, followed by a question-and-answer session. One student who enrolled in his creative writing class was surprised to find that the teacher gave little guidance on what or how to write. 'Just show me something you've done,' he would say, preferring to let the burden of proof rest with the student. The type of work most likely to catch his eye was a story or a poem with a personal crisis at the heart of it; in delicate, descriptive writing, he showed little interest.

In his course of lectures on the history of civil rights, he again improvised, as he had improvised sermons and lectures all his life. He told the students about his visit to Selma, Alabama, for the voting registration drive; how 'a black man with a typewriter in the South in those days might as well have been carrying a bomb'; he told them about his father and how he talked of Africa for the Africans, and how he 'preached of vengeance – the wrath to come'; and he explained the doctrine of non-violence by relating it to the humane influences of the church in which he had been born and bred:

The church I am speaking of, in some way, made it possible – and this is because of that subversive called the preacher, the black preacher – for black people to look on white people not as strangers, not as enemies, but as people like themselves, in *greater* trouble than themselves; because, as the Saviour had asked us all to do – '*Father forgive them!* . . . for they know not what they do.'

The lectures repeated many incidents and contradicted opinions previously recorded in essays and interviews, but their personal, penetrating character surely made the drama of the civil-rights struggle more vivid in the students' imaginations than a more orthodox approach would have done. 'The only way to teach history,' Baldwin told a reporter from a local paper, 'is to make them go through it themselves.' His most important task was to make the students feel responsible and not guilty – 'You can't be both.'

One lecture delivered at the University of Massachusetts was made the centre of an unseemly storm, involving charges of anti-Semitism. The prosecutor was himself a member of the W. E. B. DuBois Department of Afro-American Studies, and a novelist, Julius Lester. The lecture with the allegedly offending content was delivered on 28 February 1984, but the attack on Baldwin's good name as an enemy of racism in all its guises did not emerge into the public domain until four years later, when Lester – an acquaintance of Baldwin's for many years and at one time a militant black activist – published his book, *Lovesong: Becoming a Jew.*

In 1984, Baldwin had addressed his class on the then-current controversy which surrounded presidential candidate Jesse Jackson's reference to Jews as 'hymies' and to New York City as 'hymietown'. It was characteristic of Baldwin not to dodge the issue but to bring it before the students and lead a discussion on it. The question of anti-Semitism was not new to him – indeed, his first published essay, 'The Harlem Ghetto', a dissemination of that very subject, had appeared in the Jewish magazine *Commentary*:

The Jew has been taught ... the legend of Negro inferiority; and the Negro ... has found nothing in his experience to counteract the legend of Semitic greed. Here the white Gentile has two legends serving him at once: he has divided these minorities and he rules.

This was written when he was twenty-three, and Baldwin had held to the basic position ever since. In 1967, for example, he had resigned from the board of the black magazine *Liberator*, following the publication of articles which he considered to be anti-Semitic. Baldwin had then described anti-Semitism as 'the most ancient and barbaric of the European myths'.

In his book, Lester wrote of Baldwin:

He is not an anti-Semite, but his remarks in class were anti-Semitic, and he does not realize it ... At the conclusion of his lecture, he called for questions or responses. Then the real horror began. His words had given black students permission to stand up and mouth every anti-Semitic cliché they knew and they did so, castigating Jewish landlords and Jews in general. Jimmy listened and said nothing.

The lecture is recorded on tape, however, and the tape does not bear out Lester's charges. The following exchange characterizes the mood of the question-and-answer session which, to Lester, introduced 'the real horror':

STUDENT: Does Jesse Jackson's Rainbow Coalition include Jews?
BALDWIN: Of course. How could it not?
STUDENT: In the light of what he said ...
BALDWIN: In the light of what he's allegedly said about Jews. What did he say about Jews?
STUDENT: He called them 'hymies' and New York 'hymietown'.
BALDWIN: Yes.
STUDENT: How should that be construed to mean ...
BALDWIN: I can't answer that. I know that the Rainbow ...
STUDENT: What does he then think about Jews being part of the Rainbow Coalition?
BALDWIN: Well, until he said that, I had no reason to wonder about it, neither did you. Now that he has made an anti-Semitic remark, one has the right to question everything. It is a ... It's a very serious event, maybe a disastrous event. I can't answer the question otherwise.

No more of Baldwin's words are recorded after this. There follows a speech by a second student, containing bitter remarks about Jewish landlords: 'I see alliance with a Jewish group very difficult because of the experience I had . . . [with] a minority real estate lawyer.' The student then goes on to list a number of fire violations which he witnessed in the building where he grew up in Philadelphia. 'And then the building manager comes up, he doesn't even live in the building, he comes up and he says to me, oh, it's not that bad – the fire wasn't that bad. He had no idea. I wanted right then shoot that man.'

If this is the 'horror' to which Lester refers, the tape shows that it was firmly capped by another professor, with the words, 'I don't think this is going to get anywhere,' and the concluding remark of the session: 'Nobody said any kind of rainbow was going to be formed without some thunderstorms.'

Baldwin's mind was much too subtle to seek refuge in a prejudice as coarse as anti-Semitism. It is possible – though there is little evidence for it – that his experience of the adversarial relations between blacks and Jews in Harlem left the remnants of a grievance; but there is nothing on record to give substance to Julius Lester's charge – quite the contrary, in fact. Since Jackson had made his infamous remarks, Baldwin advised his students that they had 'the right to question everything' about his proposed Rainbow Coalition. And he left them with no doubt as to his own view: 'It's a very serious event, maybe a disastrous event.'*

Other things happened during his final years which were more agreeable. A lifelong ambition was fulfilled when he saw a film made at last from one of his books, *Go Tell It on the Mountain.* He witnessed a successful revival of *The Amen Corner* in London. His collected non-fiction was published as *The Price of the Ticket* in 1985, and in 1986 there was the honour of the Légion d'Honneur.

For friends, and for people who saw him on television and on platforms, he retained all his fluency, his originality, his beguiling articulacy, his wit, his command of the sermon and the anecdote. He was still 'shifting and changing and searching', as he had long ago said a writer should, looking

*When Lester's charges were made public in 1988, other members of the department promptly acted in Baldwin's defence by publishing the transcript of the seminar. The controversy continued with the enforced reassignment of Lester to the Department of Judaic Studies in May 1988.

for new ways to confront his 'traumatized country' with the graph of its emotional disorder. He seemed like one of the freest of men, one who insisted on writing his own script, who took life as a prolonged conference between him and his maker. Everything Baldwin said seemed unexpected, and sometimes his off-the-cuff remarks lay in the mind like time bombs. Twenty books and a thousand interviews were insufficient to express his moral vision, yet he could compress his ethics into a single sentence: 'People fear love more than they fear death,' he might suddenly interject in an ordinary conversation on the subject of sex or romance. Then: 'Think about it!'

His face, which could look as old as the face of Moses, would suddenly light up in pure delight like a child's. If at times he seemed to dwell in the wilderness, he found a way eventually to forge his spiritual loneliness into fresh resolve. 'We pay for what we do,' he said, over and over again; in his theology, this law – 'based on the law that we recognize when we say "Whatever goes up must come down"' – did not end in punishment but in triumph, for he also believed, and repeated and repeated, 'that people can be better than they are'.

He was as busy as he ever had been with new ideas. And yet, when he sat down to write, in 'the torture chamber', his vision would not convert into splendid sentences in the way that it used to.

Chapter Twenty-six

'It all comes back now ...'
Baldwin's last interview, 14 November 1987

Perhaps he should have died dramatically, spectacularly, as he had feared
he would. Baldwin had been accused of dramatizing the dangers of
assassination, but in the spring of 1980, in Gainesville, Florida, an
incident occurred which vindicated him. At the time it must have
seemed to herald the bullet he had long dreaded.

With the Nigerian novelist Chinua Achebe, Baldwin took part in a
dialogue at the University of Florida, under the rubric 'Defining African
Aesthetics'. Half-way through the discussion, Baldwin was interrupted
by what appeared to be trouble with the technical equipment: a short-
wave radio operator's voice came crackling over his microphone, causing
him to step back with a jocular 'Beg your pardon'. He continued
speaking, but a minute later there was a second interruption. This time,
male voices could be heard through the mike. 'I don't know what the
problem is,' Baldwin told the audience, 'but I guess the best thing is to
ignore it.'

But the next time they spoke, the voices came through loud and clear.
'You gonna have to cut it out, Mr Baldwin. We can't stand for this
kind of going on.' More threatening noises followed, again difficult to
make out.

Baldwin, shocked, spoke straight back to the microphone: 'Mr
Baldwin is nevertheless going to finish his statement. And I will tell you
now, whoever you are, that if you assassinate me in the next two minutes
I'm telling you this: it no longer matters what you think. The doctrine of
white supremacy on which the Western world is based has had its hour,
has had its day – it's over!'

The two authors then continued with their discussion and, following the final question from the floor, left the hall safely.* No one called the police. Later, Baldwin concluded that the intimidators were the police themselves.

He should at least have died suddenly. He had suffered two heart attacks – the most recent in the summer of 1983 – but had recovered on each occasion to resume a timetable of lecture tours and teaching duties, speaking engagements and official invitations to distant countries, together with a regime of alcohol and tobacco which would have long since accounted for someone half his age and twice his size.

He was in London in February 1987, and the last time I saw him he was moving across the floor of a busy room, even though his feet were six inches above the ground.

He was in the clutches of a very large man, being carried through a crowd which had just attended the opening night of the revived *Amen Corner* at the Tricycle Theatre. A wide grin, of a familiar sort, was fixed on Baldwin's face. The man who had him in his arms had sat next to me during the performance, and had punctuated every speech with '*Yes, Lord!*' and '*A-men!*' and 'Tell the *truth!*' accompanying each emphasis with a hard slap on my knee. Now he was hurrying Baldwin out of his own first-night party.

'Where are you going to be?' I asked.

'Ask *him*,' Baldwin laughed, and was whisked out the door like a piece of furniture which had been hired for the occasion.

He had not mentioned that he was due to go into hospital for a serious operation. He had cancer. Although the doctors did what they could, the operation was not a success. At the hospital in Nice, they put on a cheerful front to their patient, but informed Bernard Hassell of the seriousness of his illness. He would be doing well to last until Christmas, they said. David Baldwin crossed the ocean from New York to look after his brother, who had been taken back up the hill to St-Paul, and, after some agonized discussion, he and Bernard agreed to withhold the news.

During the summer months he was frail, walked with the help of a stick, and retired early for the night. Emblematically, he had joined together the two extreme points of his work: the epigraph to his first book, *Go Tell It on*

---

*The incident was caught on film by Dick Fontaine, and incorporated into his feature on Baldwin, *I Heard It through the Grapevine*. It is also recorded in an article in the *Black Scholar*, March–April 1981.

the Mountain, reads: 'I looked down the line, and I wondered . . .'; which echoes – from the other side of the flood, as Baldwin himself might have put it – the opening line of one of his last pieces of writing, the Introduction to his collected essays: 'My soul looks back and wonders how I got over.'

Still he talked of work-in-progress. He had a sheaf of projects and intentions, beside the novel, play and triple biography. One which would have given him satisfaction to fulfil, had he been able, came from the English publisher Chatto and Windus. Baldwin agreed to write introductions to paperback editions of two novels by Richard Wright, including *Lawd Today*, Wright's posthumously published first novel, which Baldwin greatly admired. The covers were printed, with the words 'Introduction by James Baldwin', but in spite of pledges to Wright's widow Ellen that he would get down to work as soon as he was better, this reconciliation with his old teacher and sometime adversary never happened.

His final weeks, in November 1987, were spent in the oldest part of the house in St-Paul, in a bedroom to which David had removed him from his downstairs quarters, so as to make it easier to get from bed to table and back again. It was dark and no doubt mostly restful, but the medieval floral designs and cornucopias painted on the walls inspired hallucinations. Simone Signoret and other old friends, long dead, were in the room with him.

Baldwin said many times, and repeated near the end of his life, that he was not 'a believer'. 'If the concept of God has any validity or any use, it can only be to make us larger, freer, and more loving. If God cannot do this, then it is time we got rid of Him.' These words were written in 1962, and his position had scarcely altered since.

But while he was not a believer in the sense of subscribing to a particular faith, or belonging to a specific church, his life was based on a faith that can only be called religious, just as his thought was infused with religious belief. His scripture was the old black gospel music:

> Just above my head
> I hear music in the air.
> And I really do believe
> There's a God somewhere.

He was no longer well enough to go to Bobby Short's house at

Mougins, near by, where the singer and the writer, together with David who had brought him there, would amicably compete to produce the best and oldest verses from the sorrow songs. 'Jimmy had a huge repertoire of those verses,' says David Baldwin. Lying in his sick room, he repeatedly asked his brother to play the record of Sarah Jordan Powell singing 'Amazing Grace'.

When finally he became too weak to walk, he was carried back and forward to the table by Bernard, or by David, or by Lucien Happersberger, who had come down to St-Paul from his home in Switzerland to be by the bedside.

One day, when Bernard went to fetch him from his bed, Baldwin said he didn't want to move. Bernard told David, who then went into his brother's room.

'Bernard says you don't want to come to the table.'

'That's right.'

'What's the matter?'

Like a child, according to David Baldwin, he replied, 'I'm afraid . . . I don't like it when you have to take me back here again.'

Says David, 'I almost went under at that point, looking at him lying there, all thin and shrunken. But I clung on, and then I began to shout at him, like "What are you talkin' about? Come on!", finger-jabbing and all that. I said, "*You* carried *me* when I was little. Why can't I carry you now?" And I scooped him up out of bed right there and began carrying him towards the dining-room.'

Half-way to the table, cradled in his younger brother's arms, Baldwin said, 'That old song ain't no lie.'

'What old song?'

'He ain't heavy, he's my brother.'

He died: 30 November 1987.

Abbreviations Used in Notes

Berg   Berg Collection, New York Public Library
CUL   Columbia University Library
EC   Private papers of Engin Cezzar
EP   Private papers of Edward Parone
FF   Ford Foundation
GH   Private papers of Gordon Heath
HRHRC   Harry Ransom Humanities Research Center, University of Texas at Austin
JWJ   James Weldon Johnson Collection, Beinecke Rare Book and Manuscript Library, Yale University
LL   Manuscripts Department, Lilly Library, Indiana University
LS   Private papers of Leslie Schenk
PR   *Partisan Review* Collection
Sch   Schomburg Center for Research in Black Culture, New York Public Library

Notes

page

3   'Je n'ai eu jamais d'enfance'   'James Baldwin: Entretiens'; an interview, conducted in French by Christian de Bartillat in 1974; unpublished, private collection.
    'I did not have'   Fern Marja Eckman, *The Furious Passage of James Baldwin*; New York, 1966.
    'Je suis né mort.'
    'I was born'   Introduction to *The Amen Corner*; New York, 1968.

4   According to   'Notes of a Native Son', in *Notes of a Native Son*; Boston, 1955.
    Later on   'James Baldwin: Entretiens'; the same point was made at the University of Massachusetts in 1984. I am indebted to the W. E. B. DuBois Department of Afro-American Studies for permitting me access to tapes of a set of lectures which Baldwin gave there.

5   Another son   David Baldwin junior, to author.
    'like pictures'   'Notes of a Native Son'.
    'Daddy's distant'   Part of a conversation between JB and his brother David, recorded in *I Heard It through the Grapevine*, a film by Dick Fontaine, 1981.

6   'When you go downtown'   'A Talk to Teachers', in *The Price of the Ticket: Collected Nonfiction 1948–1985*; New York, 1985.
    he told   Kenneth B. Clark, editor, *The Negro Protest: Talks with James Baldwin, Malcolm X, Martin Luther King*; Boston, 1963.
    'If it ever'   'Notes of a Native Son'.

7   schoolfriend   Eckman, op. cit.
    Baldwin remembered   'Notes of a Native Son'.
    come to the window   'James Baldwin: Entretiens'.

8   'When the sinner'   *The Devil Finds Work*; New York, 1976.

9   'I was born'   Lecture at the University of Massachusetts, 1984.
    'from church to smaller'   'Notes of a Native Son'.
    'Whose little boy'   *The Fire Next Time*; New York, 1963.

10 Arthur Moore . . . Baldwin declared   Eckman, op. cit.

12 'Is Scotland'   JB to author.
    She remembered   'Notes on My Native Son', *Freedomways*, Summer 1963.

13 'a Christian'   'Notes of a Native Son'.
    'I was physically'   Eckman, op. cit.
    On a Saturday   Information from Eckman, op. cit, and from Baldwin's essay 'Dark Days', in *The Price of the Ticket*.

15 *National Review*, 13 August 1963.

17 'It's an awful lot'   Letter to Langston Hughes, 25 March 1953; JWJ.

20 unable to recall   Eckman, op. cit.
Miller's essay on Delaney is collected in *Remember to Remember*, New York, 1947.
'The most'   'James Baldwin Comes Home', *Essence* magazine, June 1976.
'He had'   Introduction to *The Price of the Ticket*.
21 'I learned'   Baldwin's Introduction to the catalogue of an exhibition of Delaney's paintings at the Galerie Lambert, Paris, 1964.
22 'There was no'   *The Fire Next Time*.
23 'Working-class'   Letter from Capouya to author.
24 he admitted   Letter to Stephen D. James, 14 February 1963; Sch.
'It was the same'   'Notes of a Native Son'.
26 The death of David Baldwin was treated in fiction in 'The Death of the Prophet', *Commentary*, March 1950.
27 Harold Norse, *Memoirs of a Bastard Angel*, New York, 1989.
30 'I did not'   'Alas, Poor Richard', in *Nobody Knows My Name*, New York, 1961.
31 His book   Letter to Wright, 27 December 1945; JWJ.
'Dear Richard'   Undated letter to Wright, 1946; JWJ.
Wright in Charles St   Addison Gayle Jr, *Richard Wright: Ordeal of a Native Son*, New York, 1980.
32 he was   Letter to S. D. James, 28 December 1946; Sch.
a Jewish girl   Letter to S. D. James, 14 February 1943; Sch.
33 He would force   From some loose pages of a 'letter to himself', *c.* spring 1949, which JB later gave to Bosley Wilder; courtesy BW.
'It took you'   Stan Weir, 'Meetings with James Baldwin', in *Against the Current* magazine, 1989.
'He'll have to'   From a postcard written to Barbara Snader by an unknown correspondent, *c.* 1946; courtesy BS.
35 'There is no music'   *The Fire Next Time*.
36 I am indebted to David Baldwin for showing me a set of the Pelatowski photographs.
38 'I had been'   Introduction to *The Price of the Ticket*.
39 'The relationship'   *New Leader*, 24 January 1948.
40 Mary McCarthy, 'Baldwin', in Quincy Troupe, editor, *James Baldwin: The Legacy*, New York, 1989.
41 Baldwin was later   JB to author.
'not sufficiently strong'   Letter from Linscott to Rahv, 15 October 1948; PR.
'Previous Condition' manuscript   Berg.
49 Letter to Phillips, April 1949; PR.
50 'stank'   Introduction to *The Price of the Ticket*.
'Foreign Correspondent'   This information is contained in the FBI file on JB, 100–146553.
51 McCarthy, op. cit.
54 'heavier'   Undated letter to Mary Keen, postmarked 20 May 1949.
Otto Friedrich, 'Jimmy', in *The Grave of Alice B. Toklas*, New York, 1989.
56 Gidske Anderson, *Mennesker i Paris*, Oslo, 1964. I am indebted to Barbara Nordkvist for translating the relevant chapter from the original Norwegian.
'all those strangers'   Interview with Eve Auchincloss and Nancy Lynch, *Mademoiselle* magazine, May 1963.
62 editorial 'we'   Letter to Hoyt Fuller, 17 February 1953 (dated in error '1952'); HRHRC.

63 'Richard accused' 'Alas, Poor Richard'.
64 attack on Wright ... 'social situation' Letter to Rahv, 10 November 1960; PR.
65 The title of Wright's lecture is 'The Position of the Negro Artist and Intellectual in American Society'; JWJ.
67 'our early' Interview with Jordan Elgrably, *Paris Review*, Vol. 26, No. 91, Spring 1984.
68 Chester Himes, *The Quality of Hurt*; New York, 1972.
70 Schine and Cohn Ibid.
   For further information concerning Wright and the FBI, see Addison Gayle Jr, *Richard Wright: Ordeal of a Native Son*; New York, 1980.
71 one letter Information from Wright's biographer, Michel Fabre.
72 'in the womb' JB to author.
73–4 Friedrich, op. cit.
75 'I got X-rays' Letter from Happersberger to author.
77 'I suppose' 'Belatedly, the fear turned to love for his father', in New York *TV Guide*, 12 January 1985.
81 Friedrich, op. cit.
82 Knopf reader's report; HRHRC.
   pent-up complaints Letter to William Rossa Cole, March 1953; LL.
85 Ross to Keen 9 September 1953.
86 scrapped Undated letter to Cole, Dec–Jan 1953; LL.
   Abolitionists Letter to Cole, 26 July 1953; LL.
88 change of tone Letter to Phillips, April 1949; PR. Undated letter to Cole, early 1953; LL. Letter to Rahv, 10 November 1950; PR.
   'excites me' Undated letter to Helen Strauss, January 1954; HRHRC.
   someone at Knopf Letter to Cole, 13 January 1954; LL.
88–9 Friedrich, op. cit.
89 the love Letter to Strauss. See note to p. 88.
   Strauss to Vaudrin, 26 February 1954; HRHRC.
91 Efforts to have Information from an undated letter to Heath, c. October 1954, GH; also Heath to author.
92 'bombarded' 'Words of a Native Son', in *The Price of the Ticket*.
94 Hughes to Bontemps, 18 February 1953. Charles Nicholas, editor, *Arna Bontemps–Langston Hughes: Letters 1925–1967*; New York, 1980.
   Hughes to Baldwin, 25 July 1953; JWJ.
   Hughes's review of *Notes of a Native Son* *New York Times*, 26 February, 1956.
   things continued Undated letter to Edward Parone, c. July 1955; EP.
95 more meaningless *The Fire Next Time*.
   sick since Letter to Parone, postmarked 7 November 1955; EP.
   'minor crackup' Undated letter to Cole, c. January 1956; LL.
   strange microbe Undated letter to Van Vechten, 1956; JWJ.
   He confided Letter to Parone, 7 November 1955; EP.
96 *next* book Letter to Trilling, 17 March 1955; CUL.
   'thank Van' Undated letter to Parone, c. July 1955; EP.
   back in Paris Letter to Cole, 2 April 1954; LL.
   toning down Letter to Parone, postmarked 7 November 1955; EP.
97 'Give bearer' Undated letter to Heath, c. August 1955; GH.
98 'merry, merry' Undated letter to Cole, April 1956; LL.
99 'Faulkner and Desegregation' *Partisan Review*, Winter 1956; reprinted in *Nobody Knows My Name*.

101 whatever divided   Undated letter to Rahv, 1956; PR.
Baldwin referred to 'the Lucien Carr case' in his interview with the *Paris Review*, Spring 1984.
102 'If you don't love me'   See Joyce Johnson, *Minor Characters*; New York, 1982.
an actual event   Interview with Wolfgang Binder, *Revista/Review Interamericana*, Fall 1980.
103 Baldwin worried   Undated letter to Rahv, 1956; PR.
104 'burn it'   JB to author.
Schenk to Baldwin, 5 March 1957; LS.
105 'a composite'   Eckman, op. cit.
105-6 Schenk to Baldwin, 5 March 1957; LS.
106 'They picked'   BBC radio interview with Caryl Phillips, April 1984.
107 'Dreadful'   Undated letter to Rahv, June 1956; PR.
108 'bastard'   'Autobiographical Notes', in *Notes of a Native Son*.
109 Harold Isaacs, 'Five Writers and Their Ancestors', *Phylon* magazine, Winter 1960.
110 'genuine'   Undated letter to Schenk, *c.* November 1956; LS.
'weird black boy'   Undated letter to Heath, 1954-5; GH.
111 He was suddenly   Ibid.
He rehearsed   Undated letter to Schenk, *c.* November 1956; LS.
112 fifteen-year-old girl   Baldwin related the incident in *No Name in the Street*; New York, 1972.
117 'I will always'   Ibid.
119 Elizabeth Eckford   See Juan Williams, *Eyes on the Prize: America's Civil Rights Years 1954-1965*; New York, 1987.
'rust-red ... touch him'   'Nobody Knows My Name', in *Nobody Knows My Name*.
'You can take'   'A Fly in the Buttermilk', in *Nobody Knows My Name*.
120 'not even licensed'   'Nobody Knows My Name'.
'ingrown, bitter'   Undated letter to Cole, *c.* October 1957; LL.
120-21 'The Northern Negro'   'Nobody Knows My Name'.
121 'It was on'   Ibid.
123 'He seemed'   Ibid.
126 'One good thing'   Cezzar to author.
'we couldn't'   Eckman, op. cit.
127 de Liagre   Ibid.
'They get'   Ibid.
128 He was beginning   Undated letter to Cole, March 1958; LL.
129 Baldwin's review of Hughes's *Selected Poems* appeared in the *New York Times Book Review* 29 March 1959.
'women's clubs'   The transcript of the discussion was published in the *Negro Digest*, March 1962.
130 '*Uncle Tom's Cabin*'   Ibid.
Arnold Rampersad, *A Life of Langston Hughes*; New York, 1986; 1988.
'Hey Jimmy'   Hughes to Baldwin; JWJ.
In the words   See Rampersad, op. cit.
131 'I fear'   Hughes to Baldwin, 4 May 1961; JWJ.
134 Ida is a girl   Letter to W. McNeil Lowry, Director, Ford Foundation Program in Humanities and the Arts, 12 January 1959; FF.
135-6 'My film'   'The Northern Protestant', in *Nobody Knows My Name*.
136 'I'd have to'   Eckman, op. cit.

137   'The White Negro' is included in *Advertisements for Myself*, New York, 1959.
138   Burroughs   JB to author.
140   Death of the Beat Generation   JB, Cordier and Mailer to author; see also Peter Manso, *Mailer*; New York, 1985.
       'Baldwin hated'   Corsaro, quoted in Manso, op. cit.
141   There is even   W. J. Weatherby, *Squaring Off: Baldwin vs Mailer*, London, 1977.
143   'I left for'   'The Fight: Patterson vs. Liston', *Nugget*, February 1963.
       His agent   'The Angriest Young Man', *Ebony*, October 1961.
       'I am'   Ibid.
144   Cheever is quoted in W. J. Weatherby, *James Baldwin: Artist on Fire*; New York, 1989.
145   The interview with Studs Terkel was recorded on 15 July and broadcast on 29 December 1961; a transcript is published in Fred L. Standley and Louis H. Pratt, editors, *Conversations with James Baldwin*; Mississippi, 1989.
146   Phillips to Baldwin, 24 July 1961; 12 April 1960; PR.
       Fitelson's advice   Undated letter to Phillips, April 1960; PR.
       mailing rights   Letter from William Phillips to author.
147   dirty words   Undated letter to Phillips, May 1960; PR.
149   white devils   See Malcolm X and Alex Haley, *The Autobiography of Malcolm X*; New York, 1965.
150   'a kind of'   *The Fire Next Time.*
       'irresponsible'   Interview with *Mademoiselle*, May 1963.
151   'Elijah and I'   *The Fire Next Time.*
       He simply   Letter to Kazin, 15 November 1961; Berg.
152-4 A selection of passages from Baldwin's letters to Robert Mills, spanning the period September 1961–February 1962, was published as 'Letters from a Journey', *Harper's*, May 1963.
155   'The Only Pretty Ring Time'   JB to Caryl Phillips, BBC radio interview, April 1984.
       Rufus was created last   JB to author.
       It was exhausting   Undated letter to Jenny Bradley, June 1957; HRHRC.
156-7 reviews of *Another Country*   Trilling, *Mid-Century*, September 1962; Hyman, *New Leader*, 25 June 1962; Mailer, see *Cannibals and Christians*, New York, 1966; Hughes, Virginia, *Kirkus Service Bulletin*, 1 June 1962.
157-8 The FBI file on JB consists of two main parts: the main HQ file, James Baldwin 62–108763; and the New York file, James Baldwin 100–146553. The material pertaining to *Another Country*, however, is contained in a separate file, FBI HQ 145–2625.
159   'I think'   Letter to Mills, 5 October 1961.
160   Podhoretz tells   Podhoretz to author; the story is also related in Podhoretz, *Making It*; New York, 1967.
161   'shameful'   Interview with *Mademoiselle.*
162   Marcus Klein, *After Alienation: American Novels in Mid-century*; Cleveland, 1964.
       Arendt to Baldwin, 21 November 1962; Library of Congress, Washington.
164   Freedom Riders; Patterson to Seigenthaler   See Taylor Branch, *Parting the Waters: Martin Luther King and the Civil Rights Movement 1954–63*; New York, 1988.
164-5 Jerome Smith to Kennedy   Several accounts of the JB–RFK meeting exist; see Eckman, op. cit, Weatherby, op. cit, Edwin O. Guthman and Jeffrey Shulman, *Robert Kennedy: In His Own Words*, New York, 1988; also JB and David Baldwin to author; also contemporary newspaper sources.

165 'I don't know who' Guthman and Shulman, op. cit.
166 'economics jazz' Marvin Elkoff, 'Everybody Knows His Name', *Esquire*, August 1964.
    'many generations' 'What Price Freedom', *Freedomways*, Second Quarter, 1964.
167 'Mr Tolson inquired' FBI file 62–108763.
168 'By the middle of 1961' FBI file 100–146553.
    'The book section' FBI file 62–108763.
170 detained at customs Lucien Happersberger and David Baldwin to author.
    two FBI men Eckman, op. cit.
171 Wire-taps on Levinson and King See David J. Garrow, *Bearing the Cross: Martin Luther King Jr and the Southern Christian Leadership Conference*, New York, 1986, and Kenneth O'Reilly, *'Racial Matters': The FBI's Secret File on Black America, 1960–1972*; New York, 1989.
    He believed firmly JB to author.
    1,500 blacks O'Reilly, op. cit.
172 recruited as spies FBI file 100–146553.
    'investigated' FBI file 62–108763.
    'We must' *Washington Post*, 27 September 1963.
    'pervert' FBI file 62–108763.
175 King's view of Baldwin FBI file 100–146553.
176 King and President Kennedy Branch, op. cit.
    Baldwin and Niebuhr Ibid.
177 'Dear Friend' CORE Collection, State Historical Society of Wisconsin.
178 The proceedings of the round-table discussion, 'Liberalism and the Negro', were published in *Commentary*, March 1964.
    Baldwin wrote about and related his trip to Selma on a number of occasions, see for example 'Unnameable Objects, Unspeakable Crimes', in *Ebony*, editor, *The White Problem in America*; Chicago, 1966.
    'On the morning of Monday' JB related his experience at the Selma courthouse to Fern Marja Eckman, who recorded it in the notes for her book, *The Furious Passage of James Baldwin*. The notes are now housed in the Oral History Collection, CUL.
179 'to avoid the private' Interview with *Mademoiselle*.
180 'If I had my way' JB used this illustration more than once from the mid-1960s onwards; the present instance is quoted from a lecture given at the University of Massachusetts, 1984.
181 'Jerusalem' *Nothing Personal*; New York, 1964.
    'one-nighters' Interview in the *New York Herald Tribune*, 16 June 1963.
    'The Uses of the Blues' *Playboy*, January 1964.
182 'monarch' *Playbill* magazine, July 1964.
    Dupee's essay, 'James Baldwin and the Man', is reprinted in F. W. Dupee, *'The King of the Cats' and Other Remarks on Writers and Writing*; Chicago, 1984.
183 'In Birmingham' 'At the Root of the Negro Problem', *Time*, 17 May 1963.
    'the greatest poets' 'My Dungeon Shook: Letter to my nephew . . .', in *The Fire Next Time*.
184 'merely a Negro . . . anybody else': 'Autobiographical Notes', in *Notes of a Native Son*.
184–5 'Why I Stopped Hating Shakespeare', *Observer*, 19 April 1964.
185 W. E. B. DuBois, *The Souls of Black Folk*; Chicago, 1903.
190 'his lawyer' Dick Schaap, 'Green for Mr Jimmy', *New York Times*, 21 June 1964.
    black theatre *New York Herald Tribune*, 19 April 1964.

191   'leery'   Undated letter to Leroi Jones, postmarked 12 November 1958; LL.
        'Brief Reflections' in Leroi Jones, *Home: Social Essays*; New York, 1966.
        'must be given'   'Dark Bag', in *Home*.
        'If Abrahams'   'Brief Reflections'.
        Kazan regarded   Elia Kazan, *A Life*; New York, 1988.
192   Kazan's rejoinder   Ibid.
194   'This is not'   Notes to Eckman, op. cit; CUL.
196   'A' ladder   Kazan, op. cit.
        'leprosy'   Eckman, op. cit.
        Cheryl Crawford, *One Naked Individual*; New York, 1977.
196–9   JB, David Baldwin, Cordier, Corsaro, Happersberger to author. See also David
        Garfield, *The Actors Studio: A Player's Place*, New York, 1984; Eckman, op. cit;
        Kazan, op. cit.
200   'I can't go out'   Dan Georgakas, 'James Baldwin . . . in Conversation', in Abraham
        Chapman, editor, *Black Voices: An Anthology of Afro-American Literature*; New York,
        1968.
        'a big Buick car'   *My Childhood*, an hour-long television film devoted to JB and
        Hubert Humphrey, by Arthur Brown, 1965.
        'I'm probably'   Georgakas, op. cit.
        'Once I was in'   JB to author.
201   a ploy   Happersberger to author.
        'Lena Horne'   Georgakas, op. cit.
202   'ill-assessed'   The interview, which takes the form of a conversation between JB,
        Colin MacInnes and James Mossman, was originally conducted for BBC tele-
        vision; a transcript is published in Standley and Pratt, op. cit.
203   'wretched man'   Introduction to *Blues for Mr Charlie*; New York, 1964.
204   MacInnes   See note to p. 202.
206   'I'm the warrior'   Georgakas, op. cit.
207   'The hand'   *New York Times*, 23 February 1965.
209   JB to Mills   See note to pp. 152–4.
212   'helped me'   Cezzar to author.
214   The *Cep Dergisi* interview is reprinted in Standley and Pratt, op. cit.
216   'I asked James Baldwin'   *La Quinzaine*, 15–31 October 1967.
        John Hendrik Clarke, editor, *William Styron's 'Nat Turner': Ten Black Writers Respond*;
        Boston, 1968.
        'catch it'   *Newsweek*, 16 October 1967.
217   Galamison, *Freedomways*, Fall 1968.
219   Bobby Seale, *A Lonely Rage: The Autobiography of Bobby Seale;* New York, 1978.
        'I would never'   See note to p. 202.
221   Both declined   JB's defence of Carmichael was published in *Freedomways*, Spring
        1968, with a note to this effect.
222   'all known details   FBI file 100–146553.
        'He said, "Jimmy – "'   *No Name in the Street*.
223   'something has altered'   Ibid.
        'the crime'   JB and Margaret Mead, *A Rap on Race*.
        David Frost, *America*; New York, 1970.
224   'the black'   Cezzar to author.
        Life, 30 July 1971.
        'I loved Medgar'   Interview with Ida Lewis, *Essence*, October 1970.

225 'younger brother' *New York Times*, 5 April 1978.
Carmichael a troublemaker   See Garrow, op. cit.
'*no* picture'   Undated letter to Cezzar, c. August 1968; EC.
226 'That's not writing'   JB quoted the remark during his interview with Georgakas, op.
cit.
228 Irving Howe, 'James Baldwin: At Ease in Apocalypse', *Harper's*, September 1968.
229 'There is nothing'   Interview with Richard Goldstein, reprinted in Troupe, op. cit.
230–1   Melvyn Bragg, *Rich: The Life of Richard Burton*; London, 1988.
232 'certain privacy'   'James Baldwin and Istanbul: A love affair', *Ebony*, March 1970.
233 'I have'   JB to Cezzar; Cezzar to author.
234 John Herbert, *Fortune and Men's Eyes*; New York, 1967.
235 I am indebted to Engin Cezzar for supplying a copy of JB's character and script notes.
236 'If Baldwin'   Refik Erduran, in *Variety*, 1 January 1970.
237 an old friend   Stan Weir 'Meetings with James Baldwin' in *Against the Current*
magazine, 1989.
238 'I don't know'   Letter to Stan Weir, 17 August 1969, reprinted from *Against the
Current* 1989.
239 JB wrote a brief account of his introduction to St-Paul de Vence in *Architectural Digest*,
August 1987.
240 'You never know'   Bertrand Mazodier to author.
'Jeanne Faure's experience'   JB, Mazodier to author.
'Brother Baldwin'   Interview with *Black Scholar*, December 1973–January 1974.
241 'Dear Sister . . .' was first published in the *Manchester Guardian*, 12 December 1970.
244 unable to complete it   *Paris Review* interview.
'dark, dark mass'   *No Name in the Street.*
246 'salty authority'   Ibid.
'rumbling up'   *If Beale Street Could Talk*; New York, 1974.
'shrivelled faces'   *No Name in the Street.*
247 'My friends'   *Essence*, October 1970.
249 'If you depend'   Interview with David Estes, *New Orleans Review*, Fall 1986.
Said Picasso   *Paris Review* interview.
on Capote   JB to author.
250 'I cannot make'   Eckman, *New York Post*, 19 January 1964.
252 'When it comes'   David Baldwin to author.
254 'Chez Guillaume'   Baldwin, 'Giovanni's Room: Screen-play'; unpublished, private
collection.
'glad to be back'   *New York Times*, 31 July 1977.
'In New York'   Interview with Michael Zwerin, *Paris Metro*, 1977.
259 Baldwin's essay, 'Of the Sorrow Songs: The Cross of Redemption', appeared in the
New Edinburgh Review, Autumn 1979.
266 'great violence'   Interview with Quincy Troupe, see Troupe, op. cit.
270 three major projects   JB to author.
271 '*Dans une certaine mesure, j'ai vu dans Mohamed, dans ses yeux, dans sa voix, dans une geste,
moi-même et à ce moment-là je devenais l'oppresseur.*'   'James Baldwin: Entretiens', an
interview conducted in French by Christian de Bartillat, 1974.
272 Journalist Peter and David   JB to Bosley Wilder.
273 'You cannot learn'   JB to author.
'I know'   Interview with Goldstein, op. cit.
275 responsible not guilty   *Daily Hampshire Gazette*, 24 April 1984.

275   Julius Lester, *Lovesong: Becoming a Jew*; New York, 1988.
277   'shifting and changing'   'Alas, Poor Richard'.
278   'People fear'   JB to author.
        'based on the law'   *The Fire Next Time*.
280   Baldwin concluded   JB to author.
281   Wright introductions   Ellen Wright to author.
        'If the concept'   *The Fire Next Time*.

Bibliography

Works by James Baldwin, including novels, plays, essays, short stories, reviews, etc., listed in chronological order of publication.

'Maxim Gorki as Artist', *Nation*, 12 April 1947

'When the War Hit Brownsville', *New Leader*, 17 May 1947

'Smaller than Life', *Nation*, 19 July 1947

'Without Grisly Gaiety', *New Leader*, 20 September 1947

'History as Nightmare', *New Leader*, 25 October 1947

'Battle Hymn', *New Leader*, 29 November 1947

'Dead Hand of Caldwell', *New Leader*, 6 December 1947

'Bright World Darkened', *New Leader*, 24 January 1948

'The Harlem Ghetto: Winter 1948', *Commentary*, February 1948 (reprinted as 'The Harlem Ghetto')

'Present and Future', *New Leader*, 13 March 1948

'The Image of the Negro', *Commentary*, April 1948

'Literary Grab Bag', *New Leader*, 10 April 1948

'Lockridge: The American Myth', *New Leader*, 10 April 1948

'Change Within a Channel', *New Leader*, 24 April 1948

'Modern River Boys', *New Leader*, 14 August 1948

'Previous Condition', *Commentary*, October 1948

'Journey to Atlanta', *New Leader*, 9 October 1948

'Too Late, Too Late', *Commentary*, January 1949

'Everybody's Protest Novel', *Zero*, Spring 1949

'Preservation of Innocence', *Zero*, Summer 1949

'Death of the Prophet', *Commentary*, March 1950

'The Negro in Paris', *Reporter*, 6 June 1950 (reprinted as 'Encounter on the Seine: Black Meets Brown')

'The Outing', *New Story*, April 1951

'Le Problème noir en Amérique', *Rapports France-Etats Unis*, 17 September 1951

'The Negro at Home and Abroad', *Reporter*, 27 November 1951

'Many Thousands Gone', *Partisan Review*, November–December 1951

'Roy's Wound', *New World Writing*, Vol. 2, New York, New American Library, 1952

'Exodus', *American Mercury*, August 1952

Go Tell It on the Mountain, New York, Knopf, 1953

'Stranger in the Village', *Harper's*, October 1953

'The Amen Corner', Act One, *Zero*, July 1954

'Paris Letter: A Question of Identity', *Partisan Review*, July–August 1954 (reprinted as 'A Question of Identity')

'Gide as Husband and Homosexual', *New Leader*, 13 December 1954 (reprinted as 'The Male Prison')

Notes of a Native Son, Boston, Beacon Press, 1955

'Life Straight in De Eye', *Commentary*, January 1955 (reprinted as 'Carmen Jones: The Dark is Light Enough')

'Equal in Paris', *Commentary*, March 1955

'Me and My Home . . .', *Harper's*, November 1955 (reprinted as 'Notes of a Native Son')

Giovanni's Room, New York, Dial Press, 1956

'The Crusade of Indignation', *Nation*, 7 July 1956

'Faulkner and Desegregation', *Partisan Review*, Winter 1956

'Princes and Powers', *Encounter*, January 1957

'Sonny's Blues', *Partisan Review*, Summer 1957

'Come Out the Wilderness', *Mademoiselle*, March 1958

'The Hard Kind of Courage', *Harper's*, October 1958 (reprinted as 'A Fly in the Buttermilk')

'The Discovery of What It Means to Be an American', *New York Times Book Review*, 25 January 1959

'Sermons and Blues', *New York Times Book Review*, 29 March 1959

'On Catfish Row: *Porgy and Bess* in the Movies', *Commentary*, September 1959

'Letter from the South: Nobody Knows My Name', *Partisan Review*, Winter 1959

'The Precarious Vogue of Ingmar Bergman', *Esquire*, April 1960 (reprinted as 'The Northern Protestant')

'Fifth Avenue, Uptown', *Esquire*, July 1960

'They Can't Turn Back', *Mademoiselle*, August 1960

'This Morning, This Evening, So Soon', *Atlantic Monthly*, September 1960

Nobody Knows My Name: More Notes of a Native Son, New York, Dial Press, 1961

'The Dangerous Road Before Martin Luther King', *Harper's*, February 1961

'The Exile', *Le Preuve*, February 1961

'A Negro Assays the Negro Mood', *New York Times Magazine*, 12 March 1961 (reprinted as 'East River, Downtown: Postscript to a Letter from Harlem')

'The Survival of Richard Wright', *Reporter*, 16 March 1961 (reprinted as 'Eight Men')

'On the Negro Actor', *The Urbanite*, April 1961

'The Black Boy Looks at the White Boy Norman Mailer', *Esquire*, May 1961 (reprinted as 'The Black Boy Looks at the White Boy')

'Theatre', *The Urbanite*, May 1961

'The New Lost Generation', *Esquire*, July 1961

Another Country, New York, Dial Press, 1962

'The Creative Process', in *Creative America*, New York, Ridge Press, 1962

'As Much Truth as One Can Bear', *New York Times Book Review*, 14 January 1962

'Letter from a Region in My Mind', *New Yorker*, 17 November 1962 (reprinted as 'Down at the Cross')

'Color', *Esquire*, December 1962

'A Letter to My Nephew', *Progressive*, December 1962 (reprinted as 'My Dungeon Shook')

The Fire Next Time, New York, Dial Press, 1963

'The Fight: Patterson vs Liston', *Nugget*, February 1963

'The Artist's Struggle for Integrity', *Liberation*, March 1963

'Letters from a Journey', *Harper's*, May 1963

'We Can Change the Country', *Liberation*, October 1963

'A Talk to Teachers', *Saturday Review*, 21 December 1963

Blues for Mister Charlie, New York, Dial Press, 1964

Nothing Personal (with photographs by Richard Avedon), New York, Atheneum, 1964

'The Uses of the Blues', *Playboy*, January 1964

'What Price Freedom?' *Freedomways*, Spring 1964

'Why I Stopped Hating Shakespeare', *Observer*, 19 April 1964

'The Harlem Riots', *New York Post*, 2 August 1964

'Words of a Native Son', *Playboy*, December 1964

Introduction to an exhibition of paintings by Beauford Delaney, Galerie Lambert, Paris, 1964

Going to Meet the Man, New York, Dial Press, 1965

'The American Dream and the American Negro', *New York Times Magazine*, February 1965

'The White Man's Guilt', *Ebony*, August 1965 (expanded and reprinted as 'Unnameable Objects, Unspeakable Crimes' in *The White Problem in America*, Chicago, Johnson, 1966)

'To Whom It May Concern: A Report from Occupied Territory' *Nation*, 11 July 1966

'God's Country', *New York Review of Books*, 23 March 1967

'Negroes Are Anti-Semitic Because They're Anti-White', *New York Magazine*, 9 April 1967

'The War Crimes Tribunal', *Freedomways*, Summer 1967

The Amen Corner, New York, Dial Press, 1968

Tell Me How Long the Train's Been Gone, New York, Dial Press, 1968

'Why a Stokely?' *St Petersburg Times*, 3 March 1968

'The Nigger We Invent', *Integrated Education*, March–April 1968

'Sidney Poitier', *Look*, 23 July 1968

'White Racism or World Community?' *Ecumenical Review*, October 1968

'Sweet Lorraine', *Esquire*, November 1969

'Dear Sister . . .', *Manchester Guardian*, 12 December 1970

A Rap on Race (with Margaret Mead), Philadelphia, Lippincott, 1971

No Name in the Street, New York, Dial Press, 1972

One Day When I was Lost: A Scenario Based on Alex Haley's 'The Autobiography of Malcolm X', London, Michael Joseph, 1972

A Dialogue (with Nikki Giovanni), Philadelphia, Lippincott, 1973

If Beale Street Could Talk, New York, Dial Press, 1974

The Devil Finds Work, New York, Dial Press, 1976

Little Man, Little Man: A Story of Childhood, New York, Dial Press, 1976

'How One Black Man Came to Be an American', *New York Times*, 26 September 1976

'An Open Letter to Mr Carter', *New York Times*, 23 January 1977

'Every Goodbye Ain't Gone', *New York Magazine*, 19 December 1977

'The News from All the Northern Cities . . .', *New York Times*, 5 April 1978

Just Above My Head, New York, Dial Press, 1979

'If Black English Isn't a Language, Then Tell Me, What Is?', *New York Times*, 29 July 1979

'An Open Letter to the Born Again', *Nation*, 29 September 1979

'Of the Sorrow Songs: The Cross of Redemption', *New Edinburgh Review*, Autumn 1979

'Dark Days', *Esquire*, October 1980

'Notes on the House of Bondage', *Nation*, 1 November 1980

'The Evidence of Things Not Seen', *Playboy*, December 1981

'Roger Wilkins: A Black Man's Odyssey in White America', *Washington Post Book World*, 6 June 1982

Jimmy's Blues: Selected Poems, London, Michael Joseph, 1983

'On Being "White" and Other Lies', *Essence*, April 1984

The Evidence of Things Not Seen, New York, Holt, Rinehart and Winston, 1985

The Price of the Ticket: Collected Nonfiction, 1948–1985, New York, St Martin's/Marek, 1985

'Freaks and the American Ideal of Manhood', *Playboy*, January 1985 (reprinted as 'Here Be Dragons')

'Letter to the Bishop', *New Statesman*, 23 August 1985

Index